Fertility Transition

Fertility Transition

The Social Dynamics of Population Change

Loraine Donaldson

Basil Blackwell

Copyright © Loraine Donaldson 1991

First published 1991

Basil Blackwell Inc.
3 Cambridge Center
Cambridge, Massachusetts 02142, USA

Basil Blackwell Ltd
108 Cowley Road, Oxford, OX4 1JF, UK

Library of Congress Cataloging in Publication Data

Donaldson, Loraine.
Fertility transition: the social dynamics of population change / Loraine Donaldson.
   p.   cm.
   ISBN 1–55786–090–4
   1. Fertility, Human.   2. Family size.   I. Title.
HB901.D66   1991
304.6′32–dc20   90–43941   CIP

British Library Cataloguing in Publication Data

A CIP catalogue record for this book is available from the British Library.

Typeset in 11 on 13pt Plantin
by Hope Services (Abingdon) Ltd
Printed in Great Britain by TJ Press, Padstow, Cornwall

Contents

1
Population Changes: Impact and Patterns

Reproduction rates attract the attention of rulers, military commanders, religious leaders, scholars, world health organizations, and global activists. It is hard to identify another area of human behavior that has greater individual or social impact. The family, clan, nation, and world are all affected by the rhythms of fertility movements. Fecundity and birthrates, of course, influence population movements. The rate of population change affects the size, age distribution, geographic concentration, and migration patterns of world populations. All these play a central role in the globe's history and affect its future.

In this introduction I will outline briefly a few of the more important economic, political, and social results of population change in order to point out the far-reaching impact of population dynamics. I will then turn to the purpose of this study, which is to develop a better understanding of the demographic transition that nation states undergo from high, fluctuating rates of fertility to low, more narrowly fluctuating ones, as they move from uncontrolled to controlled reproductive behavior. I will give special attention to the experience of less developed countries in the period since World War II and introduce basic information and characteristics of the transition. I will also present here the format and certain basic hypotheses of my study, which develops a theory of fertility change over the demographic transition.

ECONOMIC IMPACT OF POPULATION CHANGES

Population changes are among the major variables affecting the macroeconomic performance of economies in the long run. The growth of the labor force and the average number of dependents per worker are related to birthrates. Over time, if an economy is not to have its GNP reduced by a decline in the number of workers, it must at least replace each worker who retires or dies. Moreover, changes in the rate of population growth affect the ratio between workers and nonworkers by affecting relative age-groups. Movement to rapid population growth rates enlarges the younger-age dependency groups. Declines in birthrates can leave the economy with larger numbers of elderly per worker.

Population affects market size and its composition. Improved efficiencies related to the scale of business operations are determined by market size. These scale economies can affect the pace of industrialization of an economy emerging from a preindustrial state or contribute to productivity gains that assure greater affluence in advanced economies.

Growth in the number of workers can affect investment in machinery, equipment, dams, and other physical capital. It can also affect the formation of human capital: education, health, skill levels. When workers entering the work force have less capital per laborer because of rapid population growth, their productivity drops. The interrelationships between population growth and capital formation are not straightforward, however. The effect of population growth on capital formation can be positive or negative, depending on the circumstances.

When the growth of workers keeps wages in check, thus raising profits, and when profits are a main source of funding for investing in physical capital, then high population growth can lead to more capital formation. However, if lower wages limit the growth of market purchases, capital formation may be dampened. Moreover, less developed economies will not industrialize as fast when consumption needs, in particular for food and housing, absorb more resources. This will affect output composition by lowering investment in industry. In affluent economies, baby booms or busts redirect resources among industries.

In economies where household savings finance portions of

investment spending, larger families with more young dependents could reduce national saving rates, although the evidence indicates that the impact is minor, if it exists. However, it is theorized that a rise in birthrates or a decline in infant mortality, by changing the age distribution of the populace, can affect aggregate household savings. Younger-aged households save less, while those getting on toward retirement save more. When birthrates rise, more households are made up of younger-aged members. This is more likely to have an effect in more affluent economies where personal savings are larger. Often profits are the major source of savings in poorer economies.

Human capital may also be affected by the rate at which workers join the work force and the dependency ratio per worker. One reason is that education and health needs rise in proportion to the increase in newborns; and the economy with more dependents can less readily finance these through taxation. Moreover, when lower wages accompany high growth rates in the work force, time and money invested by households in human capital return less, possibly deterring investment that is privately financed. Finally, when there are not enough jobs for the young, unemployment rates rise, and skills depreciate because unused.

Even technological change has been tied to population growth rates. When the rate of capital formation is slowed by too high rates of growth in population, advances in technology may also be slow. On the other hand, Boserup (1965) finds that sedentary agriculture may not be practised, even though it is technically superior to nomadic subsistence if population is thin. Simon (1977) relates innovation to the absolute number of people who could have talents for invention. And Kelly, Williamson, and Cheetham (1972) relate technical advances in less developed countries to profits affected by the restrained wages associated with higher population growth rates. Scale economies, too, may spur technical changes by affecting equipment utilization and type, as well as profits.

The relationship between population size and the economy that attracts the most speculation is one that foretells a shortage of natural resources. Since the time of Thomas Malthus at least, it has been noted that population growth rates affect the resources per worker, and thereby labor productivity. Focusing on the agrarian sector, Malthus foresaw a burgeoning population spilling onto land of lesser quality. He thought that this would be a factor leading to economic stagnation which in turn would also limit population growth.

Technology, of course, can overcome diminishing returns to natural resources as well as create new, man-made resources. Yet technology has negative effects connected with population and ecological fallout that can destroy or diminish the usefulness of nature's bounty. The misuse of technology, it is thought, can have harmful effects on, for example, the atmosphere, rainfall, and underground water. Such misuse may be related to population pressures, but not in all cases. It is often the outcome of poor controls in affluent economies with lower population growth rates or densities.

As technologies migrate around the globe, negative fallout intensifies; and as population increases, there are fewer unspoiled reserves of nature for economies worldwide to draw on. Thus, population is seen, particularly in the popular press, as affecting the future of the world economy. It must be noted, however, that ecology is a young science; and the interrelationships between population and environmental factors that can feed back into economic performance are just being investigated. They are as yet imperfectly understood in many cases.

The flow of populations across national boundaries, sometimes in response to population pressures, affects the work force, skill levels, dependency ratios, international capital flows, the spread of technology, wage rates, and demand patterns of an economy. There can be both benefits and costs to such flows. There is usually a net benefit in the "brain drain" situation, where the more highly skilled, highly motivated come into a country as adults. But the country which experiences out-migration of the more educated from population pressures loses.

Migration within borders also affects the economy. Sectoral transfers of labor are associated with economic development, particularly the transfer of workers out of agriculture. Rural to urban transfers are also associated with industrialization and the pull of labor into new pursuits. Population growth rates tend to be higher in rural sectors, and the young migrate in search of economic betterment. Despite contributions from migration, under- or unemployment problems develop when population grows at high rates.

Inequality in an economy can be heightened by differential rates of fertility among households. Lower income households tend to have higher birthrates. Thus the young of high fertility households receive fewer economic advantages such as education or health expenditures. This intensifies the economic dualism among such groups of people. The contrasts can be especially sharp in semi-industrialized countries such as Brazil.

POLITICAL AND SOCIAL IMPACT OF POPULATION CHANGES

Population size is interrelated with security and survival of the group. In countries where group survival in drought years depends upon numbers and where tribal rivalries exist, control of populations may be viewed as undesirable. Tribal size determines political power or possible annihilation. In such cases, birthrates tend to be high and unrestricted.

Power rankings among states are in part determined by sheer numbers. Historically this has been related to defense and survival. Modern countries, despite all their technically advanced weaponry, show concern when their population growth stagnates or declines while the numbers grow in other nations. On the other hand, densely populated lesser developed countries seeking to join the financially powerful nation-states may create policies designed to limit rates of fertility if they expect this to enhance their economic growth. Such is the case in China or India.

Political instabilities affect and are affected by international population migrations. The political process must respond to ethnic power groupings and conflicts. Ex-patriot groups or colonies abroad can affect the politics of the home country as well as those of the adopted country. History is replete with examples, while East European, Palestinian, Vietnamese, and Cuban refugees provide recent cases. Out-migrations are often influenced by population size or growth rates.

Within a country, population size, settlement, and migration patterns influence national politics. Regional vested interests can differ. Even in nondemocratic settings there are ways for regional populations to wield power. Large states can experience governing problems related to sheer size plus regional divergences. India and China come to mind here.

Countries with high dependency groups caused by population

growth rate changes can encounter tough political choices. The public purse is easily drained by education, health, or social security needs. Pressures are felt at local, state, and national levels, affecting political alignments and philosophies.

Sociologists are among those keenly interested in the flux of populations. Fundamentally the survival of the species is at stake. Population densities influence social organization, from the family to the state. Given fertility's basic importance to the group, there is group influence of reproductive rates in societies. Sexual behavior is subject to group norms and sanctions, varying from religious to legal. Marriage age, laws and customs, child custody, support, education, and labour laws all reflect group response to the impact of population upon society.

Survival of the group (family, tribe, nation) is an overriding social goal (Robinson and Harbison, 1980, p. 221). It may require high birthrates, as in the case of high mortality (whether from primitive health care or nuclear disaster); or it may require fewer people under severe Malthusian conditions (Coale, 1986; Wrigley, 1978). Once the primary goal of survival is not at stake, interrelationships between secondary social goals and population size can arise. A goal historically related to population controls is the lifestyle of families, the society, or the state. Goals may vary within cultural and/or economic subgroups. Their attainment often involves birth controls. The controls may be in the form of delayed marriages, separation of married couples, or celibate vocations, as well as more modern technical methods. A relationship between population growth rates and these goals must be perceived if controls are to be instituted.

The use of birth controls to limit population and the acceptance of various techniques of population control (infanticide or vasectomies, for example) are socially volatile issues. When societies move away from natural fertility toward controlled fertility, usually seeking a certain lifestyle norm for the group, transition leading to behavioural change is slow. In such a fundamental area of life, society is collectively cautious (Robinson and Harbison, 1980, p. 223). Religious influences in particular are slow to change in this regard. Often religious sanction of unrestrained fertility arose when survival or prosperity for the group required high fertility (Coale, 1986). Unrestrained births became an ideal that was declared sacred. Reversal of this position, which has often been adhered to for centuries, can threaten religious authority and be strongly resisted. But the fact that religions saw reproductive behavior as an important sphere for its authority testifies to social importance. The high probability of eventual change in reproductive guidelines as basic conditions change in turn testifies to the importance of population to the group.[1]

Society must organize to support its members, and in particular the dependency groups such as children, the aged, and the ill. The roles of the family and other social groups in this regard are interrelated with population growth and controls. Security of the group's well-being demands group influence of reproductive behavior of members. In fact, the idea that the group strives to maintain lifestyle norms through influencing fertility rates is central to the arguments of the fertility model to be developed here. When reproductive behavior is viewed over the long run from the perspective of the family's and society's well-being, the individual appears to be orchestrated toward conformity in this fundamental sphere of life.

AN INTRODUCTORY PROFILE OF THE TRANSITION

Having surveyed some major reasons why fertility behavior is such an important element in the study of social systems, I will now turn to some preliminary information on fertility and population change, starting with basic statistical characteristics of the demographic transition. Then I will discuss the variables most often associated with fertility in the literature and summarize different transition experiences of the period 1950–82.

It is important to keep in mind that the reliability of data on fertility, income per capita, mortality, education levels, and so on varies greatly. Thus some countries that appear to stand out from others may simply have poorer or better quality data or, in the case of income per capita in Communist countries, incomparable data. It should also be noted that income per capita rankings are not the same as economic development rankings, which are very complex

[1] See the discussion on attitudes toward family planning in Brazil in World Bank, 1984, p. 172, for an illustration of these points. A more general discussion of the ability of cultures to affect fertility under similar socioeconomic conditions is given in Knodel and van de Walle, 1986.

comparisons, difficult to design (Donaldson, 1984, chapter 1). An obvious example of this point is furnished by the newly oil-rich North African kingdoms where, for the most part, the GNP is simply generated by oil production, and this, plus small populations, produces a per capita income that is quite high. Yet the countries are not highly developed economically. Another example of data limitations is in the area of measurements of education levels or degrees of urbanization. These indices are not uniformly measured in different countries, so comparisons are rough. Nevertheless, some general demographic patterns are discernible, and some comparisons among countries are of interest.

GENERAL CHARACTERISTICS OF THE DEMOGRAPHIC TRANSITION

What is referred to as the demographic transition is the shift from high, fluctuating fertility to low, more narrowly fluctuating fertility, together with a similar (usually preceding) shift in mortality to low levels. As the transition has occurred in various countries during different historical periods, it has been characterized by certain regularities; but there are also salient irregularities that bear upon an interpretation of the causes of these shifts. The following characteristics are important to keep in mind, because explanations or models of fertility should be consistent with or bring forward an understanding of these patterns:

1 The fertility level at onset varies among countries.
2 Fertility may rise, often to new peaks, before declining; and the magnitude of the rise varies among countries. This rise is now considered an integral part of the transition in fertility rates.
3 The pace of fertility decline, and thus the number of years from onset of transition to its completion, varies among countries.
4 The timing and pace of transition varies among clusters of households identified as rural, urban, regional, or ethnically or culturally sorted. Thus, the variance of household fertility rates around the national mean often widens, then narrows. Examined at a point in time, the difference between means of

some national clusters may exceed that between means of similarly identified low-variance clusters in different countries. (See Coale and Watkins, 1986, *passim*, for details of this in the European transition.)

5 Mortality declines do not necessarily initiate transition of fertility. They can occur along with persistently high fertility rates. The lag of fertility decline behind mortality decline is large for today's less developed countries and is highly variable.

6 Fertility transition continues past the point where mortality declines slow or level off at low levels.

7 The pace of decline in fertility is usually greater in middle stages of development when growth rates in GNP per capita accelerate. Countries with higher per capita growth rates during this phase tend to have higher rates of fertility decline.

8 There is no monotonic relationship between absolute values of income per capita and fertility or economic development indices and fertility.

9 Among less developed countries today, fertility/per-capita-income groupings show Moslem countries to be atypical, having high fertility across a broad range of income levels. No other cultural or ethnic grouping shows such a consistently high fertility pattern.

10 All highly developed countries today have historically low fertility and mortality rates. Fertility rates fluctuate within narrow ranges and are below those of other countries.

FERTILITY BEHAVIOR 1950–80

Broad groupings by income, region, and the prevalence of Moslem culture help to summarize fertility rate differences among less developed countries as they evolved over the 1950–80 period of world change. In 1982 the total fertility rate was between 6.2 and 8.3 for 36 of the 45 lowest income countries of the globe where income per capita in 1982 dollars ranged from $80 to $660. Exceptions, however, were the most densely populated countries. China had a rate of 2.3, and India 4.8. Predominantly Moslem countries, no matter what their income level, tend to fall in this general range or only slightly below; thus Pakistan had a rate of 5.8.

Again, the more densely populated countries provide exceptions: Indonesia has a rate of 4.3, Egypt 4.6. African countries, Moslem and non-Moslem, had similarly high rates of 6 or above, with very few exceptions. In these lowest income countries, mortality rates were generally above 100, and often well above. Those with mortality rates below 100 had birthrates below 6.2 if they were neither African nor Moslem, Haiti being the one exception.

Lower middle income countries with incomes between $690 and $1,600 in 1982 dollars, which were not predominantly Moslem or African, had fertility rates between 3.4 and 5.6. An exception was Nicaragua, with a rate of 6.3. Infant mortality rates were generally below 100 for this group of nations.

Total fertility rates in upper middle income countries that are neither African nor Moslem ranged between 2 and 4.6 in 1982. Singapore was the one exception with 1.7. On the other hand, infant mortality rates were below 50 with the exception of Mexico (53) and Brazil (73). Growth rates in per capita GNP were the highest over the period 1960–82 for this group of countries.

High income countries (per capita income of $6,000 or more per capita in 1982 dollars) had total fertility rates between 1.4 and 2.0. Infant mortality rates were between 7 and 14. Exceptions were Moslem high income oil exporters of the Middle East.

Even in high fertility areas, a few countries showed declines in their crude birthrates between 1965 and 1982. Table 1.1 shows a World Bank selected sample by region. Figure 1.1 gives regional behavior for birth and death rates for the years 1950, 1965, and 1980. Composite graphs of this type using benchmark years mask individual country fluctuations and the tendency for fertility rates to rise before they fall continuously. Their purpose is to provide a quick overview.

China and East Asia stand out as regions experiencing dramatic drops in crude birthrates. Declines in China were accomplished through edict, in India in more subtle ways. Compared to China, India's declines have been moderate and somewhat uneven across states. They have occurred in the relatively affluent Punjab and in southern states with higher female literacy and lower mortality rates (World Bank, 1984, p. 71). China's declines have been less dramatic in the rural areas.

Fertility declines in many developing countries have been faster than those experienced in the Western world. It took about 50 years

Table 1.1 Percentage decline in crude birthrates and in total fertility rates, selected countries, 1965–82

Region and country	Crude birthrate decline	Total fertility rate decline
Sub-Saharan Africa		
Ethiopia	5.6	3.0
Kenya	+0.2	0.0
Nigeria	3.7	0.0
Sudan	1.4	1.5
Zaire	3.8	+3.3
Middle East and North Africa		
Algeria	6.0	5.4
Egypt	16.3	22.0
Iran	7.7	18.8
Morocco	20.0	18.3
Tunisia	26.5	28.6
Turkey	24.8	30.5
Latin America and Caribbean		
Bolivia	6.1	4.6
Brazil	18.6	30.4
Colombia	31.4	42.9
Cuba	51.5	55.6
Guatemala	17.6	21.2
Honduras	12.5	10.8
Jamaica	29.1	37.1
Mexico	23.8	31.3
Nicaragua	8.7	12.5
Peru	24.4	30.8
South Asia		
Bangladesh	9.6	14.9
India	19.9	18.7
Pakistan	15.8	22.7
Sri Lanka	20.2	30.6
East Asia and Pacific		
China	54.0	61.3
Indonesia	22.4	25.9
Korea, Rep. of	35.4	43.8
Philippines	32.0	38.2
Thailand	34.0	42.9

Source: World Bank, *World Development Report*, 1984, table 4.1, p. 65. Copyright 1984 by The International Bank for Reconstruction and Development. Reprinted by permission of Oxford University Press, Inc., New York.

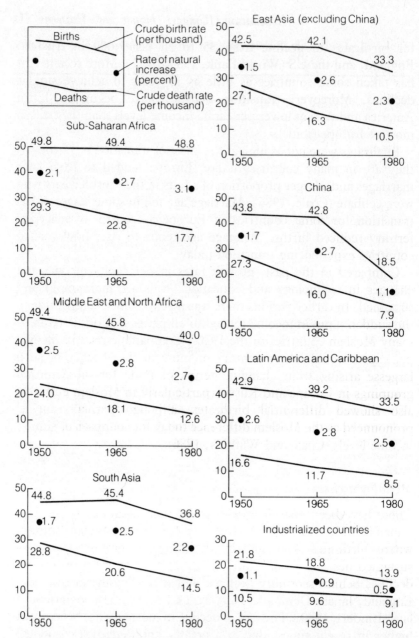

Figure 1.1 Birth and death rates and rates of natural increase by region, 1950, 1965 and 1980. In each case the upper line shows the crude birthrate per thousand, the lower line the crude death rate per thousand, and the numbers in parentheses give the percentage rate of natural increase

Source: World Bank, *World Development Report, 1984*, figure 4.2, p. 64. Copyright 1984 by The International Bank for Reconstruction and Development. Reprinted by permission of Oxford University Press, Inc., New York.

for birthrates to decline from 35 to 20 per 1,000 in Austria, England, and the US (World Bank, 1984, p. 71). More recently, it has taken some countries as little as 15 years to achieve similar declines. Moreover, transition declines have begun in Latin America and Asia at lower per capita income levels than they did in most of Europe (ibid.).

Birthrates were not as high at the onset of transition in Europe as they are in many countries today. Europe tended to have later marriages and a larger proportion of adults in their fertile years who were celibate (Coale, 1986). Marriage age fell in some stages of the transition for some countries of Europe as control of marriage fertility reduced births. Marriage age tends to rise, however, in countries experiencing transition today.

Compared to the past, growth rates in per capita income and changes in technology and education levels are more rapid and sustained. In earlier periods there was no experience comparable to the sudden jump in income related to oil prices that occurred in so many Moslem countries in the 1970s. Comparable rises in income per capita would take a century or more in the absence of such largesse arising from changing terms of trade for oil. Cultural groupings in Europe and Russia (particularly in Moslem cultures) also showed differential birthrates, although perhaps not as pronounced as the Moslem difference today for countries of similar income levels (Coale and Watkins, 1986).

Mortality declines

There have been historical cases in frontier situations in the US, Canada, Chile, Australia, New Zealand, and the Russian Empire, where birthrates were already declining as mortality began a sustained descent. Today, there is generally a long lag of fertility declines behind mortality declines, but it is a highly variable lag. England, Japan, Denmark, Norway, and Sweden also experienced lags (Lindert, 1980). The rate of decline in mortality has been much higher in recent times, due to a greater knowledge base and the international transmission of health procedures.

The fact that mortality declines precede fertility declines today and drop relatively rapidly in many cases has contributed to historically high rates of population growth. The other contributor is the high birthrate of today's pre-transition countries. Even though these rates decline faster today than they did historically, they begin their descent from a higher level, a level which tends to rise before declining. The result is that population growth rates rise in the early transition, then decline.

In the model developed here, mortality is closely related to fertility. It is a sufficient, but not a necessary, condition for fertility decline. Moreover, the effect of drops in mortality can be offset by, for example, rapid growth rates in labor productivity that allow families to support more surviving children at the same lifestyle standard. And where, over time, rapid growth leads to higher lifestyle norms, fertility may drop, even though mortality remains high. This is most likely to happen where, as in the frontier cases, health improvements are not progressing rapidly, yet labor productivity rises because of a high resource-to-labor ratio. Today in countries such as those of Africa, mortality has declined with the introduction of certain public health measures. The populace in many states cannot control lifestyles, however. Fertility remains high, limited only by long-standing institutionalized practices such as those governing the duration of lactation. There has been little change in time-use norms of family time constraints.

Education

Education levels are not closely arrayed within income groups, African countries, or Moslem countries. They show low variance only in the group of the highest income countries. The lowest income group has the highest incidence of very low education, followed by the other income groups in turn. However, studies by countries have found that education, particularly education of women, can be associated with lower fertility rates, although in poorer countries, women with a few years of primary schooling have slightly higher fertility than the uneducated. Figure 1.2 illustrates the variance in total fertility among countries for equally educated women and the relation of education to relative fertility rates within the four countries. Cochrane (1983) surveyed statistical work on the relation between fertility and education and concluded that it is not uniformly inverse.

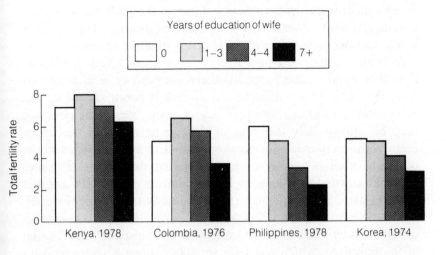

Figure 1.2 Total fertility rate by education of wife for selected countries.
Source: World Bank, *World Development Report, 1984*, figure 6.3, p. 110.
Copyright 1984 by The International Bank for Reconstruction and Development.
Reprinted by permission of Oxford University Press, Inc., New York.

Urbanization

In today's world, a concept such as urbanization can be misleading.
The rapid changes in less developed countries have been associated
with spatial agglomerations of their populace. These high population
density areas within a nation are often noted and compared to the
weaker urbanization movements in Western development. Generally,
there is a higher concentration of people in cities in today's
development experience at roughly comparable development stages.
The typical measure of this phenomenon is the percentage of the
total population living in urban areas.

Data bases vary in regard to definitions of urban areas. In fact,
for purposes other than just location of the populace, the term
"urban" can be ambiguous or misleading. Urban areas of the globe
differ drastically in regard to social and economic infrastructure,
technical and economic characteristics, per capita income, labor
force and demographic patterns, including underemployment,
dependency groups, and other characteristics associated with

development levels, government policies, and population densities. Calcutta, Lagos, Mexico City, Singapore, Beirut, Tokyo, New York, and Moscow vary greatly in many of these respects.

In some countries the poor in cities or recent migrants live better than their rural counterparts; in others, they do not. And in various countries, lives of the affluent can diverge between nonurban and urban areas to a greater or lesser degree. Lifestyles of the populace may be dramatically different or depressingly similar. Social or cultural differences may be great or small. Cottage industries on the outskirts of cities and those in villages may differ little. Families may be crowded into smaller living quarters or find government housing more attractive than the multifamily farmhouse. Overall, international comparisons based on population percentages in urban areas provide information mainly on the spatial distribution of the populace, which has different socioeconomic characteristics and causes. Thus, this variable may not be a robust proxie for lifestyle differences traditionally associated with urban-rural development in the Western historical experience. As a result, cross-country comparisons of urbanization levels and fertility rates may not be meaningful for the period under review.

The data show that the lowest income countries have lower percentages of their populace in urban areas. Above low income levels, there is no uniformity. There is a high variance among countries in the middle ranges of income, with a low in the teens and a high of 100 percent for Singapore. By contrast, the percentage of the labor force in agriculture reflects more closely the inter-country income groupings. Countries in the upper middle income group experiencing rapid growth rates showed declines in rural percentages to below 40 percent in 1980, with only a few exceptions: Malaysia (50 percent), Iraq (42 percent), and Saudi Arabia (61 percent). Moslem and African countries varied considerably in this regard. The poorest countries had over 70 percent of their labor force in agriculture on an average.

Studies of individual countries find urban fertility to be lower than rural fertility, although the gap is not large in agrarian countries. The gap tends to widen and then close again over the transition. Earlier marriages in rural areas often account for the differences in the least developed countries (World Bank, 1984, p. 112). Less disadvantaged countries have greater access to other ways of limiting births.

Family planning policies

It is sometimes said of birthrates in developing countries that each family's behavior will create an unperceived impact upon the lifestyle of the nation. High birthrates that affect national growth then affect fertility only belatedly, if at all. For example, in densely populated countries short of farming land, high birthrates are said to be a development handicap. Yet families do not perceive determinants of their lifestyles beyond their microcosm. There is imperfect knowledge.

Economists generally agree that there are some conditions and some growth rates of population that, combined, can slow progress (Donaldson, 1984, chapter 8). When the development process has advanced to a certain point, leadership groups seek to perpetuate progress. They may draw a connection between population growth rates and further enhancement of national well-being. Leaders may seek to adopt policies to change national levels of reproduction. Family health clinics may be given the additional objective of lowering fertility for purposes of national growth. Policies may be developed to penalize fertility and reward birth restriction. The techniques of birth control may be disseminated at low cost to users. In this way, it is hoped the leadership's population objectives will be achieved even among groups not currently limiting births.

The questions arise: Can forward-looking groups of policymakers change reproductive behavior in the absence of fundamental conditions leading to family behavioral change? Do a country's high fertility groups have to be ripe for such a change at the micro-level, only lacking birth control methods and information to achieve it? Or can the change be imposed by a small minority?

In Communist China, the change has been imposed. Perhaps, however, it is too early to announce complete success. In less authoritarian regimes, the outcome is mixed. In the right conditions, higher child lifestyle norms or knowledge about the health effects for mother and child of frequent pregnancies can be introduced that are accepted by the population. Families reduce fertility to achieve new norms. The transition is speeded up somewhat above evolutionary rates.

Obviously, the draconian measures needed in China reflect the fact that without them she could not have achieved the sharp change in norms needed to bring on dramatic fertility drops in the time span allotted by planners. Population policy failures in nonauthoritarian settings testify to the limits of orchestrated reductions in birthrates when the segments targeted for restraint are not receptive. On the other hand, policy success stories indicate that birth control efforts by policymakers are likely to be effective to some degree in receptive settings, accelerating the process somewhat, at least at certain stages of the transition. Usually there are changes in lifestyles or the level of risk affecting living standards before birth controls can be successfully introduced. Education, irrigation, grain reserves, transportation, and government planning are some of the changes that can affect security of lifestyles in agrarian economies. Given such changes, policies stressing a population threat to national progress may lead to transition onset. If the progress is not felt at the village level, however, the policies typically will fail.

Columbia, Indonesia, India, and Sri Lanka have had some success in lowering fertility in certain rural areas. There is usually a considerable lag between policy formulation and results, however. Sometimes there are no reductions in fertility. Pakistan and Kenya have made little progress, and family planning program indices declined in the past decade in Costa Rica, Fiji, Jamaica, and Panama (World Bank, 1984, p. 155).

A SET OF GENERAL HYPOTHESES

Having considered the importance of population dynamics and reviewed its characteristics, it is useful at this point to introduce some very general hypotheses about the behavior of fertility over the demographic transition. This can help to bring the analysis of this study into focus.

1 Fertility change over the span of the transition is a function of a set of variables; however, a change in one variable of the set may be a sufficient condition for shorter-period fertility movements.
2 The set of transition fertility determinants and the set of pre-transition fertility determinants, while to some degree intersecting sets, are arguments of different explanatory frameworks.

3 Fertility is positively related to mortality through its negative impact on expected child time needs in a situation of uncertainty.

4 Fertility is related to per capita income or a closely related income variation such as the growth rate of income per capita or changes in income per capita relative to a base period. This relationship may involve lags, and is not monotonic.

5 Fertility transition is a manifestation of group behavioral change – that is, it is a social phenomenon.[2]
   (a) Fertility is affected by the extended family.
   (b) Fertility is affected by reference groups.
   (c) Fertility is related to intergenerational interdependence and survival.
   (d) Fertility is related to a set of sociocultural values and norms.

6 The economic structure and its technical base, by affecting the use of time, influences fertility.
   (a) It affects time constraints and time flexibility, which in turn affect fertility.
   (b) It affects the amount of time needed to maintain lifestyles, which constrain fertility.

I will be utilizing the above set of hypotheses in this study, and, as the book proceeds, I will develop clarifications. For example, the analysis will give insight into why the nonmonotonic relationship between income per capita and fertility has contributed to some confusion in interpreting the data. I will also give reasons as to why the presumption that just one set of variables determine pre-transition and post-transition fertility rates can mislead the investigator and why in empirical work the two populations must be separated. I will address the seemingly loose association between mortality and fertility rates, and argue that changes in income per capita and the closely associated technical structure, as opposed to industrial indices, more clearly relate the economy to fertility. Finally, we will see that this study supports the many preceding ones that saw time use by families and societies as holding a key to fertility behavior.

---

[2] Watkins characterizes it as a "social revolution" (Watkins, 1986, p. 420.)

FORMAT OF THE STUDY

In this introductory chapter I have described the general pattern of the demographic transition and discussed the variables often associated with changing fertility. I have also introduced a set of general hypotheses about fertility behavior over the transition. In the next chapter I will give an overview to set the stage for a formal model of fertility. But before developing the model, I will discuss pertinent literature on lifestyles and family fertility behavior and review theories of fertility applicable to the demographic transition, particularly economic approaches to modelling fertility. The reason for focusing on the latter is twofold: first, the popularity of these theories has been on the rise; second, certain building blocks from these theories – experienced lifestyles and time constraints – are central ideas that have important analytical applications to fertility. Indeed, I will be incorporating them in my theory, even though my approach is that of norms, as opposed to the choice theoretic approach of economic modelling. In adapting the experienced lifestyle concept, I will broaden it to include noneconomic aspects of lifestyles.

Prior to developing the model, I will present a survey of attitudes related to its behavioral assumptions. I will then develop a rudimentary model which will bring out the relationship between the dynamics of income growth, living standard changes, and fertility behavior and show its empirical relevance. I will then go on to develop the full model and to test it. Finally, I will discuss its policy implications and make suggestions for further research along these lines.

2
An Overview

INTRODUCTION

The demographic transition refers to the gradual drop in fertility rates from high, fluctuating ones characteristic of primitive societies to low rates found in more technically advanced states. It has been associated with modernization variables (Notestein, 1945; Davis, 1945; and Kirk, 1944); but the onset of decline can begin in rural agrarian settings (Scott and Chidambaram, 1985; Coale, 1979). Moreover, birthrates fell in Europe and other areas prior to the mid-twentieth century, during times when attitudes regarding the role of women in society were not very liberal by today's standards.

Explanation or analysis of such a broad-based phenomenon must identify causal variables at work over long time periods. Analysis requires a framework or model crafted so that historically diverse cultural factors fit into a general scheme. Determinants of the fertility transition cannot be tied to just one social system, but must operate under conditions where socioeconomic variables are changing. This need is one reason why fertility behavior over the transition is a very difficult area to explore or explain.

The approach I will take here is to associate reproductive behavior with the well-being of the group over time and generations. As such, it is a behavior that responds to group sanctions, or norms. Norms can be expressed in terms of time-use categories. Norms for various catgories of time use, when combined with the productivity of time, form a constellation that can be collectively viewed as a lifestyle or living standard for the group. This standard refers to all major areas of time use and related work-time. In particular, I will emphasize time norms related to child-rearing and child welfare.

We will see that insight is gained into how norms affecting fertility change by viewing time as the constraint variable. Time limits every human's behavior over a life span and is thus a universal constraint denominator. The use of time varies as social, cultural, and economic factors change. Variables that cause the changes in time use work through norms. Two of these variables, for example, are technology and mortality. They can be examined in a preliminary way here to show their relation to time use, and thereby fertility.

The technical structure plays a key role for three reasons: it sets up conditions that lead to a controllable lifestyle (a prerequisite of the transition); it determines the hours needed to produce lifestyle components, and thereby lifestyle levels; and it can influence the flexibility of time and time constraints. For example, as technology raises the productivity of time in one category of time use, say, goods production, new norms determine whether time is allocated to other time-use categories, such as children or leisure, or affects lifestyles only in the area where time is now more productive. In some cases cultural factors determine the new usage of time. In many cases the technical change itself also dictates new patterns of time usage, setting new norms in this regard. It can cause the replacement of cottage industry by coordinated operations in a large plant to achieve specialization of tasks and other scale economies. This reduces the worker's time choices and may change his home place and time with extended family. It may require more years of education for children, setting new norms in this regard. Thus technical change can both establish new norms and place new constraints upon time available to satisfy norms for time-use categories.

In general, time use can differ among societies at similar technical levels, reflecting the impact of socioecultural factors. But the technical structure limits the divergence. And over the span of the transition, technological change enables standards of living to rise and affects time usage in ways that limit fertility.

In the model, mortality rates, especially those for infants and children, also have a strong impact upon lifestyle time needs, and thereby fertility. They affect the expected time needs per child and also the time constraint on children. They do not affect fertility prior to a situation of targeted lifestyles, though, and lose their impact as a cause of change in fertility rates once they approach low, stable levels.

Once families establish living standards they strive to maintain, then lower infant/child mortality raises the time needs per child to achieve these standards. Generally when the transition begins, death rates are relatively high, and the probability of an infant surviving to adulthood relatively low. As mortality rates drop, this probability of survival rises toward one. As it does, a greater certainty of survival raises time requirements per child.

Changes in death rates have their greatest potential impact when they move downward from relatively high levels and, at the same time, living standard increases are raising lifestyle time needs per child considerably. Over such periods, the product of lifestyle time inputs per child multiplied by the probability of survival rises. At later phases of the transition, mortality rates have reached lower levels. Further declines do not change survival probabilities greatly, and their effect on fertility changes is overshadowed by other variables. Their effect can also be eclipsed at the outset if constraints upon relatively low living standards drop, leading to increases in fertility despite falling death rates.

As adult life spans increase, this lengthens the reproductive years of women and affects the time constraints on families. Adult survival rates affect the time inputs and time needs of older family members who share in maintaining their group security since more survive into later years. Life spans change the phase of life when wealth is inherited.

It should be noted that death rates may decline to some degree without affecting fertility in natural fertility regimes. In such states, lifestyles are controlled by outside forces, especially the weather. If the states are isolated, death rates are very high. Today, however, mortality rates often decline as a result of internationally funded measures such as inoculations, even though most of the society has little control over their well-being. Limited declines in mortality associated with fewer epidemics still leave death rates comparatively high and variable due to uncontrolled diseases, poor health conditions, and bad harvests. Survival of the group may require large numbers of children, some of whom will be more resistant to health hazards and sporadic low-nutrition years. Internally generated falls in overall death rates in a society, on the other hand, are generally associated with changes that also make lifestyles controllable; and they interact with other variables to decrease fertility.

These and other aspects of the approach are best brought out by a narrative introduction in which certain basic ideas that are central to the analytical framework are laid out in a very simple fashion. Hopefully, this will prepare the ground for behavioral and other assumptions or hypotheses. The schematic presentation is a distillation of a historical process involving changes in an exceedingly complex area of human behavior. It is, of course, a simplification aimed at identifying basic causal variables that explain or predict the demographic transition. The generalizations reflect a particular interpretation of the transition that is then tested empirically.

This approach can be a framework for additional theoretical development, particularly in regard to determinants of changes in fertility-related norms. Thus the model is a scaffolding in the sense that the shape is delineated and filled in, but some structural and finishing work is left undone. Moreover, full testing of the model will require diverse empirical methods to complement those used here.

BEHAVIORAL ASSUMPTIONS

When developing a theory of fertility, behavioral assumptions are integral to the explanation of why births are limited. Motivations associated with child-bearing are numerous and include satisfaction of the instinct to love, parent, and be loved, or to perpetuate the species. Economists have identified an array of motivations related to economic needs, including the need of farm families for labor and parents' desires for support in their old age.

The motivation approach identifies why children are desired or produced, but it does not explain the number of children born. What constrains fertility? Here economists have been specific. In general, a family's wealth and income are limited, and spending on children precludes spending on alternatives. Children are viewed as a choice decision based on expected cost–benefit calculations, given an expected income and wealth constraint. The motivation in the economic approach is self-gratification, based on expected returns over costs when compared to other ways of gaining satisfaction – for example, through more goods and fewer children, more leisure and smaller families, or more insurance and fewer offspring. Choices are related to the tastes of the individual parents, somehow reconciled. These tastes are a given, although it is assumed that there is a strong desire for certain things, such as old-age support which children could satisfy. Tastes, if not a given, are related to past experience or to income in a specified way. For example, higher income brings out a desire for a higher "quality" child – one who is more educated possibly. The degree of substitutability of children for other expenditures of time and money is a matter for empirical examination.

By contrast with the individualized choice theoretic model of behaviour, in which motivation is related to personal satisfaction or utility, social scientists often adopt a norm approach to modeling child-bearing behavior. Norms are socially established and sanctioned in response to group structures and needs. There are social and psychological bases for group-sanctioned behavior. Norms are sometimes said to exist for family size per se, other times for interrelated behavioral variables that can constrain fertility. Parental behavior that determines family size in this approach is not an individualized calculation of expected relative costs and benefits. Both the utility and the norms approach, however, are general models in the sense that they simplify complex behavior for the purpose of analysis. Moreover, they both assume that fertility is controlled to a great degree and is not a function of fecundity under given health conditions.

The behavioral assumptions used here are adapted to the norm approach. In particular, as discussed later, it is assumed that norms for lifestyle time-use categories such as child care, education, health, leisure, and consumption are desired for each family member, born or yet to be born. The family acts as a group to influence the number of children so that family time-use norms are maintained. Parents are lifestyle conformists, having internalized their role as parents from their experiences within the family. Time constrains all lifestyle activities, including child-raising. Families are assumed to use time efficiently as a group, to minimize the constraints on their lifestyles and family size. And they share in pursuit of lifestyle standards. Norms change over time, in part as a result of changing time constraints upon lifestyle activities. As constraints ease, cultural factors play a role in establishing new norms. Only societies that can influence lifestyles perceptibly control fertility. In more technically primitive societies, fecundity, under given conditions and taboos, determines birthrates.

In order to develop a feel for the time constraint approach, I will give in the next section an overview of the evolution of family time-use patterns as the productivity of time rises. Improved efficiency of time use occurs as a result of technical and institutional changes.

TIME CONSTRAINTS AND FERTILITY

Across cultures and over time, people have spent most of their adult lives making a living and raising children. Even those who do not have offspring seek to secure a living standard for themselves and other family members. Time and technology constrain them in this pursuit and affect both their economic and reproductive behavior.

The way humans use time is socially structured. An individual's time allocation over a life span is to a great degree affected by the social milieu and the interrelated economic circumstances. Personal choices in regard to time use have varied historically, but have been highly circumscribed by social and economic constraints of the era. In all societies a large amount of adult time is devoted directly or indirectly to raising, educating, and providing for children, enabling them in turn to attain and secure certain lifestyles as they join the work force. Here the organization of time and its socialization are discussed in a schematic way. The plan is to develop a feeling for the changing time constraints facing the typical family in both rural and urban settings at various stages of development. The term "family" is broadly defined to include relative groupings.

Consider the use of time by a subsistence, agrarian populace. The technology level, and thus productivity of time, is low. The seasons and other climatic conditions, social traditions, and health and mortality levels are determining factors in life spans and year-to-year usage of lifetime. Children who survive childhood replenish the society's labor force hours lost to death, age, and poor health. If health conditions are poor and mortality is high, fertility must be high to ensure survival of the group. Thus survival is readily related to group size among rival groups.

In an agrarian setting, work place and home are adjoined. This proximity, plus the presence of extended family, means that many adult family members provide child time needs. The child time inputs of relatives, direct and indirect, respond to social codes of family obligations (Oppong, 1982; Weisner and Gallimore, 1977; Barry and Paxon, 1971). The needs of children in turn dictate time usage in their regard. Children place demands upon adult time allocation. Even with older children, household chores and children's farming time involve shared family responsibilities and skill training. Since many infants do not live beyond childhood, there is adequate adult time for children, even though fertility is high.

The division of adult work by age and between males and females is socially sanctioned. The total work time can vary with climate, technology, and land fertility. There are limited options for leisure time use in a subsistence setting; and leisure time is likely to vary seasonally.

Gradually, as technology advances, time productivity improves, and time allocation changes. When output per labor day is low, the satisfaction of the family's and clan's simple needs absorbs the greater proportion of available time. As living standards rise with labor productivity, the work year and day may lengthen over the simple agrarian situation where there were seasonal peaks and valleys. Life spans lengthen, and time is used in more varied pursuits.

The longer life spans mean that adults are less likely to die in their productive years. More work time is available at the same time as child survival rates rise. Once population flourishes, there can be greater division of labor time, more specialization, and interdependence. This raises the productivity of time and changes lifestyles. It also allows for the introduction of superior farming techniques, grain reserves, irrigation, and so forth that allow the community to more readily maintain its living standards in droughts or in the face of crop-destroying pests. Local self-sufficiency gives way to crop specialization for the market, and even multiple crops during the year. This requires more labor time per year per laborer and creates a dependence on market forces that structure labor time use. Mining and other primary activity outside farming or fishing also use labor time in a more regimented fashion. Moreover, with the availability of off-farm inputs there are new possibilities for productive and leisure time. Time combined with purchasable inputs may lead to better shelter or health.

As industrial activity grows, the uniform work day applies to more and more workers. Increasingly the skills needed to enter the work force are more demanding of a young person's years. Marriage age is delayed, once apprenticeship and schooling time is needed to qualify for jobs. Parents and others must give greater support time to the young before they become self-sufficient.

Expansion of the manufacturing sector means that both family businesses (as opposed to family farming) and businesses with hired workers 'absorb larger proportions of workers' total time. When women do not work in the factories after marriage, generally the home tasks are time-consuming. These tasks are supportive of the members of the family in the labor market and include home gardening, cooking, sewing, and so on, as well as child care. People tend to work as long as health permits, both in agrarian and in early industrializing situations.

Participation in the labor force or competitive business management involves increasingly rigid commitments of time. So does the corporate world as it evolves. Economic modernization is identified in part by greater control of labor hours along with specialization of labor. Time uses becomes less flexible and more compartmentalized. There is less possibility of combining activities involving, for example, work and children or elderly relatives. Kin can less easily provide direct time inputs because of similar inflexibilities.[1]

Mobility is increasingly demanded of the work force, and this perforce separates kin groups and even husband and wife to some degree. Shared family hours decline in the modern mobile society, and even children in such a society spend less time around the home place. Child care hours devolve increasingly upon the mother without relatives nearby.

Living standards become integrally related to education, even when the wife is homebound. Women maintain education, health, and other norms for children and household members. As partners in the creation of lifestyles dependent upon education, they must also be educated. Thus lifestyle standards place a limit on the gap between male and female education levels prior to the transfer of female labor hours to the market work force. This means that girls as well as boys allocate increasing segments of their lifetimes to

---

[1] Mueller (1982, pp. 60, 63) also points out that rigidities characterize time-use patterns and notes that they can affect the applicability of the choice theoretic approach to fertility, which assumes that time use is highly, if not completely, flexible.

education. Death rates continue to drop, and each child is likely to absorb education inputs in full. Parents must plan ahead if they are to have the earning time to provide education.

Productivity gains allow nonmaterial, as well as material, living standards to rise. As output per hour continues to rise, living standards improve, including leisure standards. This eventually cuts back the work week and day. But women increasingly shift more of their hours from work at home to work in a factory or office. Mortality is very low, and the elderly retire earlier. Their increased longevity raises time input needs for their support from the family and/or society.

Females as well as males are now educated for more years, and this, plus more efficient market production of goods formerly produced in the home, shifts more female hours toward market work. Goods are obtained in the marketplace for fewer labor hours than it would take to produce them at home, and a wider assortment can be had. Moreover, wives tend to work outside the home when children require more formal education and longer years of support. This is increasingly so as families are able to pay for home appliances that perform household chores efficiently and conserve the time needed for home tasks. Appliances become affordable as the economy's savings rise, reducing the interest cost of financing consumer durables.

The redeployment of female work hours, combined with isolation from kin, greatly restricts hours available to devote to younger children. Each family member feels a need to work for wages to attain an experienced standard of living for themselves and their family (Mueller, 1982, p. 79; Easterlin, 1968). Over generations these standards rise. Parents have fewer children, but they devote as many total hours to the support and nurture of offspring as parents of larger families did. They provide more for each child over a longer number of years than parents of other eras when education and living standards were lower and there was more time available from relatives. The needs of children change along with the relative efficiency of in-house production of goods and skills or education.

Parental lead time is needed to supply savings for education, housing, and prolonged support into early adulthood for both boy and girl offspring. The prolonged time needs of children, combined with dependence upon the labor market for jobs, make it harder to predict the number of children that can be supported without a drop in living standards, especially as mortality declines and raises the probability of survival. Parents defer child-bearing until more assets are accumulated. Yet these pre-family education and work years are in part raising earning potential and providing assets needed for child-rearing, just as land-clearing, a hope chest, or a dowrie did in past years. The dowrie, inheritance, or work time in preparation for raising a family are all inputs into children. The latter lengthens the time span parents can devote to a child.

Should parents with high education standards extend births into late life or have too many children too early, they would fall short of productive years and lead time for child support standards. Moreover, as mentioned, the types of goods and services provided children are less and less efficiently supplied with home time. Consequently the wife is more and more likely to enter the labor market, especially where the husband's salary is inadequate to meet family standards for market-produced goods and services. She may wait until small children are older, especially where relatives are not close by to provide substitute care. The need to earn market income, however, means that this must be balanced with the needs of small children for home time. Market work tends to place time constraints upon modern mothers and thereby limit their fertility (Donaldson, 1987). And their need to attain a balance between years at home with children and years in the labor force creates greater uncertainty in regard to potential earnings than exists for a wife employed at home.

Increasingly governments play an integral part in the process of setting and maintaining lifestyles. They, too, constrain or control time. Governments require a given number of days of labor per year. They legally dictate requirements of lifestyles such as education, nutrition, or health. Security is attained by government programs for unemployed workers, the ill, and the aged. Minimum living standards are set and maintained with public assistance. These programs and standards must be supported with taxpayers' time that could be used in other ways. They can affect the time available for raising children at a given standard of living. They can reduce certain risks, replacing the need for private family wealth to attain similar security norms. Their effect on child time of families can vary with the distribution of the tax burden, the level or type of programs, and their legal requirements. Where governments commandeer large portions of an individual's time, as in the USSR, this inevitably leads to inflexibility in family time use and interchange.

Wives in households with high income seemingly will have few economic constraints upon their time. The hours of the privileged few who inherit their wealth are used in various ways in different cultures. Where class divisions are strong, an upper class may have various social constraints upon time usage. Social obligations are sometimes interrelated with the husband's business contacts and success. The wife's time may then be indirectly regimented by economic goals. Thus, despite servants, child time may be reduced by socially defined duties to some degree for the upper class or upwardly mobile. Whenever the number of wives a man has is a function of his wealth, only a few years of each wife's life would be characterized as without work time constraints unless the wife is in a harem or can remarry into wealth.

On the whole, however, the vast proportion of the populace in their younger child-bearing age are typically not among the leisured class of great wealth, although some will eventually receive transfers from wealthy family members. Most often, inherited wealth is transmitted later in their lives, as relatives die. And those households which attain their own affluence through the market-place usually do so after years of work and response to gainful opportunities. Generally their family-forming years are characterized by work-related time constraints for both husband and wife, even though wealthy relatives provide security.

The general discussion here thus emphasizes the time constraints on those of child-bearing age who are committed to maintaining an experienced or aspired to living standard related to the technical capacity of the society and the distribution of its wealth. Time commitments are met by parents in the environs of the household and/or work place away from home. These commitments have changed with development. Children's average dependency years lengthen along with improved living standards, increased life span, and technology changes. Moreover, as I will discuss in the next section, time offered by relatives in support of child-bearing households – both income time and child time – changes across development levels. This change in family child time inputs is related to both social and economic variables. Family time constraints relative to child time needs as determined by lifestyle norms limit fertility.[2] All that is required for a limitation is that one category of child time norms by unattainable. The constraining category or categories can be expected to change over time.

FAMILY TIME (INCOME) SHARING AND SECURITY OF LIFESTYLES

Survival and security generally require group cooperation. Psychological and material inderdependence characterize every social structure. There are dependency subgroups – the aged, the ill, and the young, who contribute less than full material support – and those who support them. There is division of labor at any particular point in time and over lifetimes. There is time-sharing and time interchange leading to group identity and the psychological security it brings.

Within the social network the family is a central unit of security. Members exchange time directly and indirectly in the form of wealth, income, or other gifts that take time to obtain. Different generations and kin commit and contribute to family unity. The size of the family and the degree of time interchange vary across cultures and economies (Oppong, 1982). But even modern societies view the family unit as a central element of social structure (Levy, 1965).

The theory developed here argues that the family is a key element in understanding the development and securing of lifestyle norms. Families share so that they can achieve the nonmaterial and material living standards they have known. The historical advance of lifestyles is also protected by the tribe or nation or by international alliances. Where fertility behavior is concerned, however, it is the struggle of families to maintain their well-being that gives rise to key assumptions of the model. This does not deny, of course, that states also are concerned when too low or too high populations affect material well-being and national defense.

It may be helpful to elaborate upon this focus on family time

---

[2] The idea that time affects fertility is not new. Becker pioneered the integration of time into the household production function (Becker, 1965). Mueller surveys time-use studies and their implications for fertility, arguing for a broad approach such as the one taken here (Mueller, 1982). Easterlin notes that, more than in any other area of economics, time has come to the forefront in the analysis of fertility (Easterlin, 1986).

interchange by means of illustrations. Parents receive support from the family as they raise children. Family members offer their time directly, and indirectly in the form of income or wealth. The latter requires time to obtain, and thus can be denominated in time units. Children, in turn, provide support for aging parents directly in time units and indirectly in money or other assets. The interchange of family time across generations raises family security, enabling kinship groups to maintain living standards. This is true even where family members are fewer and live long distances from each other as modernization brings mobility. Family time interchange, however, takes place among fewer relatives as kinship groups shrink (Oppong, 1982).

Time interchange, direct and indirect, occurs in affluent as well as poor societies. Consider a simple agrarian economy again. As parents work the fields, grandparents, aunts, or older siblings care for younger children and perform household cooking and other chores. Senior family members may have cleared, terraced, fenced, or irrigated fields. The time input here is in part passed on to later generations, who in turn put maintenance hours into land improvements already in existence and add more. Where the clan exchanges time, parents find ample child care hours among relatives. Technology and living standards are at low levels. Child dependency years are limited, and high child mortality reduces the average time needed per child. Parental work time requirements do not conflict with children if a large part of child care time is provided by members of the extended family (Mueller, 1982, p. 82). In some social settings children are also looked after by community members almost in herd fashion as mothers work.

Family dispersal occurs over the modernization process gradually but steadily, reducing direct family time inputs of relatives into child care. Smaller, less extended families also lead to fewer sibling care hours. Grandparents, aunts, and uncles are not close by as in the village setting. Many have market occupations. And as women join the market work force, there is a precipitous drop in available hours of female relatives that can be shared with parents. There is also less informal community time interchange as market work gains in importance.

While modern parents find little direct child care time available to them, indirect time inputs may be substantial. Families continue to share, helping members maintain lifestyles and security in technically advanced settings where work is no longer a shared family endeavor. Education inputs are often provided by relatives, as are housing and seed money to start a business. Community time inputs become impersonal, taking the form of education and other subsidies to families, along with charitable contributions. In cultures where single-parent families occur, relatives generally give time directly and also indirectly in the form of economic support.

Changes in life spans limit how much older households can share and still maintain their lifestyles. The aging of the populace presents new risks, potentially reducing security norms of the elderly. The response by maturing households as they gain in potential longevity is to increase their saving rates. Households begin saving for their retirement years once the children have completed their education. Women in such households may enter or remain in the labor force to help build a retirement nest egg. The higher income received in middle years goes into saving needed for retirement years. These precautionary measures limit the time demands of the elderly on younger family members.

The need to maintain lifestyle security limits how much of the greater affluence of older households can be prudently shared with younger ones. Thus declining mortality diverts some resources that could otherwise be shared with family members of child-bearing age, supporting education norms and the like. Beyond this limit, sharing takes place. This indirect time-sharing in modern economies, of course, cannot relieve child time constraints that are binding because of inadequate direct time inputs.

Thus, even in advanced countries, where many aspects of material living standards are secured by the state, families also aid each other in the support of their lifestyles. Education plays an important part in securing standards across generations. Family members other than just parents share in education costs. Many "big-ticket" items of this type, including housing, require family help. Surveys also show that family members provide child day-care needs when parents work.[3] Vacations and other leisure standards often involve family interchange. And despite state-

---

[3] The US Census Bureau estimates that 15 percent of those taking care of children under age 5 for working mothers in the mid-1980s were grandparents or other relatives. See Atlanta Constitution, Friday, May 8, 1987, p. 3D. CBS Morning News reported a study showing that one-third of households received help from their families in buying their first house. One-half of families expected to have to give help for the first home (Oct. 24, 1985).

sponsored social security, elderly or ill family members can still be net recipients of family time and income. Inheritance may also be tied into lifestyle maintenance.

LIVING STANDARD NORMS

The reproduction rate is so important to family well-being and the future of society that individuals in the reproductive age-group invariably are greatly influenced by social pressures, norms, and laws. It is argued here that fertility can best be modeled as determined by the interaction of time constraints and group norms related to lifestyles rather than by the independent decision making of parents. The framework is simple, but it draws on the strong group forces that inevitably are central to reproduction behavior, given the economic and other constraints parents face in their child-bearing years.

The premise here is that once standards of living, nonmaterial and material, are technically controllable, within limits, society and the family will organize to avoid, if possible, a deterioration in lifestyles. When conditions are very primitive, most variables of existence – for example, the weather – are beyond the control of the group. In particular, fertility control will not assure living standards, because knowledge, and thereby security, is so limited. A larger family may have a better chance of surviving a plague or even a drought beyond the control of the tribe. There may be taboos or customs, such as lactation practices, that arose over time and that limit fertility. Their origin, however, will not be rooted in the need for birth control to assure living standards.

In more technically advanced societies the adoption of controls on birthrates need not occur at equivalent living standards, even among agriculturally based economies. Historical factors will affect group standards at the time society gains some control over them. The fertile soil, rainfall patterns, and technical advances in Asia gave rise to population pressures on the land. Yet as soil conservation, irrigation practices, fertilizer usage, and crop rotation led to more predictable crop yields, living standards were more controllable than those of the technically backward African economies. Reproduction rates moderated. Fertility for some periods in heavily populated regions is below levels in some Latin

American economies where economic standards are higher and less constrained.

Societies moving toward increasingly controllable living standards do so gradually, and not all regions of a nation will move in tandem. More important, a relationship between fertility levels and living standards may evolve slowly, and only belatedly be perceived by the society. Even if the relationship is understood by some, previous behavior codes may have arisen to assure survival in more primitive conditions by encouraging maximum fertility. In a traditional society, or any society for that matter, new behavior codes regarding reproduction can only evolve slowly. This is especially true where population controls are technically un-sophisticated and involve such actions as delayed marriage, opting for celibacy, separation of couples, and even infanticide. Thus there may exist unskilled workers with highly insecure lifestyles who do not control birthrates in societies where more secure workers limit their fertility.

The historical record since the industrial revolution, however, is one of rising living standards in the sense of greater security of material standards, greater choices in regard to consumption and leisure, more education, and improved health and longevity. Countries cannot always assure that they will not suffer setbacks in lifestyles. Wars and other political instabilities, disruption of international markets, financial mismanagement, and the like can cause severe dislocations. And there may be population growth that abets setbacks. Overall, the broad span of modern history shows that societies strive to maintain achieved standards, and that they control population in the process of doing so. Not every subsector of the society is successful in maintaining standards; but overall, once advance is realized, it is protected.

Even when the economy and society are dualistic and fertility is uncontrolled in some portions of the populace, those people with higher standards and lower fertility will perceive that overall continued population growth is an important factor. Growing inequality associated with differential birthrates between the subsectors can lead to political instability that threatens the more advanced sector's lifestyle. An economy must maintain its human skills, education, and health levels in order to maintain its lifestyle. Investing in this human capital takes resources and time. When the higher fertility segment of the populace has adequate survival rates, it will make up an increasing proportion of the population, and this can lead to greater dualism. The shear weight of their population growth means that the economy is composed of increasing proportions of those who have less human capital. The advanced sector will come to understand this, see that the economy cannot finance the human capital needed to protect the nation's lifestyle without lower fertility rates, and seek to curtail population growth.

Of course, human capital standards rise slowly, and there need not be abrupt changes in fertility rates to avoid intensified dualism. The point is that as standards rise and become interrelated with fertility, groups respond by influencing fertility in ways both subtle and direct to protect rising standards.

The analysis developed here draws a relationship between fertility behavior and lifestyle norms. I argue that once living standards experienced over time can be protected, lifestyle norms develop. These norms involve child care and education, security and wealth, leisure time and consumption standards. They reflect both cultural and economic factors that influence time allocation. The crucial assumption is that families seek to maintain norms (or avoid falling much below them) by limiting children to the number that they think can be provided for at experienced standards, given time constraints.[4]

Parents deciding on family size are influenced by family members, family lifestyle norms, and the input time needed to maintain them. Teenagers internalize the lifestyle and attitudes of their parents in regard to support of children (Easterlin, 1968). Norms regarding child nurture and supervision, education, security, and so forth reflect familial and social standards. These, in turn, are reflected in laws regarding education and child support, marriage age and child neglect, among others. The parents must expect to support children at experienced norms, given their own and expected family time inputs. Some will take more chances given the uncertainties of life than others. But only a very small minority will disregard lifestyle needs.

Development and rising time productivity lead to gradual changes in lifestyle norms, although not all occupations or sectors

---

[4] As Namboodiri and others have pointed out, when norms are introduced this way, there must be some minimum adherence level and associated resource allocation (Namboodiri, 1980, p. 85).

are affected positively or equally. Families are lifted by the rising tide of strong growth periods. At such times there is less need for time or wealth transfers among family members to assure lifestyles. Families overall, and in particular older parents nearing the end of their child-bearing years, and/or relatives experience wealth or income gains. When income increments outstrip material norms for couples nearing the end of their fertile years, this can change lifestyle experiences of teenagers in the family and their norms when they form their own households. Changes need not be society-wide, but can be sectorally concentrated. The increased time productivity allows cultural factors to determine how the newly free hours will be reallocated. Such productivity gains can occur in agricultural areas as well as other sectors of the economy.

SUMMARY

Lifestyle changes and shifts in time constraints of the family lead to changes in fertility. Technological advances that lead to new time-use patterns and thus lifestyles plan an important role in the fertility transition. The term "technology" is used in a broad sense to include institutional innovations that raise the productivity of time. Lifestyle changes tend to be gradual; and societies cannot utilize new social ideas or adopt new attitudes to alter living standards very much without cumulative improvements in time efficiency. However, once new ideas and knowledge lead to technical change, then the cultural and other aspects of a society's response help to determine the use of freed time. Technical innovation makes room for social innovation. The technology itself also dictates many aspects of lifestyles.

There are historical examples, however, where lifestyles are changed dramatically by new attitudes or ideas in the absence of time efficiency improvements. The Bolshevik Revolution in Russia abruptly changed time-use patterns of the society, establishing very different lifestyle norms without related gains in labor productivity at the time of the upheaval. Such a radical reorganization of a society's norms is not typical, however. Changes in time-use patterns most commonly are less abrupt, although they can quicken at times of rapid technological change. Thus, subsequent evolutionary changes in time use in the Soviet Union accompanied the technological changes and capital formation that led to industrialization.

As I have explained above, "family" is taken here to denote a group of relatives who recognize kinship ties, exchanging their time for mutual security of lifestyles. This time can be in the form of direct time commitments or indirect transfers such as earnings. Most important, there is group identity and an obligation to help any member of the group experiencing living standards below (or, more than a moderate fall below) family norms. Thus any family member would extend help so long as doing so would not place that member or his/her dependents below (or too far below) family norms. In more affluent societies there is greater scope for wealth accumulation and income increases over the adult life span. There may be life cycle standards that rise with age. Newlyweds could readily expect to live at a level lower, at least as regards some aspects of lifestyle, than they anticipate for later life. Relatives will come to their aid only when they fall below standards for that phase of the life cycle. The norms are reference levels.

Of course, some members, often beyond child-bearing years, may raise their lifestyles above the norm when there is no member in need of time transfers to avoid being below the standards. The sharing of prosperity can vary, depending in part on cultural conditioning, closeness of kinship ties, how far above the norm the family member's prosperity places him or her, among other factors. Oftentimes the better-off leave wealth to others in the family at the time of their death, rather than sooner, when needs are not pressing among other family members. They save for family security, given the uncertainties of life, rather than raising other aspects of extended family lifestyle.

Consider an extended family in which some parents still expect to have more children, others are past the age to do so but have teenagers in the household, while some have no children in the teenage years or younger. There is shared time and wealth, and all maintain lifestyles at about the family norm. The family's expected income is adequate to maintain its norms. Now assume unexpected prosperity occurs for this family, with all households sharing to some degree improved circumstances that free time from maintaining norms. Younger households will realize that they can have additional children without threatening their standards. Households beyond child-bearing years will have extra income and time to allocate to teenagers (if any), other family, or themselves. Undoubtedly for the family as a whole, both fertility and norms will rise. The new norms may reflect those of higher-norm families or classes.

When time productivity gains are large relative to living standards, constraints ease, and fertility rates will rise. This occurs most readily when family time use is relatively flexible in regard to child care time, living standards are modest, and development "takes off", so to speak. As lifestyles rise, it takes ever greater gains to raise fertility rates, since each child requires greater blocks of family time commitment. Yet family time interchange becomes increasingly more constrained, and productivity gains are less likely to accelerate as readily later along the development path. Steady increases in efficiency, however, allow incremental improvements in living standards from moderate gains in productivity. Consequently, as more and more households with lower standards move their standards upward overall, and direct child time inputs of relatives drop, fertility at the national level begins its downward path. As development first takes hold, however, the dominance of high fertility, lower standard households may push national rates upward.

In modern capitalist societies, families that became relatively rich generally need a large amount of time invested in education, complex on-the-job skills, and wealth accumulation. Even with such investment, financial success is not easily predicted; and they usually do not achieve financial prosperity until middle age. This is true of the highest income households today in America, according to census data. In midlife increased family income will for the most part raise the living standards of the children or grandchildren rather than family size, unless the father has children by more than one woman, taking in a younger mate after achieving prosperity. The effects upon family size are twofold: first, more affluent societies are often made up of families that might have had higher fertility rates if their prosperity had come in the younger years; second, because prosperity comes relatively late in affluent societies for the nuclear family, it tends to raise norms for the next generation rather than raise fertility by relieving constraints.

When time productivity gains spread to many families and sectors, norms begin to rise for all, as social standards for education, health, and so on are pulled up by the average of all households. And as a nation raises its standards, its new norms may be influenced by international lifestyles to which its leaders are exposed. In order to achieve these, time is demanded of the populace in the form of work time for taxes. The taxes are spent upon education, health, or other areas that influence standards.

People are required by law to participate in these tax-sponsored activities, since they provide benefits for the society as a whole, beyond their individual benefits. For example, inoculations prevent the spread of disease, and education raises labor productivity in general. Thus, some standards are interrelated and cannot be achieved unless the group as a whole participates. In such cases, those with higher standards and income may finance a disproportionate share of the public expenditures. Just as families share to attain standards, so do citizens of states.

Advances in knowledge certainly affect norms. Child health is one example. Historically, advances in knowledge concerning the effects of frequent pregnancies, breast-feeding, childhood diseases, and so forth have changed health care standards. Once a society's leaders perceive a need to change such norms, educational campaigns are often undertaken, and public support provided.

In this regard, the effort of birth control planning groups can be viewed as one route to changing child time standards, and thereby fertility. Of late, such groups have been transmitting international norms to less developed countries without them. In part, the motive for transmitting advanced country norms is related to fears of global overpopulation or population imbalances among countries that could affect living standards in all countries.

This point about birth control planning is brought up to emphasize that the model is not one of economic determinism. Often, however, productivity gains are needed before higher health or child care standards can be implemented. In Africa, for example, health care is very primitive because of the low development level of the country and its limited educational capacity. Advances in such countries are those that are easy to introduce, such as inoculations that are financed by international agencies to some degree. But when societies have high time productivity and education levels, ideas can more readily create new norms and lifestyles independent of economic variables. When these new norms change time needs in one or more generic time-use categories, then fertility can be affected.

Across cultures with different growth experiences, then, fertility rates can vary. They depend in part upon the rates predating fertility transition and the cultural milieu (national and international) within which new norms arose. Taking the pre-transition fertility rates as given, the model identifies determinants of *changes* in fertility over the transition. The model can be adapted to deal with aggregates. The form predicts that there will be empirical regularities associated with changes in certain aggregate variables and fertility. That is, rates of growth of labor productivity, changes in national education levels, housing per capita, and so on should be correlated over time with fertility rate changes. It is important to note that reduced form equations using aggregate data must be carefully crafted to specify the set of variables to be included in a regression, so that one variable's relationship will be revealed once the effects of the other variables are accounted for. Determining variables may not show simple correlation with fertility in all cases; it may even show the wrong sign when being tested without the full set of variables.

THE MODEL'S APPROACH: A PREVIEW

Table 2.1 gives a schematic view of fertility regimes and helps bring the approach used here into focus. The information is in part a distillation of the overview discussion. However, it may be helpful to the reader to summarize the table's breakdown.

In pre-transition states, lifestyles are not controllable for the most part, and threats to group survival can be great. High fertility is important to group survival under high risk conditions. Fertility is not constrained directly; but traditionally emphasized variables such as lactation and mating practices, sterility and other health conditions, limit fertility to some degree. This is sometimes called a "natural fertility regime."

Fertility levels in pre-transition regimes vary and can fluctuate within fairly broad limits when compared to post-transition fluctuations. The incidence of famines, epidemics, and tribal wars cause some of the variations found among pre-transition regimes. Overall, however, fertility rates are relatively high.

As technical and social sophistication begins to arise, lifestyles

Table 2.1 Fertility regimes

	Pre-transition Lifestyle not controllable	Demographic transition Lifestyle increasingly controllable		Post-transition Lifestyle highly controllable
Fertility rates				
Levels	above replacement	above replacement	close to or at replacement	below replacement
Behavior	fluctuating within broad limits	rise followed by declining trend	fluctuating within narrow limits	fluctuating within narrow limits
Direct controls[a]	not controlled	uncontrolled segments diminish toward zero	controlled	controlled
Mortality rates	typically declining[b]	declining at faster, then slower rates	small declines	small declines
Population size				
Trends	typically growing strongly[b]	growing at increasing, then diminishing rates	growing slowly or stable	declining
Factor in group survival	important	diminishing in importance	somewhat important	important
Lifestyle as a constraint upon fertility	not important	increasing in importance	very important	of lessening importance if threat to group survival perceived

[a] Refers to direct effort by families to control births as opposed to indirect results of lactation and other practices.
[b] Where mortality rates are not declining, population size grows slowly, sometimes fluctuating. Since World War II, the typical case has been strong growth rates of population with declining mortality.

are increasingly controllable, starting among more advanced segments of the population, but eventually including lagging groups. Risks to group survival diminish, aided in part by population growth related to reduced mortality, as well as greater technical control. The group's lifestyles are increasingly protected through fertility restraints: controls such as later marriage age, opting for celibacy, or more direct methods. Families view risks affecting lifestyles from an intergenerational perspective, and it becomes a binding constraint on fertility. In the early stages of transition, however, fertility rises somewhat as technical change and rising growth rates reduce the economic restraints upon lifestyles for many groups.

Obviously, fertility regimes do not emerge from a cocoon, transformed overnight. The prerequisites for demographic transition can be noted, however. They are the controllability of lifestyles and the reduced risk of limited population size posing a threat to group survival.

When the demographic transition begins, the level of fertility will be related to traditional supply-side determinants in the society. The transition need not begin at similar fertility levels in all countries. And the rates of rise and subsequent decline of fertility after transition onset are not uniform. Over the transition, however, they will converge toward the low levels of the post-transition era.

A distinguishing feature of post-transition regimes is the fact that fertility rates are close to replacement levels or even below. The table subdivides the two possibilities. It is quite possible that the constraints of modern lifestyles move societies toward declining populations. In such cases, a risk to group survival can emerge. In this stage, as in the pre-transition stage, threats to survival can affect fertility rates. The difference is that lifestyles are controllable. The fear of population decline, however, could result in the acceptance of lower lifestyles for families (for example, less education or goods per child), bringing to an end the dominating influence of lifestyle changes on fertility levels.

It should also be noted that once lifestyles are at very high levels, the time needs of an additional child to assure the family's lifestyle are large. Fertility tends to fluctuate within narrow limits as these lifestyle levels are approached. Exceptions may occur, of course. The dislocations of prolonged war or depressions may create a reduction in experienced living standards for the upcoming generation, changing fertility substantially.

In the model developed here, behavior is governed by norms and constrained by time. Fertility behavior is a decision of magnitude and commitment for parents, family, and society. Behavior in this regard is viewed as socialized behavior. Optimization and marginal calculus related to individualized or even parental welfare functions constrained by income are replaced by another behavioral paradigm. Lifestyle norms, constrained by time, limit fertility. Lifestyle is defined broadly as encompassing a family's norms for time use, including time norms per child. The pressures to conform in the complex area of human fertility behavior result in a family size predicted by changes in determinants of lifestyle norms and family time constraints.

The model gives a framework for identifying cultural, social, and economic determinants of the evolution of fertility rates from their initial levels in a pre-control setting, by relating fertility to group living standards and the capacity to control such standards. The model focuses upon changes in family time use and time constraints, changes that are affected by, for example, economic development variables, knowledge, technology modes, and social organization variables. It does not presume the same configuration is duplicated in all transition cases. The sequence and magnitude of change in variables can differ. The set of determinants for each general constraint category can be examined to identify significant historical or cultural elements in individual cases. Yet, the general level of the analysis provides a limited set of constraint categories that explain fertility changes.

Behavior involving norms and response to changing time constraints is rational behavior. It is simply a different construct from the utility maximization model.[5] If constraints are binding, then behavior changes when constraints change, thereby causing changes in fertility. Fertility behavior maintains its initial level in the model in the absence of such changes in constraint determinants. This level is related to that existing in pre-control conditions.

[5] The economist who is lost without an optimization framework, its mathematical properties, and individualized behavior assumption will undoubtedly reflect on how well he has been socially indoctrinated with the norms of the economics discipline. See Robinson and Harbison (1980) for a comparison of economic and other approaches to fertility decision making.

The model is not one that replaces or ignores the traditional supply-side determinants. Rather, it presupposes this foundation in building a model of transition. Pre-control fertility levels are not the same in all pre-transition societies. They vary with the supply-side determinants emphasized in the demographic literature. Lifestyle norms at the beginning of transition can also vary among societies. Taking these as given, the model explains and predicts changes from fertility levels at the onset of transition and the pace of such changes. Thus, in order to explain absolute fertility rates at transition onset, pre-transition supply-side determinants must be known.

3
Lifestyles and Family Fertility Behavior

THE LIVING STANDARD NORM IN HISTORICAL PERSPECTIVE

The idea that fertility is controlled in order to maintain an experienced living standard defined in economic, if not socio-economic, terms can be found in the Western literature as early as the first part of the eighteenth century. In the early 1730s Richard Cantillon produced an important economic treatise. There he wrote that men often refrain from marrying when they cannot anticipate being able to support the expected offspring at their established standard of living. He does not mention control of fertility within marriage, given his Irish heritage. His words give insight into the Irish and European solution of delayed marriage or celibacy under conditions where there is little control of marital fertility.

> When I said that the Proprietors of Land might multiply the Population as far as the Land would support them, I assumed that most men desire nothing better than to marry if they are set in a position to keep their Families in the same style as they are content to live themselves. That is, if a Man is satisfied with the produce of an Acre and a half of Land he will marry if he is sure of having enough to keep his Family in the same way. But if he is only satisfied with the produce of 5 to 10 Acres he will be in no hurry to marry unless he thinks he can bring up his Family in the same manner.
>
> In Europe the Children of the Nobility are brought up in affluence; and as the largest share of the Property is usually given to the Eldest sons, the younger Sons are in no hurry to marry. They usually live as Bachelors, either in the Army or in the Cloisters, but will seldom be found unwilling to marry if they are offered Heiresses

and Fortunes, or the means of supporting a Family on the footing which they have in view and without which they would consider themselves to make their Children wretched.

In the lower classes of the State also there are Men who from pride and from reasons similar to those of the Nobility, prefer to live in celibacy and to spend on themselves the little that they have rather than settle down in family life. But most of them would gladly set up a Family if they could count upon keeping it up as they would wish; they would consider themselves to do an injustice to their Children if they brought them up to fall into a lower Class than themselves. Only a few Men in a State avoid marriage from sheer flightiness. All the lower orders wish to live and bring up Children who can live like themselves. When Labourers and Mechanicks do not marry it is because they wait till they save something to enable them to set up a household or to find some young woman who brings a little capital for that purpose, since they see every day others like them who for lack of such precaution start housekeeping and fall into the most frightful poverty, being obliged to deprive themselves of their own food to nourish their Children.

The Increase of Population can be carried furthest in the Countries where the people are content to live the most poorly and to consume the least produce of the soil. In Countries where all the Peasants and Labourers are accustomed to eat Meat and drink Wine, Beer, etc., so many Inhabitants cannot be supported.

(Richard Cantillon, *Essai sur la nature du commerce en général*, written between 1730 and and 1734 and published posthumously in 1755. These portions from "Cantillon on Tastes and Population Growth," *Population and Development Review*, 10, 4 (Dec. 1984), pp. 729–30)

These ideas were fairly widely accepted, showing up in political tracts. In the mid-1750s Benjamin Franklin wrote a short essay entitled "Observations Concerning the Increase of Mankind and the Peopling of Countries," in which he generalizes along a similar line and relates the differential in rural/urban fertility to living standard differences. In this he states:

For people increase in proportion to the number of marriages, and that is greater in proportion to the ease and convenience of supporting a family. When families can be easily supported, more persons marry, and earlier in life.

In cities, where all trades, occupations, and offices are full, many delay marrying till they can see how to bear the charges of a family; which charges are greater in cities, as luxury is more common; many live single during life, and continue servants to families, journeymen to trades, etc.; hence cities do not, by natural generation, supply themselves with inhabitants; the deaths are more than the births.

In countries full settled, the case must be nearly the same; all lands being occupied and improved to the height, those who cannot get land must labor for others that have it; when laborers are plenty their wages will be low; by low wages a family is supported with difficulty; this difficulty deters many from marriage, who therefore continue servants and single. Only as the cities take supplies of people from the country, and thereby make a little more room in the country, marriage is a little more encouraged there, and the births exceed the deaths.

Europe is generally full settled with husbandmen, manufacturers, etc., and therefore cannot now much increase in people. America is chiefly occupied by Indians. . . . Land being thus plenty in America, and so cheap as that a laboring man, that understands husbandry, can in short time save money enough to purchase a piece of new land sufficient for a plantation, whereon he may subsist a family, such are not afraid to marry; for, if they even look far enough forward to consider how their children, when grown up, are to be provided for, they see that more land is to be had at rates equally easy, all circumstances considered. Hence marriages in America are more general, and more generally early than in Europe.

("Benjamin Franklin on the Causes and Consequences of Population Growth," *Population and Development Review*, 11, 1 (Mar. 1985), pp. 108–9)

Of course he draws conclusions from these perceptions reflecting his philosophical bent. He writes that a nation should not allow luxuries to be commonplace because "The greater the common fashionable expense of any rank of people, the more cautious they are of marriage" (ibid., p. 111). This would lead to smaller families and fewer workers for the underpopulated expanse of America. It should be noted that later, Malthus was to be greatly impressed by sections arguing that if nation-states did not seek dominance over others, reducing their means of support, their populations would flourish.

And prior to the advent of Malthus's pessimism about unbridled fecundity, Adam Smith wrote in the late 1700s of nations expanding their populations in accordance with their accustomed living standard. In particular he noted that this complement of people to resources was higher in China than England as a result of a divergence of experienced standards. Assumedly social controls of marriage age, sexual practices, and infanticide were the means of assuring the proportionate complement of people (Smith, 1937). Between East and West, the Judeo-Christian ethic, in particular Catholic traditions, influenced the form of fertility controls, favouring celibacy and delayed marriage. Ronald Lee notes that "the view is widely accepted that in pre-industrial Europe, a man could not marry without the means to support a family at a conventional standard of living" (Lee, 1978).

Gradually the use of modern birth control devices became more common. The literature reflected this by assuming that family size was planned through marital birth control and was related to a living standard norm of family and social origin.

Malthus failed to foresee living standards above subsistence for the masses in the long run. Short-term periods of improved well-being brought on by industrialization would eventually be eroded. Workers would return to a state of subsistence wages and higher potential for famine, which limits population. A complex process brings this about. Laborers living under conditions of high risk and high mortality will not have the foresight or will to forestall or prevent it. And the low fertility rates necessary to control this might result in an immoral society.

Malthus's arguments hinged on behavioral and economic factors. Reproductive behavior was not likely to change dramatically among the masses. Technology in agriculture was stagnant, and arable land was limited. These conditions eventually lead to a stationary state where no further population growth occurs and the masses receive subsistence wages.

Malthus differentiated the capitalist and landlord classes from the workers. The latter, he felt, were subject to what he called "positive checks" to their population. These included harsh working conditions, poor health maintenance, and "the whole train of common diseases and epidemics, wars, plague and famines" affecting infant, child, and adult mortality. In England at the time of the early 1800s, however, birthrates exceeded death rates, and population was growing.

Population growth threatened living standards, Malthus hypothesized. Returns to labor in agriculture decline as more and more labor crowds onto less and less fertile land. Technology was not expected to advance and offset diminishing returns in agriculture. Food could not keep up with population growth. Eventually famine would raise the mortality rate, checking population growth.

Fertility controls among the masses could only slow the pace of onset of the stationary state since, realistically, the masses were not expected to reduce fertility to replacement levels. Only "positive checks" could do that. Eventually population size would reach its limit, and the stationary state would ensue. Profits and thereby further advances in the industrial sector would be held in check by the high cost of corn needed to sustain workers.

This complex evolution of the economy is not understood by the masses. The lower class did not perceive fertility control as redounding to their own well-being. Consequently they were unlikely to opt for "preventative checks" such as later marriage or celibacy as economic conditions worsened.

Preventive checks were more likely to be used by upper classes intent upon maintaining their stations in life. Malthus himself married quite late in his thirties. He worried, however, that if this became the norm among laboring classes, it would lead to immoral types of sexual gratification, causing misery.

Malthus presents a dual fertility regime. The upper classes have the foresight and self-constraint needed to control their fertility and can influence their lifestyles by exercising them. On the other hand, population growth among the high fertility sector is unlikely to be checked sufficiently to reduce the chances of the masses falling below subsistence norms from time to time in bad harvest years. Moreover, subsistence wages and a greater threat of famines are the eventual outcomes as the stationary state emerges under realistic expectations about population growth, technology, and arable land. The death rate, not fertility control, keeps the population at replacement levels. Family planning was not necessarily the solution, since this son of a minister worried that the low fertility needed to maintain higher per capita food supplies in England would result in debasing vices, given the limited methods of controlling conception in his day. There was no viable alternative to "positive checks" in the long run.

The classical economists, influenced by Malthus, paid great attention to a minimum standard of living. They included in the subsistence wage, though, a cultural component, in the sense that wages were somewhat above the income necessary to provide the physiological limit of subsistence. This subsistence wage limited population growth in the stationary state, where wages remained at subsistence levels (Hollander, 1984, p. 141).

Interestingly Karl Marx, who considered Malthus a travesty, broke his value of labor power into two components: a physically related component associated with the minimum necessities that would allow life to sustain itself and multiply and a socially determined component. Thus, in his speech on "Wages, Price and Profit" of 1865 he noted: "Besides the mere physical element, the value of labour is in every country determined by a *traditional standard of life*. It is not mere physical life, but it is the satisfaction of certain wants springing from the social conditions in which people are placed and reared up" (quoted in Hollander, 1984, p. 141; emphasis original).

Again in *Capital I* and *Capital III* (as quoted in Hollander, 1984, pp. 141–2), Marx refers to the fact that in each epoch social definitions of necessities arise that set the value of labor above its physiological subsistence level. Thus the value of labor differs among countries. And in *Capital III* Marx related population growth to prosperity, which creates wages above the value of labor. This is turn causes more marriages, and thereby leads to an increase in population.

However, according to Marx, over historical epochs countries could see their labor value fluctuate above or below social subsistence levels as a result of the overriding forces of technological changes working through the economic system, in particular the capitalist system. In the speech of 1865 he noted: "The historical or social element, entering into the value of labor, may be expanded, or contracted, or altogether extinguished so that nothing remains but the *physical limit*" (quoted in Hollander, 1984, p. 140; emphasis original).

The standard of living argument was prominent among American demographers from the 1880s until the mid-1940s, when it was subsumed under transition theory (Hodgson, 1983). In the latter, fertility declines with industrialization; and the causal agents are to be found in the social structure transformation that occurs as society modernizes. As a part of the industrialization process, changes in the standard of living affect fertility decline, along with "an increasingly complex division of labor, elimination of ascriptive class systems, a competitive social milieu . . ." plus urbanization (ibid., p. 10). But prior to the broad approach of transition theory with its multivariables of socioeconomic modernization, demographers focused upon the inverse relationship between a society's standard of living and fertility rate. Paraphrasing J. B. Clark, Hodgson says:

> He contended that when the level of wages rose in the nineteenth century industrializing societies, the general standard of living was increased for a time period sufficiently long for people to become accustomed to it. They redefined the quantity of goods and services necessary for a satisfactory mode of living. Thereafter, they voluntarily modified their reproductive behavior to preserve their standard of living. When wages rose again, the process was repeated. A "progressive standard of living," increasing from generation to generation, became the norm, and fertility became well controlled. (ibid., p. 5)

In addition, Hodgson finds similarly grounded living standard arguments in the writings of others from 1885 to 1931 (Sumner, 1885, pp. 23–4; Billings, 1893; Ely, 1893, pp. 180–5; Giddings, 1898, pp. 306, 335; Carver, 1904, pp. 169–75; Ross, 1907, pp. 610–11; Taussig, 1911, p. 231; Fetter, 1915, chs 32–4; Willcox, 1916, pp. 1–15; Keller, 1917, pp. 129–39; Sumner and Keller, 1927, pp. 46, 70–1, 76; Bowen, 1931, pp. 172 201–02). Arguments also occur in a number of these writers linking fertility to the living standard of a family's reference group or social class. Various writers emphasized different ascribed motivations, such as the desire for children as farmhands or as old-age support. The living standard assumption is a general behavioral assumption which can subsume many particular behavioral motivations.

Gradually urbanization intensified, and this emerged as a second variable supposedly independent of the living standard constraint. Yet, indirectly it affected this constraint, since in an urban setting children were viewed as contributing less to their self-support and needing more costly inputs. Following their arguments, urban living, then, affected the living standard constraint in two ways. It raised the standard or norm for the family or class, and it reduced the ability of the child to contribute to that standard. Transition theory went beyond this, however, by considering changes in religious and other social codes, the effect of more education on ideas about family size, and the movement away from close identification with an extended family, tribe, or social class.

Yet these ideas about socioeconomic determinants of fertility posited by transition theory proved difficult to test. They failed to provide a close-knit causal sequence leading to a predictable fertility decline. Specifically, transition theory arose from empirical generalization based on pooled national data from European countries. Yet the length of the transition period from high to low fertility varied greatly among countries. Moreover, better data than were available in the mid-1940s cast doubt on the theory.

The relationship between modernization measures and fertility decline was not monotonic. There was no universal pattern in regard to the size and contour of the gap between mortality and fertility decline. Moreover, socioeconomic groups within the countries did not conform to the model. Thus, Coale's study found that subnational groups within European societies exhibited no predictable relationship between fertility decline and levels of industrialization, urbanization, literacy, and infant mortality (Coale 1969, p. 18). And historical demographers could not identify fertility decline with a specific level of economic development. Furthermore, as data became available from developing countries of the Third World, statistical profiles were no more uniform, and transition variables were still only loosely related to fertility decline.

Ronald Freedman notes that classical transition theory referred to a very broad set of structural variables of development. Yet fertility decline today has occurred where only a limited subset of development changes have taken place and where populations are still relatively poor and rural. The literature has yet to identify a subset sufficient to motivate fertility decline, and Freedman speculates that more than one combination of limited variables could suffice (Freedman, 1979, pp. 65–6). The simple form of demographic transition theory is thus refuted (Andorka, 1986, p. 330).

Along these lines, Toni Richards discusses choosing among a variety of statistical models in seeking a more specific and defensible set of variables (Richards, 1983). John Cleland finds that the results of the *World Fertility Survey* support ideational or cultural theories of transition more than structural ones, although he acknowledges that fertility-related cultural changes are them-selves usually a product of economic change (Cleland, 1985, pp. 223–52).

Variables of transition theory are socialization variables, as are those of the living standard norm. Hodgson notes that, beginning in the 1950s in America, there was a deviation from the past 60 years of accumulated research on the importance of the social structure to fertility. Davis, Notestein, and others reversed their position on causation, perhaps influenced by economic development theories of the time, and argued that population decline had to precede development. The burgeoning population growth in many less developed countries was thought to preclude a substantive rise in national saving rates. Many economists felt that a jump in the saving rate was necessary to allow for expanding investment, and thereby growth in per capita income. Suddenly demographers were arguing or hoping that rational peasants could be properly educated to reduce their fertility levels within conditions of economic poverty. Family size became a function of family planning efforts. This policy-oriented approach was spurred by the dire conditions in India prior to agricultural transformation and in China prior to the turnaround in the government's view regarding population pressures. It gained popularity despite the fact that economists have no hard data or widely accepted model simulations measuring the economic consequence of population growth. Publications by the Club of Rome and others tended to mislead those outside the field of economics.

As birthrates began to decline in many Third World countries, population explosion literature lost its appeal. And economic development theory moved beyond the population-savings centered approach (Donaldson, 1984, chapters 4, 7, 8; Lee, 1985, pp. 127–30). Thus, Hodgson concludes that most demographers are likely to return to the social scientific perspective (Hodgson, 1983, p. 29).

The contribution of economists

During the period when demographers were policy-oriented and took on a much more atomistic view of population determinants, some economists, too, were supporting an individualistic approach to examining fertility behavior based on utility maximization. Becker's seminal article in this regard spurred interest in demographics among economists (Becker, 1960). Becker used their familiar tools of consumer behavior analysis in his model of fertility, but enlarged the tool set with theoretical treatment of time allocation and nonmarket household behavior (Becker, 1976). Harvey Leibenstein used the utility approach also, concentrating upon changing tastes as income rises. Status goods become relatively more important compared to expenditures upon children (Leibenstein, 1975).

Easterlin's work, on the other hand, maintained its social science perspective, emphasizing the living standard argument and socialized behavior. He argued that the choice theoretic approach could not explain the swings in fertility, either nationally or among socio-economic groups, and was especially inadequate when applied to the demographic transition.

Easterlin then collaborated with Pollak and Wachter to produce a more tightly structured model of the demographic transition than had existed before. The authors emphasize taste changes related to experienced living standards, along with the effect of higher income upon birth control usage, nutrition, and health (Easterlin, 1969, pp. 127–56; Easterlin, Pollak, and Wachter, 1980, pp. 81–135).

The Easterlin–Pollak–Wachter model and the models building upon Becker's concept are two approaches explaining the demographic transition which are constructed in the methodological mode of economists. Given their dominance in the literature, I will give a full discussion of each in the next chapter. In the next section, I will discuss the interrelation of extended family networks with the living standard norm and tie this in with the Easterlin hypothesis.

BEHAVIORAL ASSUMPTIONS: THE ROLE OF THE EXTENDED FAMILY

Generally, an explanation of fertility transition involves answering two related questions: why is fertility controlled, and how many children will be born under a control regime. In order to answer these questions, behavioral assumptions are posited. Since artificial insemination is ruled out, the minimum number of individuals involved in the production of offspring at any point in time is two. With multiple mates, a parent's total fertility may involve more than one partner over time. Once a child is born to parents, then further births affect the siblings so that behavioral assumptions may involve the nuclear family unit or, where more than one mate is involved, the parenting group and its offspring. The behavior of those producing children may in turn be related to the influence of family members beyond the nuclear grouping(s) and to larger reference groups (Bagozzi and Van Loo, 1980; Beckman, 1978; Hollerbach, 1980; Namboodiri, 1972).

Economic models along the choice theoretic line of construction use the concept of individual utility maximization as a framework for analyzing fertility behavior. Within the nuclear family context, however, a joint utility function must somehow emerge. When an additional child lowers the economic well-being of a sibling, a common outcome, there must be trade-offs between the utility of parents, siblings, and the unborn. Generally the utility approach concentrates upon parental utility when discussing implications of the model, because prediction is more straightforward. However, logically, altruism must be posited so that group welfare of the nuclear family is somehow optimized. Thus it is assumed that parents receive utility from considering more than just their individual welfare, and this is reflected in the objective function that is maximized.

A recent altruistic approach adopted by Becker and Barro leads to a dynastic utility function that depends on the consumption and number of all descendents (Becker and Barro, 1988). Fertility is a positive function of altruistic feelings of a male dynastic head. However, the assumption is made that, for any given propensity toward altruism, the degree of this feeling drops as the number of children rises, helping to limit fertility. This expands on the Becker function, where parental utility depends on the number and "quality" of children, by indicating, if very generally, why children have utility to the dynastic head. An altruistic function in this model does not eliminate the comparison of marginal benefits of children with their marginal cost; but it does change the specification of the cost and benefit functions that determine fertility.

Are parents' preferences for children influenced by other people's preference patterns? Generally, the utility approach has avoided interdependence of preferences beyond the nuclear family because no completely satisfactory way of incorporating inter-dependence into utility models has evolved, even within the family unit context. Individualized choice reflecting established tastes is a cornerstone of the utility framework. It is not a socialization model and is thus difficult to apply to current or secular behavior where tastes are not constant and social interaction influences their evolution. See, however, the contributions of Pollak in modeling interdependent preferences in general (Pollak 1976).

The need to posit some type of group behavior or altruism has entered by another door so to speak: intergenerational transfers. Economists tend to assume that utility maximizers calculate carefully, contrasting costs and benefits over time of consumption of goods or children (Lindert, 1983). They think in terms of the expected net cost or benefit from the choice made. Looking at reproduction incentives, they naturally look for a net cost or benefit of children, usually to the parents, but possibly within a broader context. The utility of children is in part related to old-age security needs, although it is uncertain what size family this need implies. They may also be related to farm or cottage industry labor needs, where the number demanded could be affected by the law of diminishing returns. Children can be viewed as an investment that yields a return over time.

John Caldwell has hypothesized that the demographic transition is related to the direction of intergenerational net transfers. Parental behavior is one of bounded rationality where the bounds are biological and psychological. The social context of actions must be understood in order to understand their rationality. What is rational reproductive behavior in one context may not be in another. In regard to the economics of fertility, there is only one necessary condition for the transition to low rates: children must be a net economic drain over the parents' lives rather than a net contributor. This watershed sets the stage for a decline in birthrates. In particular, the nuclear family with net exenditure upon one's children must arise, among other changes, before fertility will drop. This can occur independently of modernization or industrialization as defined in classical transition theory. Social and psychological changes provide the other necessary inputs into a transition. The direction of intergenerational flows is a net cost approach, but neglects the intangible benefit components present in the usual economic calculus, perhaps considering them among noneconomic aspects of decision making. This restriction of economic benefits to the direction of income flows between parents and children gives a particular focus to the role of economics alone as an explanatory variable within the Caldwell analysis of the demographic transition (Caldwell, 1976).

The importance of net intergenerational flows to the economics of fertility transition has been acknowledged by Robert Willis and incorporated into his theoretical work on the transition. He identifies a need for an altruistic socioeconomic model of family behavior where it is possible for behavior along altruistic lines to support net intergenerational transfers in either direction. Such transfers maintain the group's well-being, of course. The techno-logical/economic regime determines the direction of flows that is optimal from the long-run perspective of economic well-being of ongoing social networks. The behavioral assumption posited is that "the parents have a positive preference for number of children and that they are perfectly altruistic in the sense that they guide and finance the wealth-maximizing pattern of investments in their children's human and physical capital so that the rate of return to capital is always kept equal to the rate of population growth." Willis turns to behavioral norms to assure transfers from children to parents. Offspring are inculcated with an obligation to make such transfers (Willis, 1982, pp. 209, 227.)

The paper concludes that, given a rate of population growth, technological changes lead to new levels of human and physical capital formation that change the net flows among generations, changing the age an individual produces his lifetime wealth relative to the age at which he consumes it in steady-state growth. The paper refers back to the work of Paul Samuelson (1958) wherein overlapping generations provide for each others' security through intergenerational transfers within a social context such as social security in the US. This transfer, however, was from the younger to the older generation to achieve the Golden Rule level of utility. Economic growth models have made much of this rule, since, under conditions where savings must be exacted from the populace to achieve a target growth rate in per capita income, one generation's sacrifices benefit the next.

The grafting of altruistic behavior and interdependent preferences onto the individual utility model produces a cumbersome apparatus for analyzing behavior relating to the dynamics of the demographic transition. The predictions of the model are not straightforward in all cases. Certainly for analytical purposes simpler behavioral arguments of greater consistency would be helpful. Obviously population behavior is of central importance to the family and broader social groupings. And since individualized choices can conflict with family or social welfare, including the welfare of future generations, a model of socialized behavior seems worth pursuing. This is a central reason why the norm methodology is used herein in lieu of the utility methodology; as with the latter, however, behavioral constraints are introduced. Constraint determinants answer the question of how many children. The concept of lifestyles is pivotal in explaining the constraints. It involves certain behavioral assumptions.

The living standard concept presented by Easterlin, while referring to the lifestyle experienced by parents in their family context, does not identify the *ongoing* influence of the enlarged family upon the parents' family size decision. For example, historians and anthropologists have typically found that income and time needed for children comes in part from the extended family. Housing and land can be shared or acquired via family wealth or time inputs. Education is another important child need that depends upon family participation in many situations. Marriage age has been related to these variables. When marriages are family-arranged or sanctioned, as occurs in many parts of the globe, the bestowing of dowries, land, housing, or education all affect the age of marriage and can also affect marital fertility. And time inputs of relatives provide important elements of child support needs.

Economists, among others, have often focused on the desire of parents to provide for their old age by raising children, while ignoring the importance of *continuous reciprocal* family relationships over each member's life, including the stage when children mature and start a family. Other social scientists tell us that a family is a socioeconomic group with ongoing interflows (Caldwell, 1983, pp. 464–5). In agrarian settings marriage age and number of offspring can depend upon housing and land shared by many relatives or acquired through family relationships. And even outside of farming, the family is the basic production and employment source well into the industrialization process (Hagan, 1984). Developing economies at early stages of industrialization are characterized by employment outside of labor markets. Here the family business is a dominant employer and affects the financial well-being of the extended family, and thereby the number of children supportable. Even larger family-owned businesses that hire labor often hire only or mainly clan members so that labor markets have a familial structure.

Consider some examples. In tribal settings, where group cohesion affects survival, the wealthier patriarch has greater landholdings, more wives, children, and dependent clan members than poorer clan heads. And if a clan "brother" has resources, these are generally shared when another member has a need as defined by custom (Caldwell, 1965, 1976). In more urbanized tribal settings such as Kenya, the financing of education is a primary motivation for remitting income to other households of the extended family. Their privately financed school fees are as high as 10 percent of household income (Johnson and Whitelow, 1974).

Usche Isiugo-Abanihe examines the high level of child time provided by relatives in his article on child fosterage in West Africa, where children are thought of as belonging not just to biological parents, but to the kinship group. He notes: "Children may be sent to live with relatives of either parent or exchanged among kinsmen who share kinship obligations and assistance" (Isiugo-Abanihe, p. 56). In return for time put into child raising, relatives receive food and other goods earned by parents freed from child-raising time. Fostering occurs at an early, even infant, age, not just at the time of apprenticeship or education fostering. Isiugo-Abanihe writes:

> The economic costs of children to parents may be lowered by the practice of fostering, while their potential value in terms of old age insurance and other benefits may remain high, leading to a positive intergenerational wealth flow from children to parents. The extended family, on which child fostering is buttressed, acts to even out the hardships of large family size. The delegation of parental roles by fostering out children entails the sharing of child rearing responsibilities, and the removal of the burdens and constraints of prolific childbearing. This also implies that fertility limitation among the educated elite does not guarantee them small family size. (Isiugo-Abanihe, p. 55)

His data show considerable variation in child relocation in Western Africa. In Sierra Leone among some chiefdoms the proportion of children fostered out by a mother aged 30–34 ran as high as 72 percent. (Isiugo-Abanihe, p. 62). The study also shows a very high positive correlation between fostering out children and the space limitations of a household as measured by the number of persons per room. The practice increases with female labor market participation. He concludes: "Fostering may have an impact, directly or indirectly, on the fertility decisions of both natural parents and foster parents, mainly because it serves to reallocate the resources available for raising children within the society" (ibid.,

p. 71). Interestingly, remnants of fostering exist among American blacks.

In rural India a bride leaves her village to reside with her husband and his family. The joint family household consists of the husband's parents and brothers, their wives and their children, all sharing a home and the produce of the farmland. Grandparents tend to look after the children as younger family members work the farm. In colonial Massachusetts the first generation of fathers controlled the land, and thereby the marriage age of sons, according to Philip Greven. And marriage required parental support. As second and third generations became less land-dependent and more urbanized, parental support of sons leaving the land lessened (Greven, 1970, pp. 75, 268).

The sharing of human and physical wealth and time inputs among extended family members is structured by codes of conduct to achieve equitable and reciprocal family relations.[1] It is probably true that a larger *percentage* of family wealth, income, and time is shared in less advanced economic settings. There is a dramatic decline in sharing of direct time as industrialization and its accompanying mobility scatter families from their hamlets and farms. Yet reciprocal ties remain, to assure family well-being and to deal with unexpected income shortfalls due to unemployment, health, and the like. And once education becomes a prerequisite for the maintenance of the family living standard, there is the probability of loans, if not gifts, of education monies from the extended family. As affluence emerges, health needs, travel, cars, and other large ticket items are familiar expenditures by more affluent adults upon children of relatives. And housing remains a large budgetary component, often involving transfers between nuclear households of a family. The transfers may be in skilled labor time of relatives needed to build or expand a shelter or in deed. In modernized Greece, the typical middle class dowry is a

---

[1] For a discussion of various models employed by social scientists in this regard, see R. A. Pollak, "A Transaction Cost Approach to Families and Households," *Journal of Economic Literature*, 23 (June 1985), 581–608. Pollak also emphasizes the importance of the extended family as a security network, concentrating on the efficiency of the family in minimizing transaction costs for many activities such as protection against old age, unemployment, divorce, illness, or death (ibid., p. 588). Viewed within this framework, it would make sense to argue that while families provide social insurance, they will economize on coverage to control costs. This indirectly supports the concept of a *minimum* living level or threshold insured by family members, as put forward in this paper.

flat. Legal aspects of dowries and marriage contracts, however, are changing along with the developing economy.

In sum, the extended family commitments vary among societies and are a result of a socialization process. However, they are not absent in the mobile, affluent societies where there is less opportunity for sharing housing or time directly. There remains even here a network of relatives supportive of a minimum floor based on their norm for deprivation. Loans among the group for housing, education, or to start a business, gifts to the unfortunate, and trust funds for the deserving are a few of the forms redistribution takes.

In the living standard model developed here a basic premise is the existence of mutual support and transfers among generations of relatives to secure family well-being. This translates into a generalized behavioral assumption that family members conform to group norms designed to assure family lifestyle defined in terms of the use of time by family members. Lifestyles often vary among societies, and similar needs such as child care can be met differently in various cultures. Specific time-use matrices of a particular culture, though, are viewed as uniformly subject to this behavioral principle.

The general assumption of ongoing group support is united with the traditional living standard premise, here related to nonmaterial as well as material lifestyle. More generally it is assumed that families have a minimum lifestyle standard or floor which triggers family sharing and affects the number of children considered supportable. The minimum does not remain constant over family generations. Rather, the Easterlin hypothesis that family norms change as their experienced living standards change is adopted. Here the norm is interpreted as a minimum, or floor, and is supportable by time inputs of relatives in case of shortfall. The family does not readily allow family members to suffer from the group-defined measure of destitution. Stated more positively, the sharing of time among relatives allows families to have more security of lifestyle and more progeny. Cultural values, along with technology and the economic structure, determine the use of time freed by increased efficiency in a society. They establish new lifestyle norms for maturing children, who become the next generation's parents. Time is freed incrementally for households and may not be adequate for another child; or time is available unexpectedly to those who are past child-bearing age. It is then absorbed into new lifestyle norms that become constraints for the next generation. The use of time must be examined in an evolutionary framework.

The constraint approach minus the demand or utility apparatus promises to simplify the causative sequence by concentrating upon changes in time use rather than motivations of parents for having children or their cost–benefit ratio to a given generation. It also answers the question of how many children a family will have, a virtue of constraint models often ignored by those unfamiliar with this methodology. Speculation about motivations for having children do not provide a clear cut-off point. This is illustrated by the idea of children as laborers or as old-age security. How many are needed to satisfy this parental concern? The constraint approach predicts a reproduction rate by examining constraint determinants.

EMPIRICAL SUPPORT OF LIVING STANDARD THRESHOLD

Empirical work supports the idea that there is family sharing related to norms of basic needs. Evidence from Africa has already been cited. There, education is to a large degree privately financed, and there is a rising rate of return to schooling. Each family, then, faces rising costs for children as years of schooling are extended. Yet completed education has risen without reducing fertility. In fact, except for the oldest women, marital fertility rises with education. (Mosley, Werner, and Becker, 1982). Large families maintain their education level by favoring their eldest children, who are then obligated to share income with parents and siblings even though they may no longer share the same abode (Gomes, 1984). In fact, in the many countries of the globe which are experiencing rapid urbanization, migrant remittances to rural relatives are well documented in the literature.

The importance of interhousehold transfers in general, some as high as 25 percent of income, has been examined in El Salvador, Columbia, and Brazil (Kaufman, 1981; Kaufman and Lindauer, 1984).) The study by Kaufman and Lindauer presents empirical support for the pivotal connection between family sharing and a living standard floor composed of goods and services. Moreover, they assume that the basic needs threshold that triggers transfers from more to less affluent households of an extended family rises for family groupings in higher income brackets. In such brackets there is more likely to be a transfer of assets as opposed to income or inkind transfers.

Evidence from El Salvador for low-income households in urban areas showed that unearned income transfers plus an estimate of in-kind transfers (probably underestimated) accounted for 11 percent of income. The transfers were from higher to lower income households, particularly to female-headed households. Statistical tests performed showed discontinuity, as would be expected when transfers occur for households below, but not those above, the needs threshold. In other words, the unearned income accrued disproportionately to lower income households.

Armed with these empirical findings, Kaufman and Lindauer propose a behavioral model of extended family networks. Their model includes reference to socially determined behavior patterns and risk, and the similarities to the line of reasoning developed in their paper and this one are brought out in the following paragraphs:[2]

> The common bond between the different family households comprising the same extended family can be considered an implicit social contract. . . . A complex array of socio-historical and anthropological kinship ties generates the contract among the various member households. . . .
>
> We postulate that the terms of the implicit social contract of the extended family are such that the member households, who at a certain point of time happen to be in a relatively more advantaged economic position, have a commitment to transfer resources to those households who happen to be in a disadvantaged position. The transfer of resources will, more specifically, be a function of the basic needs deficit of the poorer household. This commitment may be based on every household's attitude of risk aversion vis-a-vis ever falling below that threshold income required to meet basic expenditures. The assurance that, if needed, a sufficient flow of resources can be realized from other households, provides an

---

[2] After developing the fertility model, I fortuitously discovered these World Bank papers. Their orientation is the concept of "basic needs," and their behavioral motivation is not tied to fertility. While they assume that such needs vary according to income groups, they do not utilize the Easterlin hypothesis to explain the differentials among families. Moreover, the composition of a family's living standard is narrower, being identified only in terms of goods and services.

incentive for all the households within the extended family to both join and maintain the contract. . . .

A major tenet of our analysis is that a basic needs level need not be assumed to be the same across different extended families. An extended family with a relatively high aggregate income will have a higher standard for basic needs than an extended family with low aggregate income. 'Decent standards' for food, clothing, education and shelter will mean somewhat different things for each extended family since these standards are perceived by each family group. (Kaufman and Lindauer, pp. 11, 13)

ECONOMICS OF FERTILITY AND THE SECULAR PATTERN OF TIME USE

Children are generally supported through the work effort of adults. In low-technology, agrarian societies, work time is spent in the home and nearby environs, and thus in the presence of children. As an agrarian economy gives way to industrial development, home production declines. Various goods are more efficiently produced outside the household, and new goods not producible at home are sought. In addition, household production becomes more efficient with the aid of market-produced goods. However, certain tasks allotted to the female, including child care, lend themselves less readily, if at all, to efficiency gains.

The rise in labor productivity, along with technology advances, means less time is needed to produce many goods, and new goods and services can be added to the consumption set. Workers, we may assume, wish to minimize their work effort per goods set and maximize their living standard, composed of goods and leisure. Thus, with modernization, first the male and then the female shift work time away from home production toward higher productivity market production.

Monetary income and expenditures per family member rise as more work hours are spent by males and females in wage employ. Total work time does not rise, however, and eventually falls as families acquire more goods with less labor time.[3]Leisure time

---

[3] An exception is where surplus labor exists in agrarian settings. With industrial development, labor is withdrawn from the land, the available labor hours in agriculture decline, and the work hours of remaining workers rise. Those joining the industrial labor pool also work longer hours than previously.

(defined here simply as time not spent in market production) takes up the slack, eventually rising with affluence.

As economic development proceeds, fertility eventually drops, although it can fluctuate over shorter intervals. Time diverted from numbers of children is still to a great degree devoted to children, albeit indirectly in the pursuit of more goods and services per child. Increases in expenditures per child for housing, education, health, transportation, and the like absorb large portions of the increased earnings per hour of parents. And time devoted to this extends over a long portion of each offspring's life as specialization and division of labor intensify and lead to a later age of financial independence for children.

What is the relationship between these monetary, time, and goods expenditure patterns and fertility? As economic development occurs, why is more income shared with fewer children? What determines the allocation of adult time among child care, leisure activity, and market production of goods and services for parents and for children? Does affluence result in more or fewer adult hours being devoted directly and indirectly to children as fertility drops but children are provided more goods and services, not only each year but into later ages? Are increased leisure hours with affluence gained from increased productivity of work time alone, or does leisure also arise from a decline in childcare hours?[4] Do the time-absorbing education requirements of changing technology affect fertility?

An analysis of time allocation is needed to answer questions of this nature that are grounded in the economics of fertility. The Chicago–Columbia approach to modeling fertility addresses such questions within a time-use mode of analysis, and a brief introduction to this approach is presented. The reader should keep in mind that, to date, these models have been most fruitfully applied to short-run demographic changes within a given society at higher living standard levels (T. W. Schultz, 1974, p. 20 and *passim*).

---

[4] Certainly at a point in time there is an inverse relationship between leisure and the number of existing children, as household time allocation studies show. (See, e.g., Gronau, 1977, p. 1101, for a summary of US and Israel studies and World Bank, 1984, for the Philippines.) However it is not certain that over the secular development path, later generations of parents gain leisure by spending less direct plus indirect time upon children. As family size drops with modernization, the support level and duration for each child both increase. For example, in affluent economies, college education expenditures require large amounts of earnings and hence work time in many cases, while such time is not required for most children in underdeveloped economies.

4
Economic Modeling of Fertility

The lifestyle model has heretofore been considered an economic model of fertility, as has the Chicago model which emphasizes the opportunity cost of the mother's time. Both have a reputation within the demographic literature. Economic models of fertility have introduced the choice constraint approach, emphasized certain economic variables as fertility determinants, and utilized a time framework of analysis. But the methodology is fairly intimidating to the noninitiated. Moreover, its complexity can mask crucial aspects of the analysis that affect the conclusions. In this chapter I will look beyond this complexity to examine pertinent aspects of the models and contrast them with the current analysis which utilizes certain constructs of each.

THE CHICAGO–COLUMBIA THEORY OF FERTILITY

Fertility models of the Chicago–Columbia mode treat the demand for children as a function of parental tastes, household income from all sources, and the relative cost of children. Children are assumed to be time-intensive to raise and to absorb a large part of the mother's time. This time has an opportunity cost reflected in market wages. Potentially, time spent at leisure or caring for children could be used to earn income. The income the mother could earn without such competing activities is called "full income."

The Chicago–Columbia theory of fertility produces a general equilibrium model in which the allocation of the woman's time to wage employment, household work, skills training, and child-raising are determined simultaneously to maximize parental utility. That is to say, the various models have been oriented toward the relationship between fertility and the value of the mother's time in the context of labor market employment. The analytical framework is very complex, with multilayered assumptions. I propose to present here a verbal summary of salient aspects of the paradigm. In the last section I conclude that the living standard theory explains the determining element of these models: the under-explored area of expenditures per child.

The Chicago–Columbia models of fertility parallel the choice theoretic approach to modeling household behavior related to consumption of goods, services, and leisure. Utility maximization is the objective function determining time allocation. Utility arises when time is used for consumption or enjoyment of time-using "commodities" – activities such as travel, entertainment, eating, or raising children. Time, goods, services and resources are combined to produce commodities. A commodity does not have a fixed set of inputs per output level. That is, the commodity production function allows for variable coefficients of production. Children are treated in some models as themselves a commodity and in others as an input into the commodity "family life." Children, then, unlike goods, may be desired for their own sakes as utility-generating commodities.

Parents have time to "spend" in their pursuit of satisfaction or utility. Given the productivity of time, market employment will produce income at a certain rate that can be used to purchase goods and services. The parental household combines goods, services, resources, and time to create utility-generating activities such as raising children, entertaining friends, maintaining health, and pursuing intellectual and religious interests. Such commodities are produced by the nuclear household using variable combinations of goods, services, resources, and family time.

The utility functions for commodities and children are viewed from a lifetime perspective. Parents are assumed to be aware of their intertemporal welfare functions when they conceive children, since a child requires many hours of time extending over future years. This means that commitment of time to children affects time allocation to other commodities into the future. Moreover, it is assumed that parents can calculate the potential lifetime value of their work, which in turn is a constraint upon consumption of commodities. Models of this type are referred to as static, one-period models.

The utility generated by commodities cannot be measured, but commodities can be given a preference ordering. Parents then compare the satisfaction from time spent in pursuit of additional amounts of various commodities and allocate their time so as to maximize utility. Given parental tastes and time constraints, this occurs when the marginal utilities from the last hour spent on each commodity are equivalent.

As mentioned, utility arises not from consumption of goods per se, but from the more limited commodity set, which is an argument of the utility function. The household utility function is assumed to be internally consistent. Models finesse the problem of uniting the mother's and father's utility functions in more than one way. Generally, the siblings' functions are ignored, and their welfare is subsumed under parental preferences.

The degree to which individual inputs are substitutes for one another in producing commodities depends upon the technology of the household production function, a given. This technology is different for each commodity. Specifically, when costs are minimized, some commodities are more time-intensive than others for any set of relative prices of time and other inputs. As the cost of time relative to other inputs rises, households will conserve on direct time inputs into commodities. But there are limits to substitution of, for example, goods for time in the production function. These substitution constraints are more limiting for time-intensive technology. Children are said to be relatively time-intensive, as are luxury commodities – commodities that are very income-elastic so that relatively more are consumed as income rises.

Children, like goods and services, can be identified by basic characteristics and can vary according to the set of quality characteristics they have. There is a cost function for basic and quality characteristics, so that children vary in cost by their number and quality. Within limits, characteristics are producible in a more or less time-intensive way. Changes in the relative costs of inputs will change the combinations used in producing basic and quality characteristics. Children, then, like hi-fi equipment or autos, vary in quality and cost depending upon utilization of resources in their "production." As stated an important component of basic child costs is the economic value of the mother's time. Education is identified as a major cost of quality. (Of course, when education is compulsory through some level, then only part of educational spending is discretionary, and the choice model is constrained in this respect.)

While tastes for children are given, exogenously determined, it is acknowledged that when the model is applied to centuries of intergenerational behavior, changes in basic social factors affecting tastes can alter them. Tastes, then, are a parameter of the model; but an important assumption is made: as income rises, parents of any generation want children with more quality characteristics. That is, when income rises, and the relative cost of quality and quantity are constant, parents will want to spend more on each child.

Higher income arising from increased wages, then, has two substitution and two income effects upon numbers of children and/ or expenditures per child, some of which are offsetting. First, consider the substitution effects. Substitution occurs in consumption when, because the child costs more in foregone income, time is diverted from numbers of children to consumption of goods-intensive commodities. The mother in particular is said to respond to higher wages by raising fewer children. Substitution occurs in production when, as the relative cost of time rises, goods and services substitute for direct time in raising children. Consumer durables, nurseries, and summer camps reduce direct parental time inputs.

Second, turning to the income effects, note that as income rises, parents can afford more children. Normally this would tend to raise numbers and expenditures per child. But there is a second income effect. As income rises, parents have a taste for much higher quality children. The strong quality assumption reflects observation of expenditure patterns in advanced countries. In such societies, as income rises, fertility drops, and greatly increased expenditures per child occur. Many such outlays in no way substitute for direct time spent with an individual child. That is, while there are some expenditures per child that substitute for direct parental time as its opportunity cost rises, this substitution effect does not account for the preponderance of increases in goods inputs that occur in affluent families.

In fact, expenditures per child rise so much that it is thought that, as income rises, child quality substitutes for numbers. Otherwise, substitution in consumption would have to be a sufficient condition for explaining fertility declines over the demographic transition. Yet, the substitution of other commodities for children as their relative costs change is not presumed to be strong enough to account for the decline in fertility (Willis, 1973, p. 39).

Here, then, the income elasticities of quality and quantity are joined. Affluent parents want fewer children because their opportunity cost is high (substitution effects) and because of a strong preference for higher quality children. The income-quality relationship of the taste function posited in the model plays an important part in explaining the fall in fertility. And this relationship is developed along lines analogous to that between quality of goods and income, with perhaps one exception: as income rises and higher quality goods are demanded, the number of such goods consumed normally does not drop.

In sum, the pattern of commodity preferences plus the relative cost of commodities, measured by an index of goods time, determine how time is allocated between work, leisure, and children. For example, a decline in work time could be traced to a decline in productivity of such time and hence in wages, causing workers to shift toward time-intensive commodities that are now relatively less expensive. Or it could be caused by a rise in income (wages) that leads to relatively greater preference for household production of time-intensive commodities, despite their higher opportunity cost in foregone goods time as wages rise.

Becker says that the secular decline in work time as countries' income per capita rises is traceable to the preference for time-intensive luxuries as earnings rise. On the other hand, the number of children demanded declines as their relative cost rises, although spending upon each child rises, thereby raising each child's "quality." And children are produced in a more goods-intensive, less time-intensive manner. That is, less time is allocated directly to each child relative to the indirect time spent on goods per child.

Total parental time devoted to children, the sum of time to supply goods used in raising children plus direct time used to produce children, need not decline as numbers fall. However, children are not income-elastic in the sense of luxury or leisure-intensive commodities, which cause a decline in work time to accommodate increased direct time inputs as incomes rise. This is explained simply as an empirical fact. Historically, children have become more expensive relative to goods-intensive commodities, and their numbers have dropped, while their quality has risen.

Thus, while children and goods are not substitutes per se, time-intensive children and goods-intensive commodities are to some degree substitutes since a change in the opportunity cost of commodity time sets in motion adjustments in consumption patterns according to relative cost changes. When we refer to the substitution between goods, children, and leisure, then, we are referring to an indirect substitution. And unlike other time-intensive commodities, children are not highly income-elastic, although total expenditures upon children are.

In one respect children and goods are complements. For a given quality of child, there is a limit to the substitution between goods and direct time as inputs into production of children. And the goods component limit rises with quality enhancement. These supplementary goods can change over time and are a part of the cost of children, along with the opportunity cost of parental time – in particular the mother's time measured in foregone wages.

The Chicago–Columbia model predicts that the household's allocation of time by parents, particularly the mother, changes with shifts in the relative costs of goods, leisure, and children. The responsiveness of time allocation to relative cost changes must be established empirically. If these time-absorbing activities are not close substitutes in consumption, as indeed may be the case, then income/quality changes must explain most of the variations in fertility. Or, over longer periods, a whole new taste function could account for fertility changes within the choice theoretic framework. Changes in taste factors are not emphasized, however, leading Leibenstein to view changes in tastes as an alternative explanation of fertility changes (Leibenstein, 1974, pp. 468, 471).

Children as intermediate inputs

The analysis becomes even more complex in certain treatments where parental utility is a function of a commodity whose inputs include children. This output comes from the activity involving consumption of the services of goods or children or some combination. For example, combining goods, child services, and family time, the commodity "family life" is produced and yields utility that can be compared with other commodities producible with goods and time but not children. The difference between rural and urban fertility has been explained utilizing a model with children as productive agents. Their productivity is said to be higher in agrarian settings because they enter into production more extensively as farm helpers.

Here children are treated as intermediate inputs used to produce a commodity that yields utility (Schultz, 1980). Parents invest in children as productive agents. The way in which the child's behavior on the parents' behalf is controlled is not made explicit. Family life can be produced with more or less children. Parents will minimize the cost of production of this commodity by substitution among inputs. This implies a household production function whose technology determines the elasticity of substitution among factors of production, including children. The demand for children is treated as a derived demand arising from the demand for the commodity they produce. As the cost of children (not always clearly defined) rises, fewer children are demanded, and other inputs substitute in production. There is a technically defined limit to substitution. In this analysis, goods are also intermediate factors of production used to produce the commodity "family life." The production function for family life is said to be time-intensive relative to other commodities because of children.

Children of different quality would affect production differently. Presumably higher quality children have higher productivity, and thus there can be a quality/quantity trade-off in production. The trade-off would depend in part upon the relative cost of higher and lower quality children. Any rise in the cost of child quality could lead to substitution toward lower quality children.

Treating children as intermediate inputs leads to consideration of a production function for children which determines their cost. This function is time-intensive, specifically in respect to the wife's time, and presumably in comparison with goods production. Thus a rise in the wage rate of women raises the cost of children, and thereby the relative cost of the commodity "family life." Of course, the rise in wages also creates an income effect so that more commodities are affordable. This can offset to some degree the substitution effect arising from higher cost, which, by itself, reduces the quantity of children demanded as inputs.[1]

The income effect alone results in more affluent parents enjoying more of the commodity family life, among other commodities. Higher incomes accompany higher productive capacity and lead to more children, *ceteris paribus*. But, if the cost of producing children relative to other inputs rises as income rises, then other inputs will be substituted for children. Or, if the relative cost of quality rises as income rises, lower quality children will be substituted in production. Presumably as income rises, the cost of producing quality relative to quantity of children falls, leading to higher quality children and lower fertility. This presumes that quality and quantity are indeed substitutes and not complements in the production function.

When children are treated as intermediate inputs, this means the technology of the household production function affects fertility, along with the taste for family life as income changes. This technology and its parameters, however, also constitute an under-explored topic.

APPLICATIONS TO DEMOGRAPHIC TRANSITION

It will be helpful at this point to recap certain aspects of changing fertility patterns. Over generations, as economic development occurs and incomes rise, the number of children born to a woman drops, while the expenditures upon goods and services per child rise. Affluent parents spend more on goods, services, and children and have more leisure time. The drop in fertility over time is large enough to reduce family size considerably, even though development brings lower mortality rates among infants and children. This decline in family size allows much higher expenditures per child out of rising income than could occur if family size remained constant. Why do societies that could "afford" larger families have smaller ones? Do economic variables play a large part in the drop in fertility?

---

[1] As Gronau points out, for a family raising children who absorb large amounts of market-produced, as opposed to home-produced, goods, a rise in the mother's wage lowers child costs (Gronau, 1977). Such children are goods-intensive rather than time-intensive. Time intensity may vary with age.

Using the simplistic interpretation of the choice theoretic frame of reference, a decline in fertility could be explained by the dominance of the substitution effect over the income effect. This reasoning goes as follows: as incomes rise, parents desire more goods, leisure, and children. Since the source of increased income is improved labor productivity, they can achieve this with fewer hours spent producing goods. However, to the degree that wage rises increase the opportunity cost of the mother's time, the cost of children relative to less labor-intensive activities rises. Thus, the rise in wages of females results in a substitution of relatively cheaper commodities for relatively costlier children. Following this line of thought, when both income and the relative cost of children rise while fertility drops, the substitution effect is said to dominate: children are given up so as to consume more goods-intensive commodities which are relatively cheaper.

The drop in numbers does not mean that less is spent upon children. As incomes rise, expenditures upon children, other than the mother's direct time, rise. Children become more goods- and service-intensive while their numbers drop. The mother's time is devoted to earning more goods for her existing family rather than having another child. Parents, then, prefer more goods per family member as goods become relatively cheap. Presumably to some degree goods enjoyed by parents *and* parental spending upon siblings are substitutes for the additional child. And leisure may be a substitute for children, since if less time is given to offspring, some could be devoted to leisure (Oppong, 1983, p. 549). Leisure, like children, is time-intensive, with a higher relative cost as wages rise. Unlike the case of children, however, there is a secular increase in leisure. The income effect is said to dominate, resulting in less work time, even though the opportunity cost of leisure time rises.

The increase in expenditures per child as wages rise goes beyond a pure substitution effect where lower-cost goods and services substitute for the mother's time in raising children. It involves altered patterns of spending most of which cannot be related to lower costs for outlays. Education expenditures are one example. This behavior is related to the effect of income upon tastes in the Chicago–Columbia model. As income rises, parents prefer children of higher "quality," meaning children who absorb more goods and services. Since income constraints exist and tastes demand much higher expenditures per child, the number of children is reduced to allow the quality to rise (Becker and Lewis, 1974).

In fact, without the quality–taste factor, the pure income effect could dominate the substitution effect since, even though the cost of the mother's direct child care hours rises, the cost of goods and services per child drops as labor productivity and wages rise, moderating the increase in the cost of children of a given quality. Moreover, most writers using the choice theoretic approach assume that the pure substitution effect is low. This leaves the trade-off between quality and quantity as income rises as the main explanation for reduced fertility. That is, with the increased income from the father's work time and the mother's increased in-home productivity, more children are supportable. Even though the cost of the mother's time rises, with a low elasticity of substitution between children and commodities, the income effect should dominate. The fact that it does not must be due to the quality–quantity taste preference as income rises.

This approach to fertility, then, points to a need to understand the relationship between expenditures per child and fertility if the demographic transition is to be explained. In fact, Schultz noted this as early as 1974 (T. W. Schultz, 1974, p. 10). And Yoram Ben-Porath points out that the introduction of quality as a choice variable in fertility analysis still leaves the behavioral motivation "dramatically under-identified." He also notes that from an altruistic standpoint, "the decision between the number of children and their 'quality' is inconceivable without reference to the parents' standard of living" (Ben-Porath, 1973, pp. 217–18). The living standard model developed here deals with this relationship in the secular context of both less and more developed economies.

EASTERLIN'S EXPERIENCED LIVING STANDARD HYPOTHESIS

Easterlin views the Columbia–Chicago fertility models as incomplete because tastes and important "supply-side" variables such as the impact of lactation practices, nutrition, and infant mortality are treated as exogenous. Moreover, he argues that because the Chicago–Columbia models hold tastes fixed, they are not general enough even for "demand-side" analysis. And demand variables are determining in his model only for modernized societies with sophisticated birth control technology, high health standards, and good nutrition. He notes, however, that the choice theoretic framework of economics is applicable to fertility analysis and is relevant in particular to high income economies. It is simply inadequate in scope, treating important socioeconomic variables as exogenous.

Thus Easterlin accepts the idea that the relative cost of children compared to other budgetary expenditures influences fertility to a limited degree. And one determinant of the cost of children is the opportunity cost of the mother's time; although Easterlin, along with others, points out that its exact importance is yet to be empiricaly established. By contrast, Easterlin views changes in the determinants of taste as having major impact upon the behavior of modern fertility levels. In 1969 he wrote, "Perhaps the greatest obstacle so far to development of a unified socioeconomic theory of fertility . . . lies in the subject of tastes" (Easterlin, 1969, p. 133).

One problem with applying economic analytical frameworks to demography is the fact that taste formation or taste changes are generally taken to be outside the purview of economics. Intertemporal taste changes related to income shifts are specified to some degree when economists label goods as normal, inferior, or luxury. Expenditures upon normal goods rise in proportion to income. Those for inferior (luxury) goods rise less (more) than proportionately. Determinants of the income elasticity of goods are not analyzed except perhaps to note that the stomach is limited, and therefore food is income-inelastic. There is no explanation, for example, of why consumers purchase relatively more luxury goods such as yachts as their income rises even though such goods are time-intensive and thus increasingly expensive to consume as the cost of time rises. Generally the classification results on empirical observation, as opposed to, say, the sociological factors affecting this taste structure.

In fact, the sociology of taste formation is not appealing to the theoretical economist when it embraces the idea that tastes are influenced by relative income. The economists' choice theory is built upon individual utility maximization by consumers with separable utility functions that are responsive to price variations. It presumes that the taste determinants of these utility functions are stable, at least in the short run, and that short-run changes in relative incomes do not rearrange preference maps. Income, rather, enters as a constraint upon utility maximization, leaving relative prices as the stellar explanatory variable.

Even though consumption theory does not treat tastes as endogenous, the consumer choice model has proved a powerful tool of analysis when applied to goods consumption. A point to be noted, however, is that its application to fertility behavior is new. That is, prior to the Chicago–Columbia fertility analysis, goods and children were not treated as substitutes in the utility function. On the other hand, there has been a long history treating income as a constraint upon fertility. In particular, birth control is often assumed to be a response to the desire to maintain some living standard, given income potentials.

In assessing the Chicago–Columbia analysis, Easterlin accepts the idea that relative prices will influence fertility to a limited degree (Easterlin, 1969 and 1980). But he emphasizes the importance of the living standard idea, which has much broader acceptance and precedence. His approach is to introduce a simplified taste function, one that is testable and related to experienced living standards. The income constraint upon fertility then depends upon the difference between current and experienced income. The genesis of his idea is found in his 1968 NBER publication as follows:

> In other words, experience with previous higher income levels alters "tastes" and thereby consumption behavior. Young persons currently in the childbearing ages a few years before were dependent members of their parents' households, and it seems plausible that the consumption levels experienced in the parents' households among other things served to shape their current preferences in much the same way a higher income level would affect those of a given household. Moreover the situation in the parents' household when the children were in their teens would seem more relevant than when the children were quite young.
>
> In a developing economy the second generation's income at age 20–24 is typically greater than the first generation's was at that age. The second generation could thus achieve the consumption levels the first generation had at age 20–24 and have something left over for other purposes, such as saving or increased family size. But if the *desired* consumption level inherited by children from their parents relates to the parents' situation not at age 20–24 but at, say 35–44, then it is less certain that the second generation's income at 20–24 will suffice to achieve the desired consumption level. In other words,

there is an intergenerational effect tending to increase consumption at a given income level. Clearly by varying the parameters involved one could develop alternative models in which secular growth in absolute income was accopanied by increasing, decreasing or constant fertility.

(Easterlin, 1968, pp. 124–5)

The analytical insight and potential of this hypothesis have been broadly acknowledged; but the hypothesis was not formally incorporated into a general theory of fertility until the publication in 1980 of a paper by Easterlin, Pollak, and Wachter. Surprisingly, even here it is not the centerpiece of the analysis of the demographic transition. In fact, discussion of the impact of taste changes does not go beyond the earlier treatment by Easterlin.

THE EASTERLIN–POLLAK–WACHTER (PENNSYLVANIA) MODEL

Fertility decisions in what has been called the Pennsylvania model are the result of parental (married) utility maximization. The parents' joint utility function is more complex than the Chicago–Columbia function, in terms of both its arguments and its constraints. Like the Chicago–Columbia model, utility is a function of a vector of commodities produced by the household using time and goods. Given the household technology set, the commodity collection is producible from the goods collection set and the time allocation vector.

Children, however, are not included in the commodity set. Completed family size is a separate argument of the utility function. Moreover, the addition of fertility to the utility function is said to require that several "socialization" variables prevalent in sociological and anthropological studies of family size and fertility be included as arguments. Principal examples are frequency of intercourse, the use of contraceptive techniques, infant mortality, and practices such as lactation or sex taboos. Obviously some of these variables produce disutility.

A twist is introduced to utilize the Easterlin hypothesis and make taste an endogenous variable. The preference ordering over the arguments of the utility function – commodities, family size, and socialization variables – is a conditional ordering. It depends upon past experience of the parents during their teenage years as members of their parents' household (intra-family model) or as members of a social group (socialization model). Thus exposure to the tastes of their family or socioeconomic cohorts during formative years determines the preference ordering of the new generation. Such experiences set norms for consumption and family size. According to the authors, these norms can be interpreted in several ways: as aspiration levels, "bliss" levels, or "necessary" or "subsistence" levels.

Norms are parameters of the model. Thus, rather than saying that tastes are given, the Pennsylvania model takes experienced consumption and parental family size as givens. They are a function of previous generation averages and change over time. Parental preferences for goods over children then depend upon these norms.

The model sets up four constraints upon the utility function: the budget constraint expressed in time value, the household technology, and two multivariate functions, one for births and one for infant mortality. Births are constrained by social variables and by nutrition, health, and the reproductive span of the household.[2] Deaths are also affected by nutrition and health, certain social variables, and births.

Preference norms for family size may be high or low relative to the constraint upon births. If the norm is low enough, this constraint is not binding. If the norm is high relative to the health and nutrition variables that limit births, the desired family size can exceed the birth constraint level. This fact leads to a certain duality in the model. Although tastes are made endogenous to the model through norm parameters that affect preferences, the authors note that for pre-modern and early modern stages of development fertility preferences play little if any role. Families are likely to be smaller than parents would like in very impoverished economies where nutrition and health are poor. In such cases the household does not control births and does not necessarily relate nutrition or health to birthrate or infant mortality rate. Nutrition and health play an unperceived role in determining fertility. Here the authors spotlight the implications of better economic conditions for improving nutrition and health, and thereby raising fertility levels.

---

[2] Poor nutrition is thought to affect birth intervals by prolonging postpartum amenorrhea, and possibly to lower fecundity through reducing the body's stored fat level to a point of insufficient calories. For a concise discussion of this and bibliography, see Mosk, 1983, Appendix 8.

Household surveys and observed behavior document the fact that there is little if any deliberate parental control of births in the poorest underdeveloped countries among most families. Only social norms or practices limit fecundity. Societies that do not control fertility other than indirectly via social practices or norms are called "natural fertility societies." In a natural fertility society where malnutrition is not rampant, social controls – norms regarding lactation, sexual taboos, marriage customs – will limit fecundity, as opposed to nutrition or health. Rural societies are likely to be governed by social controls. Even though the authors emphasize the importance in less developed countries of socially controlled fertility, they do not explore determinants of these norms.

Natural fertility societies, then, may not have unwanted fertility. When desired family size is high, but nutrition, health, and infant mortality constrain it, parents want more children than their lifetime fertility allows. If births are above desired levels, then the absence of controls indicates that contraception costs or disutility exceed their utility. Even outside natural fertility states, where births are controlled, they may not be controlled enough to avoid all unwanted fertility. There is a trade-off indicating some drawbacks to contraception. In advanced societies with no unwanted births, the birth function's socioeconomic variables do not constrain fertility.

Over the demographic transition, actual fertility is related to the behavior of desired fertility changes and natural fertility changes. As societies modernize and nutrition and health improve, while infant deaths fall, natural fertility rises, then levels off. Desired fertility, on the other hand, trends downward as modernization takes hold, due to changes in tastes as determined by taste norm parameters and increases in the relative prices of inputs required for children. The rise in natural fertility causes completed family size to rise so long as no control is practised outside social controls. Presumably social controls are unchanged. Then family size falls as the cost or disutility of birth control techniques is outweighed by the disutility of unwanted fertility. Without controls, fertility can be thought of as "supply"-determined; with controls, demand factors are determining. Of course, societies can have subgroups in various stages of the demographic transition. This presents an aggregation problem for the empirical investigator.

The model focuses on natural fertility regimes and the transition to controls. The social or biological variables emphasized by sociologists and anthropologists are incorporated in both the utility function and constraints. Taste determinants, on the other hand, are merely introduced as parameters of the utility function. Moreover, in natural fertility regimes they play no role. In controlled fertility societies, however, they may be as important or more so than the relative cost of children.

The idea that relative costs may be overshadowed by taste changes is based on the argument that there is little research on the technology of child-rearing showing that it must be time-intensive for the mother independent of prices and tastes. That is to say, as the relative price of children rises with the mother's wage rate, children may be raised in much less time-intensive ways. Fertility may be dropping because taste norm parameters change with the higher experienced consumption accompanying rising wages over time. Of course, if the Chicago–Columbia emphasis upon the income elasticity of quality and inelasticity of quantity is treated as a taste factor, then the two theories are not as far apart, although the time intensity of children remains uncertain.

The authors hypothesize that the correlation between female education and smaller families may result from the effect of education upon the family's preference ordering over commodities and children. Others, of course, have made the same point. This counters the Chicago–Columbia hypothesis that the effect of higher education is to cause a higher wage opportunity cost of children, raising their relative cost and reducing fertility, while tastes remain fixed.

A DIFFERENT MODELING OF THE EASTERLIN HYPOTHESIS

Norms of social behavior evolve from purpose or need according to sociologists and anthropologists. This is true of norms affecting fertility. Historians have found rationales for socialized behavior, including marriage customs, sexual codes, and other variables affecting birthrates. And they have chronicled the many varieties of birth control techniques that predate modern technology. Most important, investigators have linked socialized behavior in poor economies to maintenance of living standards. Acceptance of this linkage means that the Easterlin thesis that experienced living standards affect fertility is more general than the Pennsylvania model allows. In particular, it has impact within what the model identifies as a natural fertility regime where social practices influence birthrates.

Consider the implications of the argument that fertility controls arise in response to a threat to the group's well-being. When economies are technically sophisticated enough so that families can stabilize their basic consumption level, more or less, then if this level is threatened by unlimited fecundity, social controls to limit births will emerge. Marriage arrangements are among the most common. And there is considerable literature documenting various pre-modern procedures, including separation of the couple in times of bad harvest. In many settings sexual partners do not use more direct forms of birth control. Such was the situation, for example, for periods of history in the West when, for religious reasons, direct birth control mechanisms were not acceptable. Data for European groups in the 1800s show that marriage age and incidence vary inversely with mortality (Mosk, 1983, p. 7). However, directly controlled fertility is also influenced by the group norm, as in the case of religious codes or laws. Abortion or infanticide may also be socially sanctioned responses to fertility levels that threaten the society. As Leibenstein notes:

> The high fertility rates in underdeveloped countries are considerably below their biological maximum – probably 40–60 percent below the Hutterite level. Therefore, even in instances where fertility is traditionally high, there is a considerable degree of control. Furthermore, there exists a wide variety of traditional child spacing and family size controls – deferred marriage, abortions, taboos on sexual intercourse, long periods of lactation, coitus interruptus, etc. One need not specify all possible means. Innumerable means have been known in the past. Furthermore, all means are substitutes to some degree for all other means. Finally, we can point to the fact that many of the countries that achieved their fertility decline earlier did so prior to the widespread distribution of modern contraceptive practices. (Leibenstein, 1975, pp. 2–3)

By contrast, the Pennsylvania model's explanation of rising fertility at the onset of transition emphasizes the effect of prosperity on supply-side constraints of poor health and nutrition. As these improve, conception rises. Falling fertility must await the point at which the unmet desire for larger families due to poor nutrition or health (related to family size norms) no longer exists, and tastes for children decline. In the model developed here, the living standard constraint enters at the onset of the demographic transition as a major variable. Changes in fertility do not depend on the effect of health and nutrition on a woman's ability to conceive. Rising norms for health and food, however, can affect lifestyle standards and thereby fertility.

Compared to the Pennsylvania model, the approach here extends and generalizes the importance of the living standard constraint. The latter affects less impoverished populations that do not use direct techniques to prevent pregnancy, yet limit fecundity through socially sanctioned behavior in order to stabilize their well-being. It is consistent with the fact that more densely populated, less developed countries that have been successful in supporting more people and have some technical control over their lifestyles, but are still very poor, tend to have lower birthrates. They use pre-modern or a mixture of pre-modern and modern means to lower fertility below that of less densely populated, less developed countries. This approach can also explain variations in the rise of fertility preceding its fall.

Here an argument is made for refining somewhat Easterlin's delineation of natural fertility regimes. Natural fertility regimes can be defined by the absence of socialized efforts to restrain fertility. In fact, their social goal is likely to be to maximize births to assure group survival. They may adopt behavior affecting, for example, the spacing of children that collective wisdom shows is helpful to the mother's survival and future fertility, as well as the child's health. Other behavior of socioeconomic or cultural origins may inadvertently limit births but not be designed to do so. The result is that natural fertility regimes differ in these behavior patterns. They also differ in health and nutrition. Consequently they vary in regard to fertility rates but generally have relatively high rates. Their common thread is the absence of societal efforts to limit births. There is no norm for family size.

Once poorer societies seek to control fertility, some of these areas of socially controlled behavior may evolve into useful means of restricting population. These pre-modern methods of birth control are cheap and generally available, if not equally acceptable. They have been tied to social efforts to avoid falling below very modest lifestyle floors. Presumably they are preferable to infanticide as a way of restraining population size. (At least one, marriage age, can be tied to lifestyle maintenence in affluent societies.) The absence of more direct or modern birth control techniques, then, does not establish that societies are not seeking to maintain their living standards by limiting fertility. Moreover, when such societies influence births in order to maintain living standards, periods of prosperity will ease the constraints on lifestyles and lead to more children.

In developing my model, I drop the conceptual apparatus of the Chicago–Columbia paradigm of household production of commodities and introduce a simpler behavioral constraint model. I highlight socialized standards for time expenditure per child as a constraint upon fertility in poorer and richer societies, where either social or more direct methods of limiting births are practised. Regimes without such practices to limit fecundity are thus outside the model. Hence the model does not apply to impoverished situations where nutrition and health are dominant determinants of fertility, such as certain African societies of very low technical skills where social practices affect fertility but do not stabilize consumption levels. Of course, in some poorer societies that limit births, harvest failures can still influence nutrition, and thereby infant mortality. Infant mortality is included as an argument of certain norm functions.

My model unites the relationship between expenditures per child and fertility (or what is called the quality–quantity mix in the Chicago–Columbia model) with Easterlin's relationship between experienced lifestyle and fertility in a model focusing upon norms as constraints upon family size. In doing so, the assumption is made that familial living standards are influenced and supported by the group as opposed to only parents. And time becomes the denominator or numeraire for all constraint norms. The model is in harmony with Caldwell's perspective that fertility research must encompass the use of *all* time (Caldwell, 1983, p. 464).

The time framework is adapted from Becker (1976, chapter 5), and all child inputs, including goods, are expressed in time units. That is, there is a time measure for each contribution to children, such as the father's work hours to earn goods, the grandparents' work hours to earn education funds, the aunt's supervision hours, or mother's food preparation hours. The former two are indirect time inputs, the latter two direct. By also expressing norms for child inputs in time units, the model is structured so that time constraints relative to time-denominated norms determine fertility. Generalized by this time denominator, the model reconciles seemingly diverse approaches to understanding fertility.

The use of behavioral norms with the time constraint structure avoids the controversial behavioral assumption associated with the economist's utility function that parents pursue their own self-interest, choosing between goods and children in response to their relative cost. Critics of fertility models often attack their behavioral assumptions. Even though models must make very simplified assumptions, counter-intuitive behavior in such a fundamental area affects their acceptance in general and usefulness as a policy tool in particular. The Chicago–Columbia models have experienced rather heavy attacks in this regard. In the next section I will give a short discussion of the results of statistical testing of the models.

EMPIRICAL TESTING OF THE CHICAGO–COLUMBIA AND PENNSYLVANIA MODELS

The Chicago–Columbia model has been characterized as a static, one-period model, rather than one of longer-run secular changes. As Robert Willis notes, "The static theory would appear to be better suited to the explanation of differential fertility within closely adjoining cohorts whose historical experience is held more or less constant by their common years of birth" (Willis, 1973, p. 60).

Becker and Barro reformulate the theory somewhat by introducing an altruistic utility function for the dynasty head, where altruism varies inversely with the number of children. This changes the time frame for viewing optimal fertility behavior. Dynastic families replace in subsequent generations births lost when child-rearing costs were high. They suggest that child costs were high in the 1940s relative to the postwar baby boom years because more women worked at higher wages. Moreover, family wealth was reduced by the war. Income and substitution effects shifted births to the postwar generation, they feel (Becker and Barro, 1988, p. 15). They also argue that, given altruism, fertility varies positively with the real interest rate (return to investment in human capital) and child survival rates. Lower child mortality rates lower child costs and thus raise fertility in the model. The authors say this explains why fertility rises at the onset of the transition (ibid., pp. 16–17).

Mueller and Short (1983) emphasize that in the context of demographic transition, preferences and structural variables change. And writing early on regarding the Chicago–Columbia theory's application to low income countries, Theodore Schultz notes, "the household model as it now stands has not been developed to treat the particular classes of circumstances that constrain the household in those countries" (T. W. Schultz, 1974, p. 20). Moreover, the complexity of the model has presented problems in regard to empirical refutation, especially for countries with limited data sets (Ben-Porath, 1982; T. P. Schultz, 1974, p. 259).

The model assumes that the mother's investment in her own education or training, her work time, and her fertility are all interrelated, determined simultaneously in a lifetime context. Thus, in general, two-stage least-squares regressions are specified with these as endogenously determined. Interpretation of the results and data problems both affect testing. Empirical specifications for the wife's and husband's lifetime wages, their wealth, the cost of children and quality characteristics, and labor force participation rates over child-bearing years or work life can be only roughly estimated even in advanced countries. Moreover, certain correlations are consistent with more than one model of fertility. Education may affect preferences or other norms as well as the opportunity cost of the wife's time or the husband's income. The wife who has fewer children and works more than her cohorts may be reacting to an income constraint upon living standards, rather than calculating the opportunity cost of children (Standing, 1983; Gille, 1985, p. 279). Lee and Bulatao (1983) give a thorough discussion of possible interpretations of demand-related fertility determinants in developing countries.

The Chicago–Columbia type models have been tested mainly with data from the US, Israel, and Japan. Empirical findings interpreted to be consistent with the model are the inverse relationship between fertility and the wife's education and labor force participation rate. Compared to his wife, the husband's labor force participation rate is higher, while the time spent with children is less. Thus the opportunity cost of his work hours as measured by his education level may not influence fertility. Changes in income may be either positively or negatively related to fertility according to the model. If the husband's wages rise, the number of children and/or the expenditures per child may rise. If the wife's wages rise, there should be greater labor force participation and fewer children. An increase in wealth, on the other hand, does not change the opportunity cost of the parents' time and should lead to more children. The one-period model refers to expected lifetime income from wages and wealth; and a testing of the effect of income increases alone requires that the price of time (wages) and goods be constant. The effects of income upon the number of children and expenditures per child (quality) must be separated. The choice of an instrumental variable equation for quality can be troublesome.

In sum, in advanced countries where education and work force participation are high, the economic value of the wife's time has been related to fertility in support of the model emphasizing the relative cost of children. Scattered studies in less developed countries have also emphasized education as a proxie for the opportunity cost of the wife's time and find more educated women have fewer children. However, the idea that increased market work by women in developing countries reduces their fertility is not established (Mueller and Short, 1983, p. 629). And the idea of child quality as a determinant of the income elasticity of fertility in such countries may not be applicable (ibid.). Usually these Third World studies are simple regression or correlation studies. They may find that other variables, such as urban/rural living or steel consumption per capita, vary with fertility. Investigators themselves have noted the difficulty of testing the model and the failure of these tests to generate empirical regularities.

Easterlin's hypothesis that experienced living standards affect fertility is a variation of the living standard hypothesis, which, going back in the literature, has a long base of cumulative documentation. The specific relationship between parents' lifestyle standards for themselves and their children and their familial and social exposure during their formative adolescent years was an innovative adaptation of the living standard hypothesis. It has been favorably received, not only because intuitively the idea is very plausible, but also because it provides a testable hypothesis.

Easterlin chose to test his hypothesis by the more traditional investigative route that documents socioeconomic variables in their broad historical perspective and marshalls data to support the idea at hand. Thus, in his many writings on fertility, he has investigated the impact of the open frontier in America and the land-use policies of early eras, the effects of the Depression era with its social security innovations, the impact of immigrants on labor market conditions for newly marrieds, and the particular economic features of the post-World War II period with its fluctuations in fertility rates.

The data have supported a relationship between fertility and parents' relative economic positions during high fertility ages compared to their teen years. Thus, he would argue that female labor force participation rates were likely to be high and fertility low when families suffered a shortfall from their experienced standards. On the other hand, Americans growing up in the Depression and then experiencing high postwar incomes would bear more children, and wives in the 1940s and 1950s would spend considerable time at home. He argued that the swings or fluctuations of the US fertility rates were not explained by the Chicago–Columbia models. Such models fail in particular to explain the postwar baby boom among more highly educated women able to command higher wages than women of the 1930s.

In regard to the demographic transition, Easterlin, Pollak, and Wachter stress the need to analyze reference groups independently, rather than testing their model with aggregate data. They also emphasize that as incomes rise, they expect a prolonged nutritional effect upon fertility among groups whose desired fertility is below their actual fertility due to poor health. The overall outcome is a period of rising fertility as the latter group dominates, followed by falling fertility as experienced living standards rise and birth control takes hold among all groups. Rural areas are dominated for more prolonged periods by groups with actual fertility below the desired level.

A strong relationship between nutrition and family size among the poor of less developed countries not using birth control has yet to be established (Gray, 1983). On the other hand, attitude surveys in such countries support the concept of excess fertility where people want more children, even though, relatively speaking, birthrates are high and incomes low (Easterlin and Crimmins, 1985). There is the usual problem, however, if possible determinants not covered in the attitude questions are not held constant in the minds of the respondents (McClelland, 1983).

5
Economic Constraints upon Fertility: A Survey of Parental Attitudes

FERTILITY MODELING AND ATTITUDE STUDIES

Fertility models posit behavioral assumptions that simplify reality. Yet these assumptions are not presumed to be counter-factual. Rather, they are presumed to capture an important element of fertility-related behavior so that the model may explain and predict. Testing a model leads to its rejection or modification. The latter often involves modification of behavioral assumptions.

Statistical tests of economic models of fertility have been difficult to design and execute. These shortcomings of empirical testing provide the rationale for turning to attitude studies, which examine whether behavioral assumptions are consistent with revealed attitudes. Such studies also provide additional information useful in refining or modifying models. And they can aid in identifying the more promising of alternative approaches to modeling fertility behavior, thus contributing to formulation of a more general model.

Optimally, behavioral assumptions would prove general enough to be useful in developing a fertility model that could explain or predict fertility in transition and post-transition societies. The Pennsylvania lifestyle model has been applied to both states. The Chicago–Columbia model is thought to be especially applicable to populations in advanced economies. An attitude study using data from a country as advanced as the US, then, can provide additional information about both approaches. The study was particularly set up to reflect the focus of the living standard model developed in this study. The findings indicate that the lifestyle assumptions tested are apparently general enough to apply in post-transition conditions. Specifically, questions were designed to test for the impact of the following on family size: (1) an income constraint, (2) living standard constraints, experienced and aspired to, (3) the opportunity cost of the mother's time, (4) complementarity between children and education expenditures, (5) a shortage of nurture time related to work, and (6) the support or needs of the extended family. The survey casts doubt on the importance of (3), while giving support, but to different degrees, to the rest.

Attitudes studies must be used with care, of course, since it is difficult to capture attitudes precisely and be certain how closely actual behavior coincides with the attitudes people divulge. Such surveys need to be repeated and questions formulated in different ways to increase confidence in their findings. Ultimately their usefulness lies in their ability to improve the performance of fertility models. In the interim, survey responses may help the practitioner identify success probabilities of alternative policy approaches.

ECONOMIC CONSTRAINTS UPON FERTILITY

A basic assumption of economic models is that in situations of controlled fertility, income constrains children. In the utility approach children are similar to goods in that they require purchasing power, have costs, and produce satisfaction. Given expected income and tastes, goods and children are substituted in response to changes in their relative prices or costs as parents seek to maximize utility from expenditures upon them. Even though the price elasticity of substitution may not be high between goods and children, significant rises in child costs that occur as the opportunity cost of the mother's time increases will cause lower fertility rates. And when relative costs are constant, children are similar to normal goods in that the demand for them rises with income – the demand for numbers and/or quality. Thus, while the income elasticity of fertility rates may be indeterminate, income constrains fertility, given relative costs of children and goods. In this approach it is argued that, empirically, income does not play as central a role as the mother's time cost, however, which becomes the main predictor of fertility,[1] (Becker, 1960; Becker and Gregg Lewis, 1973; Willis, 1973; T. W. Schultz, 1974). Standing (1983) surveys the methodological problems of empirical tests of this model.

The income constraint is central to the living standard model in a more straightforward way. Families wish to maintain living standards which are directly affected by real income. Changes in income and living standards are the keys to predicting fertility changes. Parents view goods and children as complements, not substitutes. Income shortfalls mean children and other family members will not attain experienced or aspired to lifestyles. Thus, the level of income relative to the costs of this lifestyle standard is a main predictor of fertility. The mother's wages are viewed as potential family income to ease the constraint upon living standards, and thereby family size, instead of a child cost that could restrict size. Of course, when both parents work, a time restraint upon fertility may arise as a derived effect of the income constraint.

Both approaches allow for a rise in education costs to affect fertility, since both treat these costs as complements to children, given income levels. In the utility approach, education is the main determinant of child quality. The taste for this rises with income. In the living standard model, education is a component of lifestyle expenditures. It determines the future lifestyle of children and extends dependency years over which living standards must be maintained by parents. Education can be substantial and thus will affect fertility.

Both approaches assume that leisure time can limit children since it limits income. In the living standard model, leisure standards are a component of lifestyle, experienced or aspired to. In the utility approach the taste for leisure relative to goods and children helps to determine lifetime earnings and affects income. But children, goods, and leisure are substitutes, and thus demand for them varies with their relative costs.

Work limits time available to children, especially if both parents work. In the living standard model, mothers will work outside the home over some part of their child-raising years if that is an option which will attain living standards for the family. While this reduces the income constraint upon children, it may create a time

---

[1] As incomes rise, consumers demand relatively more luxury goods. Declines in their prices relative to the cost of children will lead to lower fertility as incomes increase.

constraint upon family size. In the utility maximization approach, time is allocated among work, leisure, and children, based on tastes, wages, and the relative cost of children. The income constraint, then, may be viewed by parents in terms of a time constraint – either time to work so that lifestyles are maintained or to pursue wage-enhancing career opportunities for utility maximization.

Economists typically point out that income uncertainty can affect behavior that is income-constrained. Threats of unemployment that enter the expectations horizon of parents affect the income constraint upon fertility. Moreover, since children require many years of money and time outlays, parents must project future income streams in their decision making about family size. Their willingness to assume the risks of income uncertainty while undertaking responsibilities for dependents may affect their family size.

Generally economic models specify an income constraint related to the parents' earnings and wealth and assume that expenditures are related only to the nuclear family. Observation tells us, however, that families share income in crises and out of generosity. Thus the income/expenditure constraint may relate to the extended family even in affluent societies. This reduces to some degree the risk of income uncertainty.

Finally, the living standard model has two variants: one relates standards to those experienced in the parents' teenage years (Easterlin, 1968 and 1976); the other specifies a socialization process whereby peer lifestyles or upward mobility aspirations influence standards so that they may be above personal experiences (Freedman, 1963). The Easterlin–Pollak–Wachter model combines many aspects of the utility and living standard approaches (Easterlin, Pollak, and Wachter, 1980).

THE SAMPLE

The population sampled consisted of the parents of outpatient children at a children's hospital in Atlanta, Georgia. The sample of 500 was collected between August 1985 and April 1986. Parents were predominantly from the seven-county Atlanta metropolitan area which has two million inhabitants and an economy concentrated in service industries. It is one of the fastest growing areas in the US and has attracted many people from other regions of the nation. Thus it has lost its Southern identity. A scattering of patients lived in surrounding, more rural counties or more distant locations. Table 5.1 shows the composition of the sample by background.

Table 5.1 Profile of sample population

Category		Percent
One-parent households		11.8
Mother's age		
under 20		1.8
21–30		44.8
31–40		47.6
over 40		5.8
Race		
white		89.4
black		8.2
Spanish-speaking		1.0
other		1.4
Religion	*Mother*	*Father*
Protestant	51.4	48.6
Catholic	17.2	11.4
Other or none	31.4	40.0
Education	*Mother*	*Father*
high school only	34.2	27
1–2 years of college	20.4	17.5
3–4 years of college	26.2	29
over 4 years of college	17.8	23
Household income (per month)		
$600 or less		5.8
$601–1,200		9.6
$1,201–1,800		15.0
$1,801–2,400		20.0
over $2,400		49.0
Mother works		
zero hours		46.0
40 hours per week		25.6
more than 40 hours per week		27.2
no answer		1.2
Father away from home overnight each month		29.0

The sample covers those still raising a family, of course, and thus differs by age composition from the national population. It was slightly more white and more educated and affluent than the national population in part because of age and in part because the less educated and single-parent households with lower incomes were less willing to answer the questionnaire.

Questionnaire response was voluntary, in compliance with hospital guidelines. A sampling of those not responding and those filling in only a portion of the questionnaire disclosed the following reasons: inability to place themselves in a hypothetical situation, infertility, dislike of questionnaires, illiteracy, emotional tension, and religious outlook. Only a scattering of those sampled expressed the attitude that "God will provide" and that children should be unlimited. However, some questionnaires were filled in with no questions checked and written notes to this effect. Interestingly, these tended to place a limit upon the "ideal" family size. Less than 5 percent of responses were of this nature, and thus their inclusion in the sample would change the results imperceptibly. They were omitted due to an inability to differentiate religious from other reasons.

Given the private nature of the information asked, the questionnaire had to be self-administered to elicit honest responses, in addition to being voluntary. This resulted in a somewhat lower participation rate by blacks and other minorities, as well as the less literate. Ninety percent of the sample was white, with about half making over $2,400 per month.

THE QUESTIONNAIRE

Table 5.2 gives the 12 statements and their relative frequency distribution. Just prior to being given the statements, respondents were asked: "Think about an 'ideal' American family. How many children are there in this ideal family?" Instructions for responding to the statements read: "One by one, consider each of the 12 circumstances listed *as if they were true for you.* Check only the circumstances below that could cause you to have *fewer* children than your ideal American family has. Leave the rest blank." Thus, rather than ask the respondents to associate with a certain attitude – for example, that the satisfaction from children competes with that

Table 5.2 Relative frequency distribution for questionnaire responses

Statement	Relative frequency	95% confidence interval
1 I would have to give up having a lot of goods our family couldn't afford when I was a teenager and that I'm enjoying for the first time.	12.4	9.5–15.3
2 I could not give all the children an education at least as good as their parents had.	55.6	51.2–59.9
3 Another child would mean I couldn't help my elderly parents who lost their home in a fire and have no other relatives to help them.	31.2	27.1–35.3
4 I would not want to accept a loan from my parents in order to have a big enough house.	24.2	20.5–28.0
5 Both parents work long hours to support the family. They have limited time for children, and there are no relatives to give loving care to another child.	59	54.7–63.3
6 Another child for us would mean we could not help my sister and her children, who are on welfare due to her husband's ill health.	16.8	13.5–20.1
7 Having a larger family would mean the mother could not accept a high-salaried career opportunity. However, she could keep her old job and maintain living standards.	8.2	5.8–10.6
8 Because of a sharp rise in education costs, another child would keep our family from having a better standard of living.	21.6	18.0–25.2
9 Another child would drop our living standard too far below that of our friends and associates.	4.2	2.4–6.0
10 Unemployment is rising, and our family income looks quite uncertain.	38.8	34.5–43.1
11 The father would have to take a second job for a few years in order to support an additional child.	29.6	25.6–33.6
12 Another child would keep us from spending more on our children than our parents spent on us.	14.4	11.3–17.5

from goods – they were asked to respond to hypothetical situations reflecting trade-offs or constraints. This presented the respondents with less abstract or generalized propositions, making sensitive, economically based fertility choices very concrete.

PROFILE OF SURVEY RESPONSES

In order to establish if responses differed statistically by sub-groupings such as age of mother, income, and so forth, confidence intervals were estimated with a significance level of 95 percent. Results are included in the discussion below, where significant differences among subgroup frequencies were found.

Statements 1 and 12   Items 1 and 12 test parental attitudes toward having a better standard of living for themselves or their children than they experienced in their dependency years. The percentage checking these circumstances was similar (12.4 percent for number 1 and 14.4 percent for number 12). However, only 0.4 percent checked both, indicating that those checking number 12 would limit children only if they could not afford more for *them*, but not if it meant parents had to sacrifice a higher standard for themselves than they experienced. The percentage rose for working mothers who worked more than 40 hours a week compared to those not in the labor force, reaching a response level of 20 percent. It was slightly higher in families where fathers had three or more years of college and for households not planning more children. Catholics were somewhat less likely to want a better standard than others, while whites were less likely than blacks, with a possible difference of 10–40 percentage points.

Statement 2   The desire to educate children to at least parental education levels is a very strong reason for limiting fertility, with 55.6 percent of the sample checking this item. The percentage rises with the age of the mother. It was higher when at least one parent had more than two years of college.

Statements 3 and 4   Most respondents (76 percent of total households, 7–33 percentage points fewer single-parent ones) might accept a housing loan from their parents rather than curtail fertility due to a shortage of living space, especially those in higher income brackets. Almost a third would restrict fertility to provide for elderly parents in need. Thus, it is not just the nuclear family's income that constrains fertility.

Statement 5 The shortage of family time to devote to children was the most important potential deterrent to larger families. Those families in which parents had more than two years of college were much more concerned with time constraints, with an average of 68 percent checking this response when the mother was more educated and 63 percent when the father was. This is consistent with findings by Liebowitz (1975). Blacks and those not associated with the Catholic or Protestant faiths were less likely to restrict fertility because of time constraints, as were those with incomes less than $1,200 a month. Surprisingly, there was no correlation between those checking this question and the family where the father traveled in his work. Less than 10 percent of respondents checked *only* this response as a deterrent to achieving their ideal family size.

Statement 6 A sister in need is less likely to affect fertility than parents in need. While sharing family resources with one's extended family can deter child-bearing, it was less likely to do so for Catholics.

Statement 7 Very few parents of any age or income category would let a career opportunity of the mother interfere with family size. The percentage checking this item was only 3 percent for families where the mother did not work; but it rose to 15 percent if she worked more than 40 hours a week. The response did not vary significantly with education or income level. The percentage can be between 3 and 23 percentage points higher for single parents. Surprisingly, less than half of those who would limit children to obtain a higher lifestyle for themselves (statement 1) would let a career opportunity restrict family size. Only 5.4 percent checked both items.

Statement 8 In about a fifth of households a rise in education costs would restrict family size if it would restrain family lifestyle. A rise in the cost of educating children would result in 22 percent substituting a higher lifestyle than their current one for additional children. There was no correlation with education or income level. As the next item shows, this desire by as many as one-fifth for a better living standard for themselves or their children apparently is unrelated to standards among their friends and associates.

Statement 9　Only 4 percent of parents indicated that they would curtail fertility if it would result in a living standard too far below their social group, as opposed to family living standards for education and the like. Apparently families that try to keep up with the Joneses or ahead of the Smiths will not do so at the cost of another child.

Statement 10　In 38.8 percent of households, the income constraint is expected income, not current income. The uncertainty of employment-related income is important across all category subsets.

Statement 11　In about 30 percent of households there is a trade-off between family size and the father's work load when it would entail a second job. The response is lower, however, where the mother works more than 40 hours a week and among blacks. Most households, then, would be willing for the father to work a second job to support a larger family. This is consistent with studies showing household heads with more dependents work more hours per week or year (Landsberger, 1971).

PLANNED VS IDEAL FAMILY SIZE

Table 5.3 shows the relative frequency distribution for survey households' actual, planned, and ideal children. Overall, most households have had, expect, or hope to have the number of children in their ideal family. It could be that the 50 percent of households having incomes over $28,000 view themselves as the typical American family. If so, then their own income constraint may have been reflected in their ideal family size.

When looking at the difference between planned and ideal family size for most families, we are talking about the choice between one and two or two and three children, since two to three children are considered ideal by 87 percent of parents. Yet less than 1 percent

Table 5.3 Actual planned, and ideal family size as a percentage of total sample households

Number of children	Actual	Planned	Ideal
1	31.4	8.0	0.6
2	48.0	54.8	57.1
3	15.8	26.2	29.7
4	3.2	8.0	11.4
5	1.0	1.0	1.0
6	0.4	0.4	0.2
7	0.2	0.2	—
8	—	0.2	—
Others	—	1.3	—
Mean number	1.964	2.453	2.557
Standard deviation	0.897	0.915	0.757

felt a family with one child was in any sense ideal. Undoubtedly, the small range of preferences affected the number of reasons for restricting family size and the percentage for each. In particular, a choice between one and two children for those facing income constraints is a tough one to make, since one-child families are decidedly unpopular. Twenty percent of parents checked only child time or education standard constraints as possible deterrents to having their ideal-size family, omitting extended family needs, income uncertainty, and so on.

RELATIVE LIFESTYLE, INCOME, AND FAMILY SIZE

Respondents were asked to check one of five income subgroups and to rank their current living standard as "much higher," "somewhat higher," "about the same," or "lower" than that of their teen years. Seventy percent of survey households had incomes over $21,600 per year, and 50 percent over $28,800. Over one-third of the sample did not view their family as yet complete and thus expect additional children to affect their lifestyle. About 65 percent of respondents had living standards similar (the same or somewhat higher) to those when they were teenagers: 26 percent had much higher standards, and 9 percent had lower standards. The vast majority of parents viewed their lifestyles as similar to those of friends and associates. Over 80 percent of respondents checked one or more responses indicating that they would limit children to achieve a similar or higher family lifestyle than they experienced as teenagers.

Respondents' current status may or may not reflect their expected future status in regard to income and relative lifestyle, and the subgroupings are not finely differentiated. Nevertheless, with the information at hand, a few observations, while suggestive only, seem worth mentioning. But first, the expected relationships are reviewed.

The income presumed to affect fertility is that experienced over the child-raising years, not income at a point in time. And the utility approach is not falsified by the lack of a positive relationship between income and fertility unless other factors are accounted for, in particular, the child quality variable and the cost of the mother's time. There is no straightforward way to define child quality or measure the change in taste for quality as income rises; rather the preference function for child quality is an assumption of the model. Empirically, education expenditures have been used as a proxie.

Similarly, the relative living standard refers to a measure of the parents' teen years lifestyle compared to that of their child-raising years, not current income. Living standard is a fairly broad concept, and comparative measurements can be difficult. Nevertheless, the survey responses are germane.

Apparently, current relative living standards affected lifestyle expectations, and thereby the fertility behavior and goals of respondents. Thirty-six percent of those whose current relative lifestyle was lower than in their teen years planned to have a different number of children from their ideal, compared to between 16 and 22 percent for other relative income groups. Moreover, the means for actual, planned, and ideal family sizes were lower for those whose living standard was below that of their teen years than for those with similar standings. However, they were also lower for the 26 percent of the sample whose incomes had risen substantially from much lower levels. The latter finding would not be predicted by the relative income model unless, compared to other groups, a large proportion of mates had different relative incomes and, in particular, mates of these respondents did not experience higher income. The difference in means among these groups is at most 0.3 ideal children and 0.15 planned children. The groupings are broad, and not all would expect their relative standing to be fixed; but the association is consistent with the responses to the hypothetical statements, supporting the relative income hypothesis.[2]

The response patterns for the 12 items did not show statistically significant variance when broken down into subgroups by relative living standard, but with one exception: those in the lowest relative position were least likely to restrict family size to provide more for themselves than they had as teenagers. The difference was a possible 3–21 percentage points. However, they were equally as likely to curtail family size if they could not give the children more then they had.

It appears, then, that the 9 percent of households with lower relative standards are equally concerned about maintaining living standards for their children. At the time of the questionnaire they had not been able to do so. The 26 percent with much higher relative standards, on the other hand, were not significantly more concerned than others with having a higher standard. Other factors, such as divorce, years since marriage, or unexpected economic circumstances, could account for the relative income positions for these two groups. It is also possible that some families are more cautious, assuming less risk in regard to income adequacy in the face of uncertainty.

The data also suggest that current income may affect fertility goals by constraining planned family size relative to ideal. The mean planned family size for the three lower income groups was between 0.19 and 0.28 fewer children than their ideal, which was 0.14 children above the ideal for higher income groups. For the lowest three income groups, 35, 31, and 25 percent respectively did not expect to have their ideal number of children, compared to between 15 and 19 percent for the higher income groups. The presumption here is that current income affects expected future income. However, in contrast to current relative lifestyle, lower current income was not associated with lower actual, planned, and ideal family size. Lower income may cause parents to plan fewer

---

[2] An ordinary least-squares regression using $n-1$ dummy variables for relative income subgroupings as the independent variables was tested, letting the subgroup for "much higher" relative income be the intercept term. The difference between ideal and planned family size rose as relative income dropped from "somewhat higher" to "about the same" to "lower". The coefficients were significant at the 5 percent level of confidence or less, but the R^2 was less than 2 percent. The low R^2 is related to the fact that most households have had, hoped, or planned to have their ideal family size.

children than their ideal, as opposed to a smaller family size. These patterns are consistent with the findings of another study.

A survey done in 1975 by Thorton and Kim found that 25 percent of parents under 40 years old and 9 percent over that age had fewer children then they wanted due to financial circumstances. Another 18 percent would have had more children if it would not have lowered their material living standards (Thorton and Kim, 1980). This study used interviews to gather responses. Sixty-five percent were unwilling to say that they would have had a different family size had they been more affluent. However, 69 percent mentioned financial constraints as a factor affecting whether or not they had another child at a particular point in time.

CONCLUSIONS

Responses to survey items support the following findings:

1   There is support for the hypothesis that the income constraint upon experienced or aspired to living standards, particularly the education and child time standards of the parents, restricts family size. The constraint shows up in attitudes about work/leisure choices of parents to provide a certain support level for children. The certainty of the income also has an influence. There is almost no support for the variant of this hypothesis that social peer standards, as opposed to family standards, affect fertility.

2   The income constraint that is applicable involves extended family income. The needs and financial aid of relatives have the potential to influence fertility considerably even in affluent societies.

3   Time constraints (which are related to the income constraint) have the greatest potential for limiting fertility among those tested, with as many as 68 percent of the more educated indicating that a shortage of family time to devote to the nurture of children would restrict their family size. Parents working long hours to achieve living standards would have fewer children, especially if there were not other relatives to fill in. A potential shortage of parental time was not related to women pursuing higher living standards via careers, but may

be correlated with mothers working to achieve experienced living standards for children.

4 As many as one-fifth of parents would lower their fertility rate to attain a better family living standard for their children than they experienced. For these families, rising education costs will limit children more than it will for families seeking only experienced lifestyles, other things being equal. The ratio for blacks may rise to twice this level.

5 The opportunity cost of the mother's time appears to reduce fertility very little, although it is somewhat more likely to do so if the mother has had the experience of being the sole support of the household.

In looking at economic constraints, it is interesting to note that parents indicated a desire for upward mobility in terms of their own lifestyle (12 percent) or that of their children (22 percent). In part this may reflect mixed marriages in the sense that one partner has higher experienced standards than the other. Whatever the cause, this means that lifestyle standards for a certain number rise for reasons other than just experience, giving a further thrust to upward movements in the standard. For such households, conflict could easily develop between lifestyle standards and the seemingly unpopular result of a one-child household. In fact, the rising tide of delayed child-bearing and greater work force participation by women may reflect this quandary for some. Women enter the work force in order to be able to afford another child. The political maneuvering for education subsidies in the 1980s may be another indicator of how binding the income constraint is.

The importance of education as a complementary expenditure for children is confirmed here. This is consistent with earlier findings in the 1965 National Fertility Study, in which over 80 percent of parents indicated that they would undergo severe financial hardship if the situation required it to send qualified children to college (Thornton, 1978). This means that the parents would sacrifice goods they might consume to attain education standards for existing children when there is an income shortfall. The survey here shows that they would limit children under such conditions if a larger family would lower education standards.

The uniformity of the survey responses indicates that experienced living standard, adjusted for upward mobility or divergent parental backgrounds, is an important variable that must be included in multivariate analysis of fertility. This means that income constrains fertility; but nuclear family income is too narrow an income measure even in affluent economies where smaller households are the norm. Younger parents may expect to share income or inherit wealth from their relatives, and this can affect their ability to obtain housing, educate their children, and so forth. Or they may support elderly parents. This means that the expected incomes of parents are interrelated to some degree with the incomes of their lineal households. Thus, ideally, in statistical tests of the hypothesis, measures of parents' adolescent living standards should be compared with their expected attainable standards as supplemented or depleted by family sharing, rather than the usual approach of using the father's relative income.

The living standard is also broader than normally calculated. Leisure, security or wealth, time needs of children, and education standards should be a part of the family living standard measure, not just material goods standards. And since as many as one-third of parents will upgrade their lifestyle goals (either for themselves or their children), the standard should be adjusted for this. In other words, the Easterlin concept of living standard, as well as the income that constrains that standard, have been too narrowly defined in empirical work.

The mother's earnings must be included in measuring the income constraint. Empirical studies which try to estimate the household's expected lifetime income typically extrapolate only the father's earnings based on current status, occupation, and wage. This treatment arose in part as a result of the utility maximization approach, in which studies use the woman's education level to stand for her wages and thus the opportunity cost of children. Yet, apparently the relationship between women's wages, labor market participation rates, and fertility reflects a desire by mothers to relieve the income constraint upon experienced or aspired to lifestyles and thereby children, rather than to substitute material goods for children as the time cost of children rises with improved job opportunities for mothers. The mother's educational level, on the other hand, may represent the education standard for her children, or nearly so (Smith, 1983, p. 502 and references therein). It is a very crude measure of the time cost of children (Easterlin,

1978, p. 66). And demographers emphasize that education affects attitudes and norms related to reproduction.

The straightforward inclusion of the mother's wages as part of the household's income constraint is consistent with other studies appearing in the popular press. In a survey of 2,000 households by Ethan Allen, the furniture manufacturer, three-quarters said that mothers with young children should go to work only if earning more money was a necessity. In a *Redbook* magazine survey of 500 respondents, 90 percent said that women work because they need money. More mothers working outside the home (96.4 percent) felt this way than stay-at-home mothers (86.5 percent). *Redbook* summarized the spontaneous responses as indicating that most felt "needs," as opposed to "wants," caused mothers to enter the labor force (*Redbook*, Aug. 1986). In other words, the mother is not making conscious substitution choices between material goods and children based on relative costs. And a survey by a Chicago-based executive placement firm of over 400 high-salaried executive women working for one of the 1,000 largest US firms found that, even for this highly professional group, only one-third said careers affected their decisions about whether to have children (*Atlanta Constitution*, Dec. 8, 1986, section B).

Such a view of work does not conflict with an attitude by women that it is important for them to be more career-oriented, especially given the divorce rate. Of course, constraints such as those related to job choices, time inflexibility within jobs, and job market re-entry costs may mean that careers aimed solely at income standards in actuality interfere with the mother's optimal allocation of her time between work and children. Many times real world conditions mean that the best obtainable solution will be a time commitment beyond the optimal to her career and less time for children or leisure. In other cases, the constraints may cause time to be allocated more toward children, especially for the large numbers of those in lower-skill jobs, if their living standards are also modest.

Finally, it can be argued that in the affluent two-child culture, fairly large percentage changes in expected earnings relative to those experienced in the teen years must occur to produce a statistically significant effect on fertility. Year-to-year income changes, even when lagged, are too small to affect fertility in the modern family with a costly lifestyle. The income constraints would need to lessen over several years by sufficient amounts in order to affect subsequent fertility. This means that more proximate causes, such as those examined by demographers, may be the best predictors of short-run fertility changes in the two-child culture. As Easterlin has noted in this regard, his original articles were concerned with longer-term swings in fertility over periods of dramatic changes in relative economic status (Easterlin, 1984). This perspective is especially applicable now, when the society's choices are mainly between one and two children. Moreover, the relationship between fertility and income changes is probably not a simple linear one. Moffitt makes a start in regard to incorporating some of these ideas and finds support for the Easterlin hypothesis (Moffitt, 1982).

6
Fertility Patterns of the Transition Onset: Insights of the Living Standard Model

The lifestyle concept is a cornerstone of this treatise, of the full model to be developed in the next chapter. In this chapter, I will present a more naive model, so that the explanatory powers of the living standard concept can be singled out. The emphasis here is on the transition onset, and dynamic aspects of the experienced lifestyle approach will be brought out. The empirical results are supportive of hypothesis 4, which states that there is a nonmonotonic relationship between fertility and the growth rate of income per capita, which involves lags.

A consensus is developing around two aspects of the transition from high, fluctuating fertility rates to low, narrowly fluctuating ones. First, fertility rates may show a fairly prolonged increase to peak levels prior to the transition to low, fluctuating rates. Latin American countries in particular show evidence of this (Dyson and Murphy, 1985). Thus, disproportionate population growth accompanying the transition is not traceable only to mortality declines. Second, fertility rates vary among countries in regard to peak, trough, and average levels prior to the transition, and are not uniformly associated with a similar modernization or development level at the onset of a declining trend to low rates (Scott and Chidambaram, 1985; Coale, 1979). Explanation is needed of why fertility rates fluctuate at both higher and lower levels, why they may show a pronounced peak prior to the transition to low rates, and the timing of the onset. By explanation is meant an insight into the basic causes, as opposed to the proximate causes.

THE LIVING STANDARD CONCEPT

Interestingly, insight into these fundamental questions can be gained from one of the oldest ideas relating to fertility: the living standard concept. The idea that lifestyle norms affect fertility predates Malthus. Hodgson (1983) has surveyed its history. This idea was superseded by the theory of the transition attributed to Davis, Notestein, and others working at Princeton's Office of Population Research in the 1930s and 1940s. However, in the light of more recent data, transition theory does not appear to answer the basic questions posed above. On the other hand, the living standard concept as updated by Easterlin gives insight.

Easterlin introduced the idea that growth, which raises experienced living standards for the next generation's parents, will, along with incomes of that generation, greatly affect fertility changes (Easterlin, 1968, 1969). Empirical work done by Easterlin and others has lent support to this idea (Easterlin, 1976). And Easterlin, Pollak, and Wachter incorporate the concept in their general theory of the demographic transition (Easterlin, Pollak, and Wachter, 1980). Interestingly, they do not develop it fully as an integral explanatory variable of the model. And Easterlin has in fact concentrated upon measurements of "excess fertility" and "supply-side" factors such as malnutrition and health in Third World countries to explain their fertility behavior (Easterlin and Crimmins, 1985).

Here, the Easterlin concept is developed more fully to show that it can shed light on the three basic questions above. The model is not presented as a complete theory of fertility. Other variables are held constant in order to trace the impact of experienced lifestyle norms upon patterns of fertility. But its powers to explain the more recent empirical findings are quite strong, and therefore of interest.

The living standard model is one of controlled fertility. It assumes that birthrates are constrained either by marital behavior – age, incidence, and so on – or by historically diverse birth control techniques within marriage to allow lifestyles to be maintained. Thus, for the model to be applicable, there must be a perceived relationship between fertility and the achievement of living standard norms. When this occurs, norms regarding reproductive behavior arise to protect the general well-being of families and society.

In the lifestyle model, unlike the traditional theory of the demographic transition, fertility may fall in mainly agrarian settings. Historically, of course, there has been and is a range of incomes and lifestyles among agrarian economies. The lifestyle model assumes that, in part at least, this reflects the historical timing of socially evolved fertility constraints. Arguably, these constraints would arise as groups perceived a connection between their reproductive behavior and lifestyle. Norms for housing, education, and goods can easily vary among societies when they evolve in different historical conditions. As a result of rising norms, fertility rates may fall below the high rates typical of uncontrolled fertility regimes, even where a large majority of the populace is in agriculture and related pursuits. These rates may also rise again if income constraints are lessened. A fuller development of the Easterlin lifestyle model can explain why. To do this, we will examine how economic constraints and income changes affect norms and fertility under different growth scenarios and with all other variables affecting fertility held constant.

METHODOLOGY

Demography touches on many disciplines, and therefore draws on diverse methodologies to analyze important questions about fertility. Studies of the demographic transition in particular give us a legacy of cross-disciplinary approaches that provide insight into its causes. Demographers with strong statistical training provide sophisticated empirical techniques, whereas others trained in social sciences methodology provide additional avenues for advancing our knowledge base. Invariably when scholars have different backgrounds and methodologies, communication problems arise. Given this fact, some comments about the methodology of this and the following two chapters seem in order.

The models developed in this book show the logic of the analysis, identifying all crucial assumptions and relationships. The focus of the model in this chapter is narrower than that of the full model, but allows preliminary exploration of a crucial relationship of the full model. This type of model-building findings its roots in the sciences. It requires simplifications and abstraction to gain generality and establish the internal consistency of the arguments of the theory. It is a very different approach from that of the demographic historian. Yet, theorizing is always present when we seek understanding of a complex social phenomenon such as the demographic transition. Historians invariably have informal, albeit less technically complex, models that guide their explorations.

Theories sometimes persuade on logic along, despite their abstraction; but to find broad acceptance, they must be testable and illuminate empirical regularities. Thus a model, in addition to providing an analytical structure, should generate testable hypotheses. This latter requirement invariably affects the model's structure.

Hopefully, the framework developed in the book will generate further modeling and will be testable in diverse ways, using different disciplinary approaches. The type of empirical work done in this chapter and also in chapter 8 uses data from different countries at an aggregate level and follows the precedent set by econometricians working in the area of economic development. This area of study uses cross-country, ordinary least-squares regressions and pooled time-series regressions extensively to identify general patterns of the development process.

The use of cross-country aggregated data has limitations that are well known. The data lack the homogeneity of a cross-section of data from subareas of a single country, for example, and usually fail stringent statistical tests for pooling. However, a sufficient span of national time series data for tracking determinants of fertility behavior over the transition generally do not exist. Cross-country studies are one technique for dealing with inadequate country observations. The assumption is that pooled observations of countries at different stages of the transition can represent, at least approximately, any country's fertility patterns. Empirical work of this type is accepted based on the argument that, when carefully interpreted, it may help to reject certain hypotheses; and that when the hypotheses cannot be rejected, further testing is warranted. When available, country data for part of the transition time span can be examined to see if they are consistent with the cross-country results.

Moreover, limitations exist for all data on the transition. For example, parish records have been used to document fertility behavior. Yet historians question the accuracy of parish bookkeeping due to fires and unrecorded births of those born out of wedlock or to religious dissenters from the established faith. Even official census data for certain years or countries can be misleading. Such information is all we have, however, and is superior to no information. In fact, by using a pooled cross-section of many countries to establish patterns, the shortcomings of a single country's data are often circumvented.

The models developed herein are consistent with information from the literature about the demographic transition. The aggregate tests provide information that arguments of the model cannot be rejected based on cross-country regression. Further testing, of course, could falsify some of the arguments of the model.

BACKGROUND

Growth can be gauged by the average annual rate of increase in GNP per capita for 5- or 10-year intervals over the growth span. This, of course, is the economy's average rate. It does not imply that the growth or development process raises all family incomes in lockstep with changes in this average. Different sectors, geographic areas, skill specialities, or even industries are favoured at different periods. And those receiving benefits from growth do not receive equal benefits. Moreover, those areas or jobs with advancing incomes in one phase may not experience continuous increments, but remain on a plateau reached in earlier periods. Most important, income growth may or may not accrue proportionately to the set of households which are in their most fertile years. The sharing of income among extended families will not offset completely the distribution of growth proceeds among fertile and infertile households. Incomes of fertile households through generations of the same or new occupations, then, do not necessarily show a line of continuous growth or closely track the average change for the economy. Income growth for families and their progeny will be uneven, and there can be income declines with sectoral or occupational shifts, among other factors. And as the standard of living rises, the increase in income necessary to support another child at the new standard also increases, so that even where income rises, it may be insufficient to allow for an increase in family size.

Families with varying income levels over generations can minimize the effect upon each generation's lifestyle by adjusting their fertility. However, couples with completed or almost completed families who experience income changes will have a greater change in living standards than newly fertile couples. In particular, mature couples raising their children can experience unusual growth in their incomes and be unable to adjust their total fertility upward greatly. In fact, income growth is often at its peak at that stage of their lives. Their children will experience higher lifestyles than the parents. This sets the stage for a new living standard norm for the next generation. In turn, norm changes affect fertility.

The effects on aggregate fertility are more easily grasped with the help of a simple multi-period model. The analysis assumes that all other basic variables affecting fertility are unchanged. And the form of birth control is left open. In fact, it is more tractable to assume that fertility is controlled within marriage or cohabitation, rather than by adjustment to age of unions. The analysis holds for either case, however.

THE MODEL

Express the set of household norm incomes for newly fertile couples at time t as: $A_t = \{a_t: a_t > 0\}$. Norm incomes are those needed during child-raising years by newly fertile couples to attain the lifestyle experienced in their teenage years *if* the woman has the same fertility as her mother. (Where lifestyle experiences of mates differ, assume that the higher standard prevails.) Groups of families experiencing similar lifestyles in the past will have similar norms so that their norm-sustaining incomes, that is the elements of set A_t, will cluster.

It is helpful to compare past and current norms. Mother and father are descendants of households of earlier generations (stem-households of time zero). The term "stem-household" is now defined as the parent's lineal household with the higher norm at time zero, so that each current household's norm is compared with only one stem household norm. Norm incomes, of course, must be compared in constant prices. Each current household's norm incomes $\{a_t\}$ can be mapped onto norm incomes of a stem-household $\{a_0\}$ in set A_0, which, of course, contains fewer households. The stem-household paired set $A_t \rightarrow A_0 = S_t = \{(a_0, a_t): a_0 \, \varepsilon \, A_0, \, a_t \, \varepsilon \, A_t\}$.

Let C_t be the set of household incomes available to each newly fertile couple over their family-raising years when these begin at time t. Elements of C_t for each household $\{c_t\}$ can be paired with $\{a_t\}$ for the same household to form a set of ordered household income pairs, $D_t = \{(a_t, c_t): a_t \ \varepsilon \ A_t, \ c_t \ \varepsilon \ C_t\}$. When the pairs are plotted on a graph with $\{c_t\}$ on the vertical axis and $\{a_t\}$ on the horizontal, then any households that plot below the 45° line will face an income constraint that will lower their lifestyle if fertility is the same for the newly fertile as for the previous generation. Those women in households above the 45° line can have higher fertility than their mothers and retain their experienced lifestyle.[1]

Now let B_t be a subset of A_t. The elements $\{b_t\}$ are the norm incomes of newly fertile couples in set A_t who experienced higher lifestyles than the families of time zero from whom they descended: $B_t \subset A_t$; $B_t = \{b_t: \ b_t \ \varepsilon \ A_t; \ b_t = a_t > a_0$ stem-households$\}$. The elements of subset B_t will include more above modal than below modal lifestyle income norms. As growth proceeds, more norms of set A_t exceed those of stem households in A_0. And as the constraint $(a_t > a_0$ stem-households) changes, so does subset B_t. This subset will include more and more of the higher elements of set A_t. This results in the norm income pairs $\{(b_t, c_t) \ \varepsilon \ D_t\}$ having a greater chance of falling below the 45° line, given the development-generated pattern of incomes over time. As the plotting of all households moves closer to the 45° line and below, measures of aggregate fertility drop. But in the early phases of growth, aggregate fertility may readily rise as the income constraint on households eases.

THE MODEL UNDER DIFFERENT GROWTH PATTERNS

Several simplified growth scenarios can be useful in analyzing fertility behavior, and several outcomes are possible. It is helpful to consider a limited number of sets of newly fertile couples beginning at different time periods over which growth is traced. Sets will be identified by time period subscripts 0, 1, 2, . . . as in A_0, A_1, and so on. The economy at time period zero is assumed to have low labor productivity and high fertility rates.

---

[1] If fertility is not controlled within marriage, then age of union is varied. This changes set A_t for each t, and thereby aggregate fertility.

First, consider a stylized situation of a constant, uninterrupted growth rate in labor productivity. A percentage of households in each period receive higher incomes. The growth creates the potential for rising, then falling fertility as an ever-enlarging subset of households (B_t) experience higher lifestyles. This can be seen by beginning at period zero, prior to the onset of growth, when B_0 is a null set. In period one, growth occurs, elevating a percentage of the populace with complete or nearly complete families to a higher lifestyle experience as their labor hours attain more goods. Couples in this group are not at the age to have many more children. Teenagers in such households who become parents in period two will have higher living standard norm incomes (subset B_2). Whether or not their fertility is greater than, equal to, or less than that of their parents in set A_1 depends upon the level of their own and their spouse's labor productivity, and hence household income over their fertile years compared to the one-time increase in norms.

Assume income increases in period two are not disproportionately distributed to households of subset B_2. Some households experience the same or lower income than their parents. Fertility for households in subset B_2 will be lower on average than for families in $(A_2 - B_2)$ because norms are higher. Even though fertility for some households in subset B_2 will fall, overall the outcome will be rising fertility, since relatively few households in set A_t belong to subset B_t, and incomes are higher for these households with unchanged norms.

In period three, newly fertile couples in subset B_3 can be children of any households in set A_2. Constant rates of growth set the stage for rising norms in a percentage of lower and higher norm households. As a result, the proportion of couples in set A having higher norms than those of period zero enlarges as growth continues. Eventually, as norms continue to rise, fewer and fewer couples experience the norms of A_0 households, and more and more experience norm increases from higher lifestyle *bases*. The higher the norm, the larger the income increment needed to support another child. Thus, even with a constant growth rate in income, the number of children per household drops, since only a percentage of households each period experience higher income; yet each period the number of households in subset B_t enlarges as a percentage of A_t households, and the level of their norms is higher.

·Different rates of continuous growth will change the pace of fertility increases and declines. The income increment must be sufficient to support another child at the established living standard if fertility is to rise. With faster expansion, household sharing in that growth that are members of set A_t but not subset B_t will lie further above the 45° line. Rises in fertility rates can occur at a faster pace, reaching peak levels earlier. However, norm levels per period for all households in subset B_t will be higher. Thus, when such households do not share in growth, they will lie further below the 45° line. As subset B_t enlarges, the rate of decline in fertility will be quicker, since norms are higher in the case of more rapid growth. On the other hand, with very low growth rates, norms will adjust upward only very gradually. Lifestyles do not rise significantly for many, and their norms remain the same. Fertility declines will eventually occur if growth is steady, but the transition will be prolonged. Obviously, there can be periods under rapid and slow growth rates where households above and below the 45° line offset each other's fertility changes and aggregate fertility remains constant, other things also being unchanged.

Second, consider a situation of a continuously accelerating growth in labor productivity, starting from the same growth rate as case one but reaching rates much higher. This will result in norm levels being higher per period compared to case one, but this will also be true of incomes. The income constraint will be lessened, since household incomes are increasing more rapidly throughout the fertile years, while norms change only once per generation. Fertility will be higher than in the case of constant growth in labor productivity, but will exhibit similar dampened progression given realistic assumptions about the rate of income acceleration. The probability that fertility rates will rise in earlier periods is stronger here than in case one.

Third, assume a similar growth rate as in case one, but that growth is interrupted by periods of stagnant labor productivity or declines in its rate of increase. Consider the case where there is growth in period one, creating a subset B_2, followed by stagnation in period two. In this situation, some households in set B_2 will not receive incomes as high as their parents. Fertility in period two will fall modestly from that of period one, since families of subset B_2 as a whole will haver fewer offspring, while the number of children will remain more or less constant in the households with unchanged norms. The more households there are in set B_2 relative to A_2, the greater the downward adjustment in birthrates.

Fertility will remain near the level of period two until growth resumes. A decline in labor productivity growth rates in period two could also reduce fertility, but by less than outright stagnation. The more A_2 households included in subset B_2 and the sharper the decline in growth rates, the lower fertility will be in period two relative to period one. In period three, experienced lifestyles will be unchanged in the case of stagnant income. In the case of slowed growth, subset B_3 will have a lower norm increment than in the case with higher growth. The increment will be moderated by the growth slowdown. Thus, interrupted growth will create a one-time fall in fertility as movement occurs from positive to zero growth in income. Over similar growth spans, fertility rates may be higher on average than in a situation of constant growth, since subset B_t will tend to include relatively fewer households of set A_t. Figure 6.1 illustrates the cases discussed.

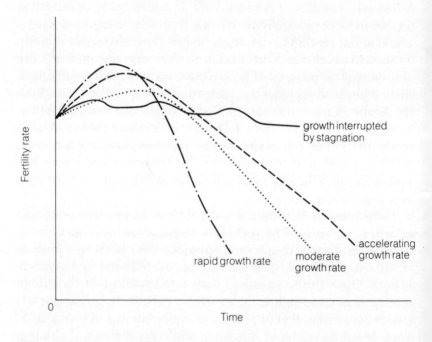

Figure 6.1   Growth patterns and fertility rates.

Actual declines in income per capita for prolonged periods will produce the opposite outcome of increases. It will reverse the rise in norms as children of households experiencing lower lifestyles subsequently lower their norms and no households experience a rise in norms. Households will have lower fertility rates at first, due to income declines.

From this brief schematic discussion it is obvious that income distribution is also important with respect to the behavior of fertility, since it determines the dispersion of $\{a_t, c_t\}$ around the 45° line. If, starting from low levels, income growth is concentrated in a very few sectors and/or higher-income households, the number of households in subset B_t will be relatively small. This will moderate rises in lifestyle norms and slow the decline in fertility for a given growth rate. Fertility rates, on the other hand, will not tend to rise as much, since less goes to A_t households with low norms. However, if the gains of growth are concentrated at first, then accelerate, and spread rapidly, birthrates can surge among the many poorer, low-norm households with rising incomes. It is common for inequality to worsen, then lessen, as development proceeds (Chenery and Syrquin, 1975). Such an outcome can affect the pattern of fertility change.

The fact that fertility declines in less developed countries are slower in agricultural areas and for those more recently migrating from rural areas (Haines, 1979; Repetto, 1979) is explicable by their relative income experiences. Growth in income per capita in agriculture is more moderate than growth in other sectors and is subject to high fluctuations due to weather, blight, and related conditions. Many times governments control agricultural prices, causing income growth there to lag behind that of other sectors. The behavior over the growth path of demand (foreign and domestic) relative to supply changes is a main cause, however, of the slower rate of income growth in this sector. Norms do not rise as rapidly as in other sectors, explaining the more moderate fertility declines. Recent migrants from rural areas will arrive with lower norms and will experience income growth in most cases. Their fertility will reflect the lessened income constraint. The next generation or so will experience higher norms; but compared to longer-term residents, the fertility rates will be higher for more recent arrivals.

And, of course, as has long been noted, children may be cheaper to support in rural areas for a given living standard. This is in part due to lower food or housing costs, in part due to their ability to offset some of their own cost more readily as producers on the farm compared to child laborers in town. For a given rise in income and norms for agricultural households, then, the income constraint is less binding.

Summing up, continuous growth will eventually lower fertility, but can easily produce rises in fertility rates prior to the onset of the transition to lower rates, assuming other factors do not offset this effect. The higher the rate of growth, the higher the rate of fertility rise prior to onset and fall in transition. Stagnation leads to constant fertility levels after a one-time decline when growth stops. Uneven or interrupted growth moderates the rise to higher norms. Accelerating growth can give rise to periods of rapidly rising fertility that will eventually fall as lifestyles move quickly to higher levels. In general, relatively high levels of fertility prior to the onset of a declining trend can be related to accelerations in rates of income growth. Uneven distribution of the income gains generated by growth will slow the decline in fertility rates compared to situations of continuous growth with broadly spread gains, since lifestyle norms rise for fewer households over time. Changes in income distribution can also affect the pattern of the transition.

This simplified discussion ignores the fact that other variables may restrict family size even though the income constraint eases. Nevertheless, the results are helpful in interpreting the effect of income constraints combined with gradually rising norms over the long-term growth path. Fertility is a function of past income levels and their patterns of change, which affect both norms and their constraints. Put another way, income and changes therein are not a simple constraint upon fertility, but also determine the evolution of living standard norms which they constrain. Norms at later stages of development are affected by earlier lifestyles, including those experienced on the eve of social controls of fertility. Not surprisingly, countries (and families) that develop different lifestyle norms will not have similar fertility levels, even though income levels are roughly similar at a particular time.

EMPIRICAL APPLICATIONS

The model predicts a relationship between growth rates of income and fertility, but not between income per capita and fertility. A statistically significant relationship between income per capita and fertility has long been sought. Generally, affluent countries have lower fertility than less developed countries with lower incomes. Despite this rough overall pattern, empirical studies of the demographic transition linking income per capita or other income measures such as household wages to fertility measures have not produced the expected correlation. Most studies are ordinary least-squares regressions, sometimes of log form. These are mostly cross-section studies with no selection of countries according to transition stage. Some are micro-, some macro-studies. The set of determinants used varies. (A summary of this type of research is given by Mueller and Short, 1983.) Macro-level studies sometimes show a positive income effect, particularly in rural areas. However, here too, many insignificant coefficients occur. Mueller and Short note that the relationship is apparently not monotonic, and that there is a fair amount of evidence of a positive relationship over some lower income ranges.

The above analysis implies that for longer-run time spans, average growth rates in per capita GNP should have an impact upon fertility rates. Once the transition to lower rates has begun, higher growth rates in income per capita should accelerate it. Table 6.1 lists a number of countries experiencing drops in birthrates between 1960 and 1982. The countries are listed by level of income per capita, starting with the lowest, Sri Lanka. Sri Lanka stands out because most nations with her relatively low per capita GNP have not begun transition. Yet her response to income growth is within the range of other countries. Her lifestyle norms for education, in particular female education, are quite high, while her mortality rate is low for an agrarian economy.

Brazil is a case of interrupted growth rates that accelerated to very high levels during growth spurts. This contrasts with the postwar Mexican expansion which, once begun, was relatively continuous and steady until the late 1970s, when oil revenues entered the picture. Thus Brazil's percentage decline in birthrates was no more pronounced than Mexico's, even though her average

Table 6.1   Twenty-year changes in incomes and birthrates

Country[a]	Annual change in GNP per capita	Crude birthrate		Percentage change in crude birth rate[b]
	1960–80	1960	1982	1960–82
Sri Lanka	2.4	36	27	−26
Bolivia	1.7	46	43	−7
Honduras	1.1	51	44	−14
Egypt	3.4	44	35	−22
El Salvador	1.6	48	40	−17
Thailand	4.5	44	28	−36
Philippines	2.8	47	31	−34
Guatemala	2.8	48	38	−21
Costa Rica	3.2	48	30	−37
Peru	1.0	47	34	−27
Ecuador	4.8	47	37	−20
Turkey	3.4	43	31	−28
Columbia	3.0	47	29	−39
Paraguay	3.7	43	31	−27
Malaysia	4.3	44	29	−34
Korea	6.6	43	23	−47
Panama	3.3	41	28	−32
Brazil	4.8	43	31	−27
Mexico	2.6	45	34	−25
Venezuela	2.6	46	35	−24
Hong Kong	7.0	35	18	−47
Singapore	7.5	39	17	−55
Trinidad & Tobago	3.0	38	29	−22

[a] Countries are listed according to the level of their 1982 income per capita, starting with the lowest.
[b] Computed from unrounded members.
Source: The World Bank, *World Development Report 1982, 1984*, Annex tables 1, 20. Copyright 1982, 1984, by the International Bank for Reconstruction and Development. Reprinted by permission of Oxford University Press, Inc., New York.

growth rate in per capita GNP was on the high side. The distribution of income in both countries reflects economic dualism, particularly in Brazil. Relative to Brazil, Korea, Singapore, and Hong Kong experienced steadier and higher growth in per capita GNP and larger percentage declines in birthrates.

Figure 6.2 plots the percentage declines in birthrates versus income growth rates for various countries. There is a statistically

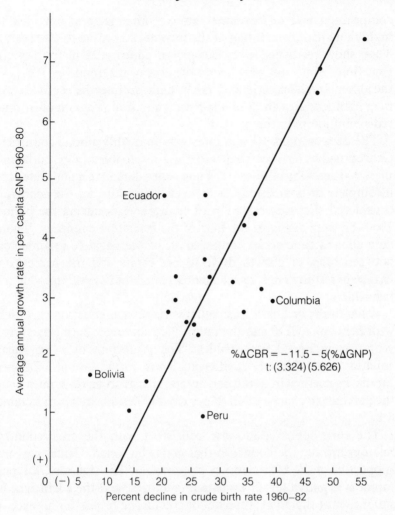

Figure 6.2 Rates of change of crude birthrates and GNP per capita
Source: World Bank, *World Development Report*, combination of tables 1 and 20.

identified relationship showing that higher growth rates in income per capita over a 20-year period are associated with higher percentage declines in birthrates. (The regression has an R^2 of 0.60; t distributions are significant at the 1 percent or less level.) Income per capita, on the other hand, is not correlated with birthrates for these countries, as the model would predict. And interestingly, outliers such as Ecuador and Bolivia are cases where ethnic composition and oil revenues, among other factors, have led to highly unequal distribution of the income, according to observers.[2] They show relatively lower downward adjustment in fertility. In fact, Bolivia may not have begun the downward trend yet. Peru, on the other hand, experienced fairly high declines in reproduction rates, but low growth. She underwent a radical program of income redistribution over this period.

The data on reproduction rates vary in quality among countries. Conceptually, fertility rates are superior to birthrates, although these too are subject to error. Time series data for fertility rates are incomplete or nonexistent, with a few exceptions for the countries considered. Fertility rates for 10 or more years during the period 1960–82 were available for four of the transition countries. These data allow a time series confirmation of the negative relationship between rates of growth of GDP per capita and the percentage change in fertility rates, using a more refined measure of reproductive behavior.

A log-linear ordinary least-squares regression equation was used with per capita GDP and the infant mortality rate (both lagged two years) as independent variables. The coefficient of a log-linear equation is an elasticity coefficient. Thus, in the case of GDP per capita, its coefficient is the percentage change in fertility rates over the percentage change in GDP per capita. Results are given in table 6.2.

The time series results are consistent with the cross-country relationship for the countries that could be tested. Thus they are supportive of the cross-country relationship. The sign for GDP per capita is negative for all transition countries, and the coefficient is significant at the 5 percent level of confidence or less for all except Mexico. Mexico's fertility rate did not start to decline continuously until after 1973; but using a 2-year lag, there were insufficient observations to restrict data to the post-1972 period. Thus Mexico's time series results are affected by the mixture of onset and transition periods. The coefficients for the other countries indicate that for every increment of 1 percent in the growth rate of GDP per capita, the percentage change in fertility rates is between 0.6 and 0.8.

---

[2] This is based on discussion with economists familiar with the countries and their tax bases. Brazil is another country with high inequality and lower downward adjustment of birthrates over the period.

Table 6.2 Log-linear OLS regressions with fertility rate as the dependent variable, using available data 1960–1982

Country	Coefficient		DW	DF	Adjusted R^2
	GDP per capita	Infant mortality rate (lagged two years)			
Transition					
Guatemala	−0.607[a]	−0.361[b]	3.5	8	0.75
Mexico	−0.179	0.546[a]	1.1	17	0.71
Venezuela	−0.798[a]	−0.058	0.8	12	0.59
Singapore	−0.630[a]	0.154	1.1	13	0.98
Post-transition					
Chile	0.047	0.463[a]	1.0	10	0.78
Italy	0.297[a]	0.726[a]	1.8	17	0.97
Japan	0.853[a]	0.902[a]	2.4	18	0.40

[a] 5% level of confidence or less.
[b] 10% level of confidence.

The model implies that for post-transition countries with stagnant economies there would be no relation between changes in fertility rates and the small fluctuations in GDP per capita. Data for Chile show that the rate of decline in infant mortality rates is significantly associated with the percentage change in fertility rates, but not with the behavior of GDP per capita, which registered a growth rate of less than one over the period.

By contrast, countries such as Japan and Italy could be expected to show a positive relationship between percentage changes in GDP per capita and percentage changes in fertility rates. These countries experienced fairly strong (3.4 percent in Italy) to strong (6 percent in Japan) growth rates in GDP per capita after recovery from wartime and postwar deprivations and prewar depression that held living standards down for a prolonged period. Fertility could be expected to respond as it does in countries during the early phases of rapid growth at the onset of transition, rising in proportion to the strong upward swing in growth rates. This is the case for both countries. Of course, the absolute change in fertility for a given percentage change is lower than for less developed countries which have a higher base fertility level. In all three countries the drop in infant mortality rates is significantly associated with fertility rates.

Sequential combinations of the stylized growth cases discussed could produce fertility patterns similar to those identified by Dyson and Murphy (1985). In particular, their major finding – that fertility often rises to its highest peak prior to the onset of the demographic transition to low rates – is readily derived from situations of constant or accelerating growth or of periods of strong growth followed by a slowdown in the rate of increase. Accelerating growth is typical of certain stages of development when industrialization and technical change take a firm hold (Donaldson, 1984, chapter 1). Thus, the authors Dyson and Murphy find that it is the Latin American countries, which are more advanced than other Third World regions, in which the pattern of fertility rise and decline (measured by crude birthrates) is pronounced. In table 2 of their article, reproduced here as table 6.3, we find that several Latin American countries (Columbia, Venezuela, Costa Rica, El Salvador, Mexico, and Ecuador) attained their peak in the more rapid industrial growth era following World War II. These countries started industrializing in the 1930s and 1940s and were able to accelerate this process in the 1950s. Growth was helped along by the rapid expansion of world trade after the war. With continued growth in the 1960s, gains spread among the populace. Taiwan, South Korea, Malaysia, and Hong Kong, Asian countries with strong postwar development, also peaked in the same period. And looking back to the European experience in Dyson and Murphy's table 1, we see that Europe was in the stage of fairly rapid development and income growth in the 1800s when fertility peaked (Mitchell, 1976). North America, with strong growth performance, had higher fertility rates than Europe; but fertility began to decline earlier.

The historically high level of the postwar peaks in reproduction rates may also be tied to economic performance. Compared to the preceding decades, growth rates in per capita GNP were very rapid in the period following World War II, slowing down only in the latter half of the 1970s. This pattern of income growth could produce relatively steep rises in fertility rates followed by sharp declines, as occurred in many countries in the 1970s. The rapid falloff in fertility can be related to the quickly rising norms for more and more newly fertile couples, followed by the slowdown in growth in the late 1970s. And in some countries income distribution was relatively skewed. In fact, income distribution in postwar Latin

America has been highly unequal gauged by historical standards. As growth spread eventually to poorer, low-norm segments, their fertility rose. And Dyson and Murphy carefully document the proximate causes of these changes. In a 1986 article, Alba and Potter document for Mexico the rise in the socially perceived need for fertility control to maintain norms. This research also traces the postwar increase and then decline in Mexican income growth rates. The sharp declines in fertility parallel the income growth slowdown and the spread of modern birth control techniques in response to social concern over living standards. Prior to the slowdown, Mexico enjoyed continuous, high growth rates in per capita GNP unparalleled in Latin America.

Undoubtedly the behavior of other variables – decreases in infant mortality, for example – lessened the rise and/or contributed to the fall in birthrates along with living standard changes. These factors will affect the timing of changes in fertility. But even though other factors may have offset to some degree the effect of a lessened income constraint upon birthrates, they do not explain the rise of the latter to levels as high as those of some states of uncontrolled fertility, after being at much lower rates.

Compared to countries experiencing transition onset in the postwar period, nations such as Chile and Japan, whose birthrates peaked in the prewar era, exhibited fluctuating fertility rates that did not have as strong a pre-deline surge, and rates did not fall as precipitously. As Dyson and Murphy point out, "even in populations where the manifest contribution of birth rate increases to faster [population] growth appears to have been minor, the factors that brought the increases about must have acted to brake the speed of subsequent declines in fertility and [population] growth rates" (Dyson and Murphy, 1985, p. 430). Within the living standard framework the prewar pattern is explicable by erratic income growth – sequences of growth interspersed with drop-offs in rates of growth, stagnation, or, in the 1930s, even income declines. The income constraints for those with unchanged norms did not lessen as quickly as they would have in a case of stronger and more continuous upward swings. And norms did not rise as rapidly, thereby slowing the rate of fertility decline. Yet the existence of income constraints upon rising norms is evidenced by the moderate drops in birthrates over shorter time periods prior to continuous decline.

Table 6.3. Reference chronologies for crude birthrate movements in selected

	1901–9	1910–19	1920–9
Latin America and Caribbean			
Colombia			-----
Guyana	--------28▽	+++32△--27▼++	+++++33△---32▽
Venezuela	28▽++	++27△-------	--27▼+++31△--
Costa Rica	37▽+++++++	+++43△------	-38▽++++++47△-
El Salvador			++
Guatemala			
Honduras			
Mexico	34▲-----		31▼++++
Panama			
Surinam			
Ecuador			
Paraguay			
Peru			
Argentina		-------	---------
Chile	+++++++++	+++++40△----	36▽++++++43▲--
Uruguay	----30▽++++	32▲---------	---------
Barbados		----31▼++	+35▲-------
Cuba			
Guadeloupe			
Jamaica	40△----38▽+++	39△------35▽++	++38△------
Martinique			
Puerto Rico		+++++++	++++++++++
Japan	+++++++++	34△-------32▽++	++35△-----
Taiwan	+	++41△-----39▼+	++++++++++
Sri Lanka	+++++++++	+++++++++++	+++++++41▲--
Malaysia			
Philippines	30▼+++	+++++35▲----	33▽++++++35△--
Singapore	+++++++	+++++++++++	++++++++++
Brunei			
Hong Kong			
Kuwait			
Europe			
Eng. & Wales	---------	-------19▽++	++21▲------
Germany	---------	-------17▽++	++23▲------
Italy	---------	-------23▽++	++30▲------
Spain	++31▲-----	-------29▽+	++30△------
Sweden	---------	----------	---------

[a]For the algorithm that produced this figure see text and n. 40 of article cited in source. All CBR series. Numbers given above the symbols △ (peak), ▽ (trough), ▲ (highest peak), and ▼ (lowest trough) estimates, but are given solely to convey a rough idea of the scale of CBR movements indicated by or constant within a falling phase. Some countries have major gaps in their CBR series, especially evaluated separately. To help in interpretation, we have attempted a tentative regional subgrouping of under "islands" (e.g., Hong Kong and Malaysia) the label is not strictly correct.

Source: Excerpted with the permission of the Population Council, from Dyson and Murphy, 'The table 2.

1930–9	1940–9	1950–9	1960–9	1970–9

on which this figure is based are unadjusted (i.e., not detrended).

are the 5-year moving average values of the CBR for that year. We stress that they are not

the registration data. + denotes CBR rising or constant within a rising phase; – denotes CBR falling

during 1940–9. In such cases ▲ and ▼ symbols may appear twice, since the two subseries have been

countries within the broad regional groups. Of course, in the case of some populations listed

Finally, Europe, albeit in a less technically advanced era, had attained higher living standards and income per capita on the eve of the industrial revolution than today's less developed countries. In other words, norms rose with the gradual rise in incomes accompanying the agricultural transformation. The growth of the industrial revolution allowed changes in marriage behavior as the income constraint lessened. Growth was gradual and cyclical, but with periods of acceleration. The more gradual rise of incomes and norms over the agricultural and industrial phases of development led to a relatively late and modest pre-decline increase as compared with the postwar experience of industrializing less developed countries, which borrowed technology and expanded with the comparatively fast-paced world growth of the postwar era.

SUMMARY OF ANALYSIS

Insights of the naive living standard constraint model presented in this chapter and of the consistent empirical evidence can be summarized as follows. Logically, living standard constraints upon fertility can occur in mainly agrarian economies so long as fertility is perceived to affect well-being. The living standard determinants are treated as inoperative in technically primitive societies where birthrates have no predictable effects upon maintenance of lifestyles. There, basic determinants include some factors that are proximate causes in the transition stage.

Conditions under which transition takes place today are distinguished by periods of more rapid acceleration in growth rates of per capita GNP and reduced incidences of stagnation, as well as more rapid drops in mortality rates. Accelerations in per capita GNP often begin when living standards are below those experienced in Western development and fertility levels are higher. The model shows that strong reductions in income constraints during onset of the transition can create rises in fertility rates prior to their decline.

Once declining fertility trends occur, the rate of decline is faster, the more rapid the growth rate of income per capita, since norms are higher. Whether or not growth rates are steady, interrupted, or accelerated will also affect the pattern of fertility changes. The model also implies that the distribution of income along the growth path affects the outcome. Higher inequality can slow the trend to lower fertility, and lower inequality can accelerate it, other things being equal. Certain data supportive of these analytical findings are presented.

Drops in mortality rates tend to precede the falloff in fertility rates. The basic living standard analysis presented, although not a full model of fertility transition, can explain conditions of rising or stalled fertility rates when mortality rates have already begun their downward trend. The analysis provides insight into why the population explosion is traceable to factors other than just mortality declines. It also predicts that there will not be a monotonic relationship between per capita income and fertility rates.

7

A Lifestyle–Norm/Time Constraint Model for Analysis of Long-run Changes in Fertility

THE APPROACH

The model that I will present here draws upon several key ideas in the literature about basic fertility determinants and utilizes a methodological approach that treats household activity as constrained by time. Behavioral premises are very broad and general. They avoid specific (often controversial) motivational assumptions about the desire for, or benefit of, children. Moreover, the origin of fertility decisions extends beyond the nuclear family or couple to the familial group and society.

The model reaches back to the economic living standard idea; but it greatly broadens this concept to include *nonmaterial* lifestyle components, in particular those that relate to children. Behavior is explained using the concept of norms as opposed to individual utility functions. The lifestyle standards are expressed in norms and their time determinants and are anchored to Easterlin's idea of experienced lifestyle. The constraints are expressed in time. Norms and constraints change over time. This approach presupposes the use of socially sanctioned birth control methods (which may be more or less sophisticated technically) to limit fertility when additional children would reduce living standards below a minimum.

The outcome is a general model that identifies a limited set of basic variables or behavior categories that determine reproductive behavior. Many variables identified in the literature are classifiable as subsets of the generic categories. Seemingly competing ideas are often reconciled within this scheme. The framework guides the researcher in regard to types of information that would be included under these categories. The model lends itself to qualitative as well as quantitative testing by social scientists.

FAMILY COHESION AND SECURITY

Group-determined behavior is a basic building block of the model, reflecting the fact that humans exist as members of a social matrix. Procreation is treated as an innate behavioral trait constrained by socially determined limits to fecundity. Although the model's behavioral premises are simple, they are presumed to arise from tap roots of the behavior tree. The idea that reference groups exercise leverage over fertile individuals in regard to the number of offspring they will produce is a common one in social science studies (Davis and Blake, 1956; Lorimer, 1958; Freedman, 1963; Blake, 1972; Lee, 1974; Hill, 1974; Mason, 1983). Therefore, in this background section we only suggest, in a general way, certain reasons for group cohesion that are interrelated with fertility. Essentially the reasons emphasized reflect the need for security, broadly defined. In particular, the family ensures that group well-being is secured by influencing fertility.

Stated more forcefully, the family – a kinship group broader than just mother and father – is the crucial reference group for unraveling the decision-making behavior relating to birth constraints. The roots of this premise are grounded in the fact that children are part of an intergenerational nexus that assures perpetuation of the species. They are supported by parents, family, and society as they mature. The crucial role that offspring play in assuring a future for the human race inevitably generates group identification with their needs – needs which are socially defined. Further, group responsibility leads to influence upon their number (Ryder, 1974, p. 77). When examining limitations upon the number of children, the most important group of reference is the family. It is the scaffolding upon which a theory of fertility must be built.

The family is a mutual support network of relatives that provides a basic source of emotional, material, and physical security for the individual from infancy through old age. Societies may differ with regard to the depth of family cohesion and the breadth of membership, but all families extend beyond parents and their offspring (Levy, 1965). Mutual obligations are instilled and enforced through group pressure. One such obligation important here is the support of family members whose standard of living – that is, the way their lives are organized and their time utilized – is threatened by loss of health or death, unexpected child care needs, or income shortfalls. When circumstances dictate, kin with higher lifestyle levels are expected to help relations living below the norm. Such group pressures extending to relatives with higher levels of time and/or wealth redistribute income to some degree and require time commitment from kin. In turn, their contribution creates reciprocal obligations for their potential needs. The importance of the family in determining and securing the living standard level of its members is the key to its influence upon fertility. In the model developed, it is clear that the lifestyle constraint upon fertility is much more complex than the simple income constraint that limits consumption of goods.

In sum, children are a regenerative link in the intertemporal family security network. They affect psychological and material security. Security is a function of group acceptance and of sustained maintenance of living standards. Children raise the sense of belonging and acceptance, in part by generating genetic identity. They solidify intergenerational interdependence of family members. Families support their lifestyle by sharing time and wealth over life spans, and this creates mutual obligations within the group. Such reciprocity raises the probability that family living standards will be maintained despite age or incapacity affecting an individual's goods time productivity. That is, commitment to family time interchange raises security.

Control of births need not raise security in states of very primitive technology and high mortality. In some poorer economies technical know-how is very rudimentary, and the number of children does not decrease the fluctuations in materials goods or affect the meager living standard. In fact, uncontrolled fertility will increase security by raising the probability of survival in droughts, plagues, or conditions of ongoing tribal warfare. Fecundity determinants, rather than family constraints, dictate the number of offspring in such societies. On the other hand, poorer agrarian economies that are technically able to control output fluctuations to some degree through farm practices will limit the number of offspring if additional children would lower material security below the accepted norm. Thus we find historical cases of heavily populated agrarian countries with lower fertility rates than countries with more land per capita.

In affluent economies, material security norms are higher, and achieving these norms is a function of human capital, or education. This fact affects the education norms that society establishes. In such economies large numbers of offspring are more likely to reduce security below established norms, since education and saving per family member may both decline as the number of children increases. The effect of more children upon security in wealthier economies will be tempered by social support of education and social programs for unemployment, retirement, and the like.

In conclusion, the family maintains a higher, more secure nonmaterial and material living standard on average through mutual support in terms of direct or indirect time interchange. The kinship group is a source of psychological as well as material security; therefore, family cohesion is important to the individual. The family as a group influences the behavior of members in order to maintain the well-being of all. Customs or mores that affect factors such as marriage age, wealth transfer, income sharing, and time obligations are examples of areas where the family influences individual and parental behavior. And, most important here, the family not living under the most primitive technical conditions will constrain fertility, since the expansion of family size through additional children affects group welfare.

BEHAVIORAL ASSUMPTIONS

The term "family" refers to a kinship group broader than the nuclear family, whose members share their time, income, and wealth. The family, along with society, establishes living standard and child support norms and acts to secure these norms for current members and the unborn. The family wants to prevent a decline in its well-being below its lifestyle floor. The time constraint model explains the linkage between maintenance of these living standard norms and the fertility rate. In this section we specify crucial behavioral assumptions that tie constrained fecundity to the family unit providing mutual support and security.

The model makes a central, simplifying assumption about behavioral motivation of the family in regard to mutual support: namely, that family members will support the perpetuation of the family but, through group sanctions, seek to control fertility in order to maintain (secure) family lifestyle norms for goods, security, and leisure and norms for child care.

As an extension of this idea we note that family goals are reflected in the social organization beyond the family, which also supports lifestyle norms through subsidies, laws, and social control. Laws affecting marriage age and child neglect, poor laws, and subsidies to schooling, housing, medicine, and the like are examples. Laws will reflect modal norms of the population. Parental decisions regarding family size must be understood within the context of social and family enforcement of norms for child support and inputs by society and the family into child support. Fertility is constrained indirectly by the need to conform to socially sanctioned lifestyle norms, not directly by a norm for family size per se (Mason, 1983, p. 396).

A second major assumption of the model is that the great majority of parents are social conformists in regard to lifestyle norms and hence the number of children they will seek to have. This implies that the decision to produce additional children is rational, in that methods of birth control, which may be more or less sophisticated technically, are socially sanctioned and/or enforced and are practiced when additional children threaten family living standards.

A certain number of parents will defy social influence. Parents not conforming are a small minority and are referred to as deviants. The number of children born to deviant parents is assumed to vary randomly above and below the average born to conformist parents. The analysis, then, concentrates upon determinants of fertility for conformist parents, assuming that the effect of deviant parents upon demographic trends will be imperceptible.

Family lifestyle and child support norms are defined in relation to minimum levels that are enforced through group pressures and inducements. Lifestyle norms are established in relation to experienced rather than aspired to living standards. In particular, the assumption is made, following Easterlin (1966, 1969) that lifestyle norms for new children and the family are those experienced by potential parents in their teen and early adult years. Thus the family may desire a living standard for current children above that which bound older family members at the time they had babies. Sustained prosperity, for example, raises goods and/or leisure living standard norms for the next generation as income rises above norms in years after child-bearing. Reference groups are assumed to influence the new norms adopted by households in this situation. Unexpected income drops persisting over teenage and young adult years of parents will lower lifestyle norms.[1]

In sum, the power of the group (family, society) to influence behavior is treated as a constraint upon the decision of parents to propagate. Parents will seek, with family approval, the maximum number of children that constraints allow. In order for the model to be significant to the explanation of long-run trends in fertility, the constraints must be limiting over different historical settings. This turns out to be a workable assumption, since norms change with familial and social response to changing socioeconomic conditions experienced by the group. They can be specific to social groups or classes and change as the economic status of the class changes. Secular changes in time use are highly influenced by changes in work time organization and its interrelations with the family unit.

Inevitably models of fertility greatly simplify the complexities of human behavior involved in order to explain the main forces at work succinctly. Here the analysis is structured differently from the utility-maximizing models that postulate a trade-off between the quantity and/or quality of children as income and/or relative prices change. The standard of living model treats children and goods as complements rather than substitutes. Yet it explores in some detail the relationship between expenditures per child and fertility, which is at the heart of the quality/quantity discussion. However, the emphasis upon a choice response by parents to economic stimuli is absent. Instead, the analysis proceeds from the above set of basic behavioral assumptions about perpetuation of the family and concentrates upon determinants of group constraints as predictors of

---

[1] It is possible that the psychology of this group-determining behavior is a ramification of the basic drive for food and shelter to survive. In sociological terms, the Easterlin assumption is compatible with the social identity approach to norms, where individuals infer applicable rules of behavior. The role model for parents includes their responsibilities as lifestyle providers. Parents infer applicable lifestyles based on those they experienced more recently. See Mason, 1983, p. 392.

fertility. These constraints are related to secular forces affecting fertility. In this respect, then, the model is within the traditional approach of sociologists, anthropologists, and demographic historians. Moreover, fertility behavior is modeled at a very general level, with the result that explanation or prediction emerges from a frugal set of assumptions.

A CONSTRAINT MODEL OF FERTILITY

The two main variables determining fertility are living standards (defined in terms of time usage, including child time norms) and the time constraint. The time constraint affects the maintenance of lifestyle and the time that can be allocated to child care. The health and age structure of the populace are treated as parameters.

Living standard (also referred to herein as lifestyle), Z, is a function of goods and services (hereafter referred to as goods) per family member (G/F), economic security per family member (S/F), and leisure per family member (L/F) per time period. Leisure is defined as time not spent obtaining goods and services or raising children. The relationship can be noted as follows:

$$Z = Z(G/F, S/F, L/F) \tag{1}$$

Family time, T, is a main constraint upon Z and is used to produce goods, security, and leisure, and to add to the stock of family members by raising children, C. The family minimizes the time constraint on its living standard by efficiently allocating hours, given Z categories and their proportionate size for the reference group.

Family members, as mentioned, desire to attain/maintain lifestyle norms and to perpetuate the family. Following Easterlin (1966, 1969) lifestyle norms that are desired for children are, at the minimum, those experienced by the parents in their teens, $Z^\star$, and considered the lifestyle minimum for the existing family. For simplicity of notation, the families of both maternal and paternal lineage are assumed to relate to the same living standard norm. The family norm will also reflect the lifestyle standard most commonly experienced in the family's reference group. We note this lifestyle floor or norm as follows:

$$Z^\star = Z^\star(G^\star/F^\star, S^\star/F^\star, L^\star/F^\star, \lambda \bar{Z}^\star) \tag{2}$$

where the asterisks refer to the previous time period when minimum standards were established, $\bar{Z}^\star$ is the modal lifestyle level of the family's reference group, and $\lambda \leq 1$. Family can now be defined as relatives who are present or potential contributors of time to maintaining mutual lifestyle levels of $Z^\star$.

Because children absorb family time, a constraint on lifestyle, they affect the time available for G, S, and L, as well as the denominator, F. Additional children, then, affect Z and can cause lifestyle norms to be unattainable. More will be said about child time requirements later.

Family time spent at work will have a known goods output per time unit, β, where output is measured in general purchasing power over goods. The composition of lifestyle goods, assuming that there are substitutes within categories of goods sets, is a function of relative prices at any time. Thus, given relative prices, there will be a least-cost goods set that meets lifestyle norms for shelter, nutrition, and so forth. However, the focus here is only on broad categories of goods sets that are complements, not substitutes, when minimum living standards are not met. Important categories of lifestyle goods are housing or shelter, food, and education.

Family time is allocated among work, leisure, and children. Location of kin, age, work requirements, and the like will limit the ability of family members to exchange hours freely among time category sets. Family members strive to keep $Z/Z^\star \geq 1$, where $Z^\star$ is the lifestyle norm. Children are time-intensive and affect G/F, S/F and L/F. The time absorption of children is composed of specific time category norms. The time needed to meet these category norms must be calculated in order to determine the number of children that can be added to family size without reducing family living standard below $Z^\star$.

The family is enumerated at time t and changes as mating, births, and deaths occur. In anticipating family time available to newborns over their dependency years, we have to assume perfect knowledge or assign probabilities to family time sets and speak of expected time sets. So long as $Z/Z^\star > 1$ for the family, there is a potential time matrix for the support of additional children. As will be explained subsequently, each family member will have a category-specific time matrix arranged so as to maintain $Z^\star$ and minimize the constraint upon new children. The category time matrices are then compared with child support norms expressed in time input requirements. Binding constraints in one or more categories limit pregnancies.

THE SECURITY NORM: A DIGRESSION

At this point I will digress slightly from the model's development to explain that the security norm is satisfied in large part by attainment of the goods and leisure norms; thus direct reference to this norm can be dropped. (Of course, this presumes that family lives are not threatened by ongoing hostilities among groups or nations.) As discussed earlier, the effect of children upon security is complex. Security is identified with perpetuation of the family and optimization of intergenerational time flows so that lifestyle norms are maintained. Both are related to the age structure of the family at a point in time. Time allocated to children can now reduce time devoted to work and thus current goods, while providing future support for the kinship group. Family wealth diverted to education of children creates an alternative form of income security, with a different stream of returns over time and net present value.

Security, to a large degree, requires that goods, services, and leisure per family member per time period over the present family's planning horizon not fall below the lifestyle floor or norm which relates to a previous time period. We can express this as follows:

$$S/F = f(G/F - G^\star/F^\star, L/F - L^\star F^\star)\Big|_{\substack{\text{min.}\ (G/F - G^\star/F^\star) = 0 \\ (L/F - L^\star/F^\star) = 0}} \tag{3}$$

A closer look at G/F is helpful in understanding conditions of fertility control. The maintenance of the lifestyle goods norm per time period is a function of the ratio of productive labor hours to total family members, k, output per labor hour, β, assets or wealth per family member, w, and the asset productivity ratio, ρ. Thus the security function can be reformulated in terms of these variables as follows:

$$S/F = f[(\beta k + \rho w) - (\beta^\star k^\star + \rho^\star w^\star), L/F - L^\star/F^\star] \tag{4}$$

A change in lifestyle norms among generations requires a change in one or more of these variables. As economies advance, education and technical change raise β and ρ, while the composition of w changes, becoming dominated by ownership or other rights to capital as opposed to land. Education levels and the population growth rate affect k through their effects on dependency ratios.

The above equation defines security in terms of the other two living standard components. For a given lifestyle norm, sustaining the goods and leisure norms satisfies the economic security norm and provides time for nonmaterial aspects of security such as psychological needs. Thus we proceed to analyze the relationship between fertility and maintenance of these norms, keeping in mind that this relationship also defines most aspects of economic security. Before doing so, we state more explicitly a point made previously.

In technically primitive agrarian economies, mortality, especially for infants and children, constrains family size and affects dependency ratios, k. There may even be excess leisure hours where children do not survive to absorb adult support time. In this type of economy the main productive asset, land, is not a limiting factor in many cases, in part because, using primitive tools, the worker can farm only a very limited amount of land. The weather, not population density on the land, determines fluctuations in efficiency ratios of land and workers for rain-fed crops. Under such conditions, β and ρ are uncontrollable variables, and limiting fertility does not affect economic security (Donaldson, 1984, chapter 9). In fact, the opposite may be the case when the high mortality rate threatens group survival.

In this type of economy a decline in mortality, other things remaining the same, will not necessarily lead to a drop in birthrates. If the situation remains one where fluctuations in β and ρ are still the determining factors and are greatly influenced by outside forces, living standards do not vary inversely with birthrates. Reduced mortality simply brings more land under cultivation through the use of off-season excess leisure hours, so that w rises as k declines.

Two things may change to bring on fertility control in agrarian settings. As mortality continues to decline, land becomes more densely populated and less augmentable. More importantly, fluctuations in efficiency ratios may become controllable through improved modes of farming, so that fertility restrictions will contribute to a controllable living standard. In the absence of these factors in societies experiencing early drops in mortality, populations soar, and bad weather continues to create famines without leading to fertility control.

This digression was necessary at this juncture to explain the handling of the security component of lifestyle in the analysis. We return now to the model's development.

ANALYSIS OF TIME SETS

Let $T_{z^\star}$ be the expected time set needed over the foreseeable future to provide the existing family with minimum lifestyle norms. Then the expected total family time set, T, minus $T_{z^\star}$ is the maximum expected time for additional children available from family members other than parents, T^f, the father, T^p, and the mother, T^m; that is,

$$T - T_{z^\star} = T^f + T^p + T^m \tag{5}$$

It is also expected that society will provide support for children. This is denominated in time set inputs as T^b. Thus the expected maximum time set that could be available as inputs for additional children, T_c, will equal the sum of these four time source sets.

$$T_c = T^f + T^p + T^m + T^b \tag{6}$$

Because we are concerned with blocks of time reaching into the future, it is helpful to arrange time in matrix form. Time subdivision units, t_{ij}, such as hours of a particular day/year, are elements of the matrix of expected time inputs from family, parents, and society. A zero element indicates no time input for a particular hour/day/year. T_c now becomes the union or sum of the disjoint time sets from all sources:

$$T^f \subset T_c = \{t_{ij}^f : t_{ij}^f \ \varepsilon \ T^f \text{ and } t_{ij}^f \ \varepsilon \ T_c\} \tag{7}$$

and so forth for T^p, T^m, and T^b.

Now we introduce four uses, or categories, for time spent on children: goods production (T_g), nurture (T_n), supervision (T_v), and education (T_e) time. Each time category set is the union of time-use sets from all child time input sources, so that we can write:

$$T_g \subset T_c; T_g = T_g^m + T_g^p + T_g^f + T_g^b, \text{ all disjoint sets} \tag{8}$$

and so forth for T_e, T_n, and T_v, except that it is assumed that society does not provide nurture time. T_n^b is a null set.

The family and society allocate their time efficiently, designating the categories, for which time will be used as well as the specific hour/day (t_{ij}). Two factors make potential time inputs to additional children from various sources imperfect substitutes among time-use categories: first, efficient allocation of time by parents, family, and society requires specialization according to comparative advantage, which raises efficiency per time unit supplied for specific categories; second, structural factors tied to logistics, economic organization, existing time commitments, closeness of kin, and the like will mean that time inputs potentially avaiable are imperfect substitutes among specific child time needs.

Given variations in time efficiency by source and structural constraints to flexible use of time, optimal time allocation will result in category-specific time constraints upon fertility. To some degree it is impossible to transfer time inputs among categories that are oversupplied to others undersupplied so that child time constraints are reduced. Structural factors and the degree of specialization change over historical periods, affecting which categories of constraints are binding.

The four categories of time use are not necessarily disjoint sets. A father or mother in, for example, an African economy may supervise, nurture, and/or educate a child at the same time that the parent farms. A child strapped to a mother's back as she hoes is being nurtured by the closeness of the mother. The mother may talk to the child, teaching the child to communicate while she works. Education, supervision, nurture, and goods production all occur simultaneously. Many other examples, of course, would be less inclusive than this. We will return to a discussion of determinants of the degree to which time categories overlap, producing joint output. Now we simply note that T_g, T_n, T_v, and T_e can be intersecting sets.

T_c can now be defined as the union of all expected time category sets from all child time input sources. Because time-use sets for different categories are overlapping, the sum total hours in these sets will exceed the sum total hours in sets of child time input hours identified by the source of time inputs.

The time matrix expected by a particular set of parents will contain zero elements. Moreover, there can be null sets for time-use categories, depending upon specialization and existing structural constraints upon the individual supplying time. We have already defined T^b_n as a null set based on the assumption of zero social inputs into nurture. Parents are aware of the time set category designations. The certainty of near-time input matrices is greater than expected distant-time matrices. Thus near-time matrices have more weight in fertility decisions.

All monetary or goods inputs from savings or other assets for child support are denominated in time. For example a dowry or shelter provided from shared housing is the equivalent of specific t_{ij} use time needed to provide these inputs. Time inputs into supervision of children and education can be direct time inputs of parents and family who actually supervise and educate and/or indirect time inputs which represent the income earning time needed to purchase supervision and education time. Efficiency arising from specialization and division of labor between the family and society can affect the allocation of time between direct and indirect inputs of time into both areas.

The time matrix is highly influenced by the level of development and technology – by the required specialization and mobility of labor. This important point will be discussed below. Here we note that when development brings separation of work time from the family farm or business, plus formal education, T^f, T^p, and T^m all tend to contain fewer elements. In addition, time category sets have fewer time units that can serve more than one purpose or use. Thus intersecting sets $T_g \cap T_n$, $T_n \cap T_v$, and so on contain fewer hours as the level of economic development rises.

CHILD NORMS

We proceed with the fundamental idea that there are norms in any society regarding lifestyle level. The family seeks to assure $Z^\star$ for all family members, including children. Children, then, must be assured minimum lifestyle goods, including education. These norms can vary among groups and over time.

In addition, we assume that the family and society set minimum standards regarding child care levels of supervision and nurture. We designate these norms for goods, nurture, supervision, and education in time units per child as A_g, A_n, A_v, and A_e.

Let

$$A_c = A_g \cup A_n \cup A_v \cup A_e \tag{9}$$

As explained below, labor productivity, β, will affect these time norms; so will infant-child mortality rates.

Norms are enforced by a subtle mixture of controls and inducements embedded in group interaction. Society sets laws regarding schooling, marriage age, child support, and parental responsibility for children's behavior. Families bond group members to behavioral codes through the use of psychological and material rewards and penalties.[2] The pressures upon parents to maintain child norms will succeed except in the case of deviant behavior. Conformist parents will not produce additional children when there are inadequate support hours to meet child norms.

In order to maintain family lifestyle and achieve nurture and supervision norms, the following constraints must be met for each additional child:

$$A_g \leqslant T_g; \; A_n \leqslant T_n; \; A_v \leqslant T_v; \; A_e \leqslant T_e \qquad (10)$$

That is, the expected time category sets from all sources must equal or exceed the child norms for each category. More than one of these constraints may be binding. Moreover, different constraints are likely to be binding at different levels of economic development, in part because norms change, in part because inputs for time categories and/or the productivity associated with input hours change, and in part because of a decline in the degree to which sets of expected time-use hours overlap.

Comparing different spans of transition years, then, the set of variables that determine fertility can change as different time categories are binding. In particular, it is expected that the education, nurture, and supervision constraints are binding only in more developed economies that show certain patterns of time allocation and education support. The goods constraint, on the other hand, is expected to be binding in economies at varying levels of income per capita, but not among some affluent groups in more advanced economies where the education and/or nurture time constraints are expected to determine fertility.

The model developed here provides a framework adaptable to different disciplines for theorizing about the determinants of both child norms and family and parental time constraints. It is very

---

[2] Mason notes that norms operate as constraints but are also internalized by the individual. There is disagreement over how this socialization process is achieved. See Mason, 1983, pp. 391–3.

general in the sense that social, cultural, and economic variables can be considered and tested; but all are expressible in the common denominator of time allocation determinants. Ideally, this focus upon time will prove to be a unifying link for the different disciplinary approaches to population studies. Moreover, the framework can be applied to various population groupings and/or the family unit. In fact, the idea that time can be a fundamental building block in understanding fertility is basic to the time usage studies that occur in the area of demographics, as well as the Becker approach, where time is introduced into a household production function.

In the rest of the chapter we will explore child norm and time constraint determinants at a very aggregated level and from a secular perspective, choosing proxie variables that will make the conceptual model empirically operational for national data sets using statistical testing procedures such as regression analysis. It is presented as one approach to testing for the variables determining time constraints and norms. In the process of making the model empirically operational, there is discussion of the reasoning behind the choice of proxie variables and their possible influence upon fertility over different socioeconomic settings.

DETERMINANTS OF CHILD NORMS

Mortality rates   Infant and child mortality rates affect all expected child time norms. The death rate in less developed countries is highest among infants and children. Child and infant mortality levels introduce uncertainty into the estimation of A_c. A decline in child and infant mortality rates raises A_c, since the probability of the child reaching adulthood and thus absorbing time is greater. This, in turn, will reduce fertility by raising the time on the average that each child is expected to need to meet norms. For the moment we omit mortality in examining determinants of specific norm categories since it affects all of them.

Education norms   Child norms for formal education change as technology and living standards change. The time norm for education is affected by the degree to which jobs require formal schooling, which in turn is related to the knowledge base and technical sophistication of the economy. In technically advancing economies, education costs rise more rapidly than income per capita and lengthen a child's dependency years, thereby raising the goods costs of children. In particular, introduction of education for the female represents a quantum leap in living standard expenses, since it doubles education costs or nearly so. (Moreover, female schooling reduces time inputs of older girls into housework and supervision of other children.) Not surprisingly, then, rising education norms can readily raise living standards in excess of the growth in income per capita. Of course, education norms can reflect both investment in job skill needs and learning for personal enjoyment, the former being indirectly, the latter directly related to lifestyle.

The education level of parents, in particular the parent with the most years of schooling, will be the major factor influencing the norm adopted for the offspring (Heckman and Hotz, 1987, p. 531). The time-consuming nature of education and the slow growth in labour productivity of education hours have a bearing upon the time inputs needed for each child to satisfy his or her education standard. In addition, changes in technology affect the required years of schooling. For empirical work the determinants of the education norm are specified as follows:

$$A_e = f(\overset{(+)}{E^{p,m}}, \overset{(+)}{\text{government education subsidies per child}}, \overset{(-)}{\beta_e}) \quad (11)$$

A_e is the product of the years of schooling and the time costs of each year. The latter will reflect the quality of education and the former the additional goods time needed to support children past their childhood dependency years. Since male and female standards differ and the sex of the unborn children is not known, A_e will be an average of the sex-specific norms. The calculation of $E^{p,m}$ will be similar to that of A_e. $E^{p,m}$ is an average of the sex-specific family education level for the parent who grew up in the family with the higher average level. Selection of the higher norm is another route whereby living standards, and hence norms, rise over time.

Private time norms often exceed public. However, the education level of parents will be influenced by the education standards that governments set, which are represented by government subsidies. The change in government subsidies will reflect the education requirements of changes in technology as perceived by the state. In poorer societies, the education level of parents and government subsidies will be highly correlated. The statistical problem is resolved, however, since the time inputs of the state will roughly offset their impact on the time norm for education; hence government subsidies drop out of the constraint determinants. As we will see later, $E^{p,m}$ also affects time inputs of family members, and thus there will be an asymmetry in its constraint impact. When the education constraint is binding – that is, when the coefficient for $E^{p,m}$ is statistically significant – the effect of education levels upon time norms exceeds its impact upon family time forthcoming. This constraint becomes more restrictive as the education years needed to support the family lifestyle lengthen (Cochrane, 1979, 1983). Finally, the productivity of education time changes very little and is probably most influenced by scale.

Goods norms　The goods time norm will reflect the consumption standards of parents (or the parent with the higher standard) in their teenage years and will be reduced by gains over time in labor productivity. Goods time needed is enlarged by prolonged dependency years as education norms rise. However, this may be treated as part of education-determined time input costs. For empirical work we can state:

$$A_g = f \left[\overset{(+)}{\frac{1}{\beta} \left(\frac{G^\star}{F^\star} \right)^{p,m}} \right] \qquad (12)$$

where $1/\beta$ is labor time per unit of goods output. Shelter and food time needs dominate this norm.[3]

Nurture–supervision norms　The time input norms for nurture and supervision are determined by the dependency of children, by requirements for safety and loving care. Most societies have some methods of conserving on supervision time, but little can be done to raise the productivity of such hours perceptibly. Of course, there are some scale economies to be gained as family size enlarges. The statistical equations in the next chapter, in order to simplify,

---

[3] Supporting the importance of housing standards today is the finding by Kelley and Williamson (*What Drives Third World City Growth?* (Princeton University Press, Princeton, 1984), p. 108) that low-cost housing accommodation in urban areas was an important determinant of in-migration to cities.

assume that A_n and A_v are constants. Of course, sociologists and anthropologists may readily explore causes of changes here that will affect fertility. Hopefully the framework presented will instigate further analytical work of a complementary structure.

The four norm functions specified above reflect time input needs under the premise that the child survives to adulthood. Later, we make all four a function of the mortality rate among younger age-groups.

DETERMINANTS OF CHILD TIME SETS

Family time The input time of the family, meaning relatives other than the mother and father, varies greatly from agrarian, lower-income societies to urban, higher-income societies. This has long been noted and studied by social scientists, often with an eye to its impact on fertility. Here the secular changes in family time usage become more fully identified with fertility through the structure of the model developed. An important determinant of T^f is the degree to which extended families share living space – land for housing and housing units. The extent to which the family must provide security, as opposed to socially provided security, for disability, old age, or unemployment also affects the amount of family time parents can expect in support of children. When the family is a major source of security, norms, not an extensive legal framework, achieve group needs. Family bonds and obligations must be established. This occurs through shared family time inputs into successive generations. When the security is socially provided, this diverts family time from children to earning taxes to support government security programs.

In agrarian economies it is common to see the family labor force working family-owned or tenant land. The goods production in such agrarian societies generally involves relatively large amounts of shared family time for production and consumption. And economies in earlier stages of industrialization are often characterized by the family business, in which family members share goods production time and income. This shared family time for goods production declines dramatically in urban, specialized economies with larger inputs of physical and human capital, a mobile population, and large corporations.

The increase in labor productivity with development enlarges the goods production per input unit of family time. However, there is eventually a fall in the work week that raises the leisure standard of family members, thus cutting work time for maintaining the family's goods standard. Both leisure and goods standards restrict the expected time for shared family input into an additional child. These standards are related to a minimum family norm experienced when current parents-to-be were in their teens. Optimally, we could unravel the causal strands to explain how these standards change form one generation to the next. A less ambitious tack is taken here, and these norms are simply represented by leisure time and labor hours to sustain goods acquisitions by households at the experienced level. The analytical framework identifies the importance of studies of changes in these norms, however.

Some family members may be living above the norm as a result of favorable economic conditions, so long as no family member is living below the minimum standard. The norm provides a reference point for calculating expected family time inputs into additional children. These expected inputs may be in time equivalents for shared housing, dowries, land, inheritance food and other goods, and education or in nurture and supervision time. However, the family will not provide time to support additional children if proferring such time would lower family living standards below the norm.

As explained, time input matrices are catregory-specific in many instances. For example, grandparents who do not share housing space and those in another geographic region will perforce have more limited time inputs into nurture and supervision but may use their time to earn income to provide education and goods for their grandchildren. Nurture and supervision time, and even shared family goods time, can reflect the nonmaterialism of a society. This outlook is often encoded in religious precepts that define the role of the family and family members and, in particular, male–female roles.

Finally, an educated child can substitute for wealth assets in other forms by providing future family income or security. Family savings, then, may be more readily available for education than for goods consumption. And the introduction of family savings as well as family income means that national income and wealth distribution can affect the national fertility rate. (Unfortunately, reliable data on their distribution within a national population are scarce.) In the model, wealth is measured in time units needed to earn goods and services purchasable with the wealth.

The parents' time Even when time inputs from all sources are treated as homogeneous, this does not make them perfect substitutes, since there are exogenous constraints upon each individual's time set. Such constraints – whether time inputs are homogeneous or nonhomogeneous – dictate the need for a highly flexible time source to minimize the time constraint upon additional children. Here the mother's time over her child-raising years is assumed to be more flexible than the father's.

Some background discussion can expand upon this highly simplified treatment of the mother's time. The parents' time is generally most efficiently allocated to allow maximum offspring by making the mother's time adaptable and committing relatively more of the father's time to work that perforce separates him from the children. This is particularly true once labor markets, as opposed to self-employment, dominate employment opportunities. In part, commitment of more of the mother's time to child care relates to the nurture needs of a nursing infant. In part, it stems from the physical differences in strength and the traditional division of labour toward nurture time by the female. Because this division of labor limits market employment for the woman, it has resulted in relatively greater allocation of education to males since the return is relatively higher.

However, when standards of living rise to a certain level in more technically advanced societies and less goods time is available from the family, relatively more of the mother's time is allocated to meeting living standard needs. This restricts nurture time input from the mother at a stage when nurture time from the family is also low. Even when the mother does not work, in more affluent marriages, the shortage of nurture time can limit children, since the father's time and family time for nurture are relatively limited. The modern female's alternatives for time commitment sharply delineate the conflict between child nurture norms and the upholding of family lifestyle in more prosperous economies. Society can substitute time inputs in day care and schooling, organized sports, and the like for the reduced supervision time of family and father, but not for increasingly scarce nurture time. Nurture requires family time inputs. And as economic security becomes less interrelated with children and family, divorce may rise and family cohesion drop, thereby lowering nurture time. (Oppong, 1983, gives a summary and bibliography of works related to the above discussion.)

More highly educated women will be in social groups where the education and goods standards are higher. Optimal time allocation to minimize child constraints may mean that such women enter the labor force in relatively greater numbers than women with lower education and living standard norms. Empirically this holds for the US. In some cases highly educated fathers earn enough that the education–goods constraint is not binding. The woman without a job who is married to a higher-income earner is likely to devote time to maintaining and increasing the husband's income through entertaining and maintaining other social contacts necessary to a professional man's career advancement. Such engagement of time by affluent women can be a requirement of the husband's career development and limit child time and hence fertility, especially when nurture time inputs from relatives are low. In general, social, cultural, and economic institutions will affect family and parental time inputs. A full understanding of lifestyle maintenance requires the tools of various disciplines.

Public time   The determinants of publicly provided time inputs to satisfy child time norms vary with the affluence and ideology of a society. In particular, taxes are not readily collected from poorer economies. As the ratio of taxes to GNP rise, there is more scope for social spending that can affect fertility. Publicly provided health services come to mind. Also, the need to provide social inputs into children rises as technology levels, and hence education levels, rise. Education has externalities in more technically advanced, specialized economies, and thus taxation for education is legitimized as incomes rise.

Ideological outlook can have strong effects upon the total social time input. Socialist or Communist societies will have greater levels of T^b at given income levels. Typically, however, other characteristics of a centralized regime will reduce fertility. Their tendency to encourage, if not require, high female work force participation reduces nurture time. And where the Communist regime limits investment in housing while eliminating land and home ownership on private property plots, there can be a housing constraint upon additional children. In fact, the greater controls of centrally planned economies over their citizens' time allocation will reduce flexibility of time use by families, and thereby intensify fertility constraints.

CHILD TIME DETERMINANTS

Seeking determinants of child time, T_c, that are measureable and reflect the complex socioeconomic forces at work over the long run, we set up the following functional relationships, based on the previous discussion of family and parental time constraints:

$$T_g = f\{ \overset{(+)}{\text{rural/urban residence}}, \overset{(+)}{\frac{1}{\beta_g}\left(\frac{G^t}{F^t} - \frac{G^\star}{F^\star}\right)}, \overset{(-)}{\text{housing per capita}},$$

$$\overset{(+)}{\text{maximum work week}}, \overset{(+)}{\text{family employment/total employment}}\} \quad (13)$$

where G^t/F^t is current family goods consumption per capita, and $1/\beta_g$ is labor time per unit of goods products. The family leisure standard will also affect time for goods acquisition. The maximum work week can be used as a proxie for the leisure norm for the family.

$$T_e = f(\overset{(+)}{E^{p,m}}, \overset{(+)}{\text{family savings}}, \overset{(+)}{\text{government education subsidies}}$$
$$\text{per child}) \quad (14)$$

Time (money) inputs for education from grandparents and others of the family will be greater when family education norms and savings are higher.

$$T_{n,v} = f(\overset{(+)}{\text{rural/urban residence}}, \overset{(-)}{\text{housing per capita}}, \overset{(-)}{\text{social security}},$$
$$\overset{(-)}{\text{female labor force participation rate}}, \overset{(+)}{\text{religious outlook}},$$
$$\overset{(-)}{\text{mobility}}) \quad (15)$$

Notice that some determinants affect more than one time-use set.

TIME CATEGORY CONSTRAINTS

Variables positively (negatively) related to A_c raise (lower) time constraints and will be negatively (positively) related to fertility. It is helpful to organize determinants of constraints by categories as follows:

$$T_g - A_g = f\left\{ \overset{(-)}{\frac{1}{\beta_g}\left(\frac{G^\star}{F^\star}\right)^{p,m}}, \overset{(+)}{\text{rural/urban residence}}, \overset{(+)}{\text{max. work week}}, \right.$$

$$\text{housing per capita}, \quad \overset{(-)}{\frac{1}{\beta_g}\left(\frac{G^i}{F^i} - \overset{(+)}{\frac{G^\star}{F^\star}}\right)^{p,m}},$$

$$\overset{(+)}{\text{family employment/total employment}}, \overset{(+)}{\text{government}}$$

$$\left. \overset{(+)}{\text{subsidies per child}}, \text{mortality rate}\right\} \tag{16}$$

Housing per capita may serve as a proxie for the goods standard norm, $1/\beta \ (G^\star/F^\star)^{p,m}$ in empirical testing. It also influences nurture and supervision time constraints. Moreover, rural vs urban residence and family employment vs total employment will both reflect shared goods time and may be correlated. In other words, empirical testing may reduce the number of proxie variables retained.

$$T_e - A_e = f(\overset{(-)}{E^{p,m}}, \overset{(+)}{\text{family savings}}, \overset{(+)}{\text{mortality rate}}) \tag{17}$$

Government education subsidies affect both T_e and A_e and cancel out. The productivity of education hours is assumed to be constant. The sign for $E^{p,m}$ is negative when the constraint is binding. When education standards are very low and costs are minor relative to income, the education coefficients will not be statistically significant. And when family savings available for education are high relative to the norm, fertility will be restricted by other constraints.[4] Over

---

[4] This explains the mixed results in the literature regarding the relationship between years of schooling and fertility in countries with varying average years of schooling. Also, since there is a correlation between education, earnings, and labor force participation rates, simple correlation studies can be misleading (Cochrane, 1979 and 1983).

some stages of the demographic transition, education is expected to be a significant determinant of fertility declines.

$$T_{n,v} - A_{n,v} = f(\overset{(+)}{\text{rural/urban residence}}, \overset{(-)}{\text{housing per capita}},$$

$$\overset{(-)}{\text{social security per capita}}, \overset{(-)}{\text{female labor force}}$$

$$\overset{(+)}{\text{participation rate}}, \overset{(-)}{\text{religious outlook}}, \text{mobility},$$

$$\overset{(+)}{\text{mortality rate}}) \tag{18}$$

The mortality rate is the variable most likely to prove statistically significant as A_c rises, at least until it reaches lower levels and changes are small. It is positively related to all categories, because the higher the infant and child mortality rate, the lower the probability coefficient for A_c – that is, the lower the probability that the infant or child will live to absorb the full-time norm hours. Notice that "rural/urban residence" and "housing per capita" are common to both $T_g - A_g$ and $T_{n,v} - A_{n,v}$. As these variables change, they affect the degree to which the time sets T_g and $T_{n,v}$ overlap. The model is a constraint model where:

1 One or more constraints will be binding over the female's reproductive life span, except in situations of very primitive technology where the group cannot influence living standards by restricting children.
2 One or more constraints will be binding for groups of families at a given time, since a percentage of reproductive females in the group will face binding constraints on additional children even if the remainder do not.
3 Over the transition, the constraint categories that are binding can change, so that not all variables are significant over shorter time spans.

Empirical studies must be designed to deal with the ramifications of the third generalization.

CONTRIBUTIONS OF THE NORM/TIME CONSTRAINT APPROACH

The norm/time constraint approach to modeling fertility transition builds on a broad cross-section of the literature. A large number of variables associated in the literature with fertility transition, but not necessarily in an interrelated way, are brought under a common analytical structure that fits the pieces together so that the larger picture emerges. The model explains how cultural aspects of time-use patterns and mutual support systems, education, housing and consumption standards, female and male work force participation rates and conditions of employment, mortality, and technological change affect fertility through their impact on norms or time constraints. Analytically, the approach has several noteworthy features:

1 The model yields generalization from a frugal, intuitively appealing set of assumptions which are consistent with the literature's discussions of fertility behavior over historical epochs of demographic change.

2 The analysis is interdisciplinary. It assimilates a broad array of frequently identified fertility variables, both economic and social, into a single framework that explains their interaction over the transition and suggests further modeling and empirical exploration.

3 The model extends and broadens the living standard approach of Easterlin and others, incorporating norms for child and adult lifestyles expressed in time use.

4 Intergenerational interdependence as it affects time use by the extended family, prominent in studies of fertility, is incorporated into the model. Family time, a universal denominator, constrains fertility and is thus a central construct of the analysis. Specifically, time from contributing generations is modeled as inflexible to some degree, and determinants of its inflexibility affect fertility.

5 The model explains why the relative importance of determining factors can shift over the transition. Time-denominated norms constrained by imperfectly flexible time from extended family members are grouped into lifestyle norm categories that affect fertility. Norms, time constraints, and time flexibility change over the transition. Thus the norm categories that are binding on fertility shift. This helps explain why different variables prove important in various more narrowly focused studies.

6 The roles of mortality rates in the pre-transition and

transition cases are clarified. Infant and child mortality rates are central to the model through their effect on expected time needs to meet child norms. This treatment of mortality rates, along with (5), explains why their impact varies over the transition. In pre-transition regimes, high mortality simply reflects the minimal controllability of lifestyles and contributes to making survival of the group a cause of high fertility.

7 The framework can readily be adapted to generate testable hypotheses at both the aggregate and disaggregate levels, using various disciplinary *modis operandi*.

8 The model differentiates between pre-transition and transition regimes. In testing for fertility transition variables, pre-transition societies must be excluded, because fertility analysis there requires a different model. Some variables may operate in both regimes, but in different ways. Moreover, nations at early stages of transition will generally have dual regimes, so data from them must be handled carefully.

SUMMARY AND CONCLUSIONS

The drive for procreation, for growth of the family and the species, is constrained by norms or standards related to child care, health, security, leisure, goods, and services. In fact, some norms help to assure survival. Norms are affected by technological advances and economic growth, which change time allocation of the family, educational needs, and security interrelationships of the family and society. In control regimes, population growth is sought so long as experienced living standards of parents-to-be are supportable. As time allocation needed to maintain lifestyles changes, so does the number of children supportable at new standards. There is a cultural content to lifestyles that is expressed as time constraints are eased during periods of growth in labor productivity. New norms then arise, although they may also occur as a result of infrequent exogenous influences such as political upheavals or religious transformations.

In the model, changes in time allocated to children and hence fertility do not arise because of changing taste for, or utility of, children relative to other areas of time absorption as the productivity of time changes, but because norms for lifestyle categories of time inputs and time constraints upon them change. Individual tastes are expressed *within* categories of lifestyle time inputs. And families with fewer children may absorb just as much child time as larger families of a previous era, because their standards of living are higher, especially education norms. In fact, these smaller families may absorb more of the parents' time in many constraint areas, because of the lack of time input of other relatives available in another era.

The framework is general. It encompasses variables mentioned in the demographic literature as determinants of fertility and ties them into the secular evolution of birth rates. Arguments associated with fertility are infant and child mortality rates, security and survival of the species, education, a normative standard of living (broadly defined), the role of the extended family, norms in regard to time needs of children, time constraints, technology levels and productivity, religious outlook, rural vs urban population proportions, and family work relationships. Time, it turns out, is the unifying link setting constraints on achievement of norms expressed in time, which in turn limit fertility. Results from a pooled time series test which we will look at in the next chapter, are found to support the model.

8
A Test of the Living Standard Model

ORIGINS OF THE DEMOGRAPHIC TRANSITION

Explanation of the demographic transition must identify determinants of controlled fertility – fertility that increasingly falls below biological maxima for given health levels. Judging from the experience of many countries, such reductions enter the picture prior to the phenomenon of continuous decline. Here I will posit an explanation for the movement of fertility rates away from high fecundity levels and their eventual fall to low ranges. The origin of the decline lies in the social control of fertility to maintain group well-being. The watershed is when social controls enter, not the onset of continuous fertility decline.

Once a group moves away from uncontrolled reproduction to socially conditioned fertility levels, there will be a gradual, but not necessarily continuous, drop in the total number of children born to a woman. Fertility can fluctuate, but it drops below fecundity levels for the conditions of improving health. Eventually a continuous, more precipitous decline takes place, moving fertility rates to much lower levels. Often this decline is preceded by an upswing. Then, once the decline is completed, the rates may fluctuate around these lower levels just as they did around earlier, higher levels; but they do not rise or fall more than a relatively modest amount.

Attention has been riveted upon the stage of precipitous decline. Yet it is equally important to explain the behavior of fertility rates as they begin to fall below very high levels, where variations reflect mainly supply-side factors such as nutrition, health, and the unplanned effect of evolving sexual practices upon fertility.

Comparisons among countries indicate that there is a fairly large difference in fertility rates between uncontrolled fertility in highly fecund African states and societies that are still relatively poor but have greater technical control of their agricultural output, and hence per capita income. The latter have lower fertility but have not yet experienced a continuous decline of birth and death rates. Coale has found that European populations obviously controlled fertility "to an extensive degree prior to the widespread development of literacy, prior to the growth of cities, and prior to the establishment of low levels of infant and child mortality" (Coale, 1979, p. 9).

In poorer societies with lower fertility levels, group guidance of the incidence and age of marriage, breast-feeding, separation of couples in bad harvest times, even group-condoned abortion and infanticide, are some of the socially developed behavior patterns that moderate population growth to maintain experienced living standards. These standards are rising, especially among some groups, but not as fast as they will at a later stage of development. Modest increases in lifestyles prior to more rapid rises in per capita GDP are associated with reproduction rates below uncontrolled levels. The pace and distribution of changes in living standards and associated health conditions can vary among countries at early stages of development, so their fertility levels may not cluster closely around the group mean. Eventually, however, they enter the transition period of continuous decline to similarly low, but fluctuating, reproduction rates. Variables that influence fertility need not weigh equally in all phases of the transition.

In sum, the first downward movements in fertility occur as lifestyles improve somewhat, and new standards are maintained. Literacy and the level of basic education, while modest and variable across societies, can affect lifestyle standards at this stage. Infant and child mortality remain high. Given relatively rudimentary living standards, fluctuations in both income per capita and death rates for the young can be substantial and can lead to fluctuations in fertility rates. In contrast, the phase of continuous decline in fertility rates to low levels is associated with substantial movements in one direction of several key variables: (1) continuous, precipitous drops in young mortality rates, (2) a stage of accelerated development arising from an industrial thrust adequate to raise material lifestyle norms for significant portions of the population, (3) sharply rising education norms related to technical changes accompanying development, and (4) increasing constraints on family nurture time. Once major movements in these variables are completed, fertility rates stabilize around low levels, fluctuating mainly in response to income and family time constraints relative to norms for consumption, wealth, and education.

CROSS COUNTRY VS TIME SERIES TESTING

The demographic transition involves a prolonged secular movement of death rates and birthrates spanning more than half a century. Variables influencing movements in fertility rates may lag changes in these rates by a generation. It is unusual to find sufficient time series data sets for single country statistical analysis. In particular, data are scarce for the countries of the globe currently in the midst of transition.

The test of the model performed here utilizes variables common to the multi-country experience. It is thus a limited testing of the model, one that is compatible with the use of cross-country data profiles for regression analysis. The data used in testing the time constraint model are pooled time series from ten countries. The use of pooled data was necessary to achieve sufficient sample size to test the model. Moreover, yearly observations were not available for all variables over similar time spans in all countries. Thus the data constitute an unbalanced sample, with some countries more heavily represented than others. Restriction of the observations to reduce imbalance produced similar results, yet it restricted the degrees of freedom.

COUNTRY SELECTION

A theory of demographic transition must explain fertility behavior that shows a distinct pattern from pre-transition periods. In the model here the turning point occurs when societies are sufficiently sophisticated technically to control to a given degree their material well-being, an important component of their general living standard. At that point, the number of children born into a family affects its living standard. Prior to such technical advancement, population densities are relatively low, and material living standards are determined by exogenous factors, including the weather, pests, floods, and so on; shortfalls cannot be prepared for adequately, or disease contained to any degree. Once a relationship between children and well-being evolves and is understood by the group, socially conditioned birth constraints upon marriage age or incidence, sexual mores, and the like are geared toward population control. Families move from a condition where group survival depends upon uncontrolled fertility to one where maintenance of experienced living standards depends upon limiting fertility.

At this point the determinants of fertility constraints will predict the transition behavior patterns. However, these variables will not predict fertility in pre-control societies. There is a need to recognize the change in status of pre-transition variables as transition conditions develop. Pre-transition determinants of fertility, such as sexual practices or marriage age, become proximate causes in transition states and are viewed as methods of birth control. Malnutrition affects the mother's fecundity and is a basic factor in pre-transition states. It soon loses significance as a random influence in early transition states, since societies are controlling births to prevent or reduce its incidence. Mortality levels may be a basic determinant in both states. But, for the most part, a new set of basic determinants emerges when, because of technical advance, well-being of the group and fertility are interlocked so that social controls of fertility emerge, and the pre-transition variables become instruments of control or proximate causal factors.

This means that testing of the transition determinants requires a population of countries that excludes pre-transition states. Of course, there can be pre-transition subgroups within dualistic developing countries which have not experienced a broad spread of technical knowledge to all groups. Countries should be picked to avoid a dominance of pre-transition conditions when transition determinants are being tested. In other words, most African societies, Bangladesh, and countries of similar technology levels are most properly excluded from a population designed to test determinants of fertility over the demographic transition. In this research, data limitations restricted the country list to ten, with Japan the only Asian representative.

DATA LIMITATIONS

The previous chapter specifies variables expected to affect fertility based on the analytical models. Data at the national level exist for a subset of these determinants for several countries during phases of their transition. Pooling them provides an adequate range of data in the absence of extended time series for each country. And use of pooled data is consistent with the level of generality of the model.

The final ordinary least-squares regression equations require country data for the following variables:

INF3 =   Infant mortality rates for babies aged 0–1 lagged 3 years behind fertility rates. This is the number of infant deaths per 1,000 live births per year. Fetus deaths are excluded from the data.

ENR =   Secondary school enrollment ratio. This is the number of children enrolled in secondary school as a percentage of the eligible age group.

MPL =   Female employment ratio. This is the level of female employment as a percentage of total employment.

DGDP3 =   The change in gross domestic product per capita over the most recent three years as defined by the year of the fertility data.

CHOP =   Annual increase in living space per capita in square meters.

FER =   The fertility rate. This is the number of all live births in a year pre 1,000 women aged 15–49.

Countries from which data for all variables for various years were available – Chile, Italy, Finland, Venezuela, Panama, Tunisia, Portugal, Japan, Puerto Rico, Costa Rica – do not have equally accurate data sets. Yet, because the sample does not include the most poverty-striken countries of the globe, estimates of fertility and other variables are of a generally acceptable quality for the purpose at hand. However, comments on certain measurement problems are in order.

The use of a cross-country sample required translation of per capita GDP for each country from its own currency into a common currency, here the US dollar. The exchange rates are not all equilibrium rates; nor do they reflect exactly equivalent purchasing power between countries. Restriction of the sample to the years of more flexible exchange rates starting in the 1970s avoids the severe distortions of the era of rigidly fixed rates. However, even where GDP estimates are highly accurate and exchange rates in equilibrium, the data will be an imperfect measure of income purchasing power (see Kravis, Heston, and Summers, 1982).

The change in housing space per capita may not capture completely changes in more modest rural housing. And the proportion of housing that is rural varies from country to country, thereby allowing for some understatement in more rural countries.

The number of children enrolled in secondary school as a percentage of the eligible age-group will be highly affected by the education levels of females. In less developed countries, males compose a larger percentage of secondary education students than is the case as a country advances. As more females are educated, a larger proportion of them join the work force. Thus, not surprisingly, there is some correlation between ENR and MPL. For the sample, these variables appeared to function as alternate proxies for education norms and family time constraints, rather than as independent measures. Consequently final equations treat them as such. Moreover, inclusion of both limited sample size.

Finally, data on government social expenditures for families and family wealth statistics were not available, nor were suitable proxies. The change in personal saving per capita was correlated with the change in GDP per capita and could not serve as a proxie for changes in family wealth. Thus these variables were omitted from the regressions. Data on the percentage of the population in urban centers was available, but with gaps for most countries. However, it was not found to be useful, as we will see below.

SUPPLY-SIDE VARIABLES

The model identifies fertility constraint determinants. Birth control techniques, including socialized behavior such as marriage age, are not included. Their correlation with fertility simply reflects changes in basic determinants. Yet controlled fertility regimes are never perfectly controlled. In part, this is because there are costs and disadvantages to the control techniques or practices. Moreover, infertility exists, and has various causes. As the demographic transition proceeds, couples have a broader choice of control techniques. However, at the same time, they have greater need for contraceptives, since their desired family size is declining, and, given better health, their ability to conceive is rising.

The question arises as to whether the availability, affordability, and/or acceptance of more varied forms of birth control result in families more closely approximating their target births. In other words, is there a systematic downward movement in the percentage of children in excess of the target? If so, and if this were caused by additional forms of birth control, then certain supply-side determinants would affect the transition, since target family size would be more closely approximated.

However, there are equally strong offsetting forces at work. The probability of conception in unprotected intercourse rises as nutrition and health improve in modern societies, while infertility falls. At the same time, the target number of children drops, enlarging the margin for error. An extra child in a targeted two-child family is a 50 percent error rate; another child in a six-child targeted family size is a 16.7 percent error rate.[1] Moreover, under conditions of high infant and child mortality, an extra child in *probability* terms moves the family beyond their target by less than one whole child. For these reasons, variables related to the biological aspects of fertility or the shortfalls of contraception techniques are not presumed to create a downward bias in unplanned fertility and are omitted from the cross-country regression analysis. They are pertinent, of course, when disaggregated household data are used.

REGRESSION FINDINGS

Table 8.1 gives ordinary least-squares regression results. As explained in the section on changes in per capita GDP, the relationships are log-linear. All five variables have a statistically significant impact upon fertility. In each regression, only three affect the drop in fertility levels of 80–85 percent: secondary school

[1] Thus, as many as 27 percent of white married women in the US in the 1970s said they had one or more unwanted children (Rosenzweig and Schultz, 1985, pp. 1–13, 992–1015).

Table 8.1 Determinants of fertility pooled time series log and semi-log OLS regression results[a]

Equation form	Constant	CHOP[b]	DGDP3[c]	INF3[d]	MPL[e]	ENR[f]	DF[g]	Adjusted R^2
Log	4.1802 (9.90)	-0.0394 (-2.350)	0.0419 (5.505)	0.3791 (7.694)		-0.2417 (-3.691)	30	90
	3.6170 (20.759)	-0.0751 (-4.009)	0.0460 (6.073)	0.4006 (10.694)	-0.1194 (-4.112)		57	74
Semi-log (independent variables log form)	134.6112 (3.293)	-4.6206 (-2.818)	4.0869 (5.492)	29.0304 (6.033)		-32.6254 (-5.100)	30	90
	36.4287 (2.242)	-7.5479 (-4.322)	5.4251 (7.677)	35.4067 (10.138)	-15.3754 (-5.680)		57	74

[a] Numbers in parentheses are t distributions. All coefficients are significant at the 0.01 level except log equation CHOP coefficients which are significant at the 0.03 level. The signs are as expected.
[b] CHOP = Annual increase in living space per capita in square meters.
[c] DGDP3 = Three-year change in GDP per capita.
[d] INF3 = Infant mortality rate lagged 3 years.
[e] MPL = Female employment ratio.
[f] ENR = Secondary school enrollment ratio.
[g] DF = Degrees of freedom.

enrollment (ENR) or its alternate, the female employment ratio (MPL); the infant mortality rate lagged three years (INF3); and annual increases in living space per capita (CHOP). On the other hand, the change in per capita GDP over the previous three years (DGDP3) accounts for fluctuations in fertility due to a tightening or easing of the goods constraint upon living standards. Over the transition, its effect is to slow fertility decline.

The coefficients for the log form of the equation can be interpreted as elasticities showing the percent change in fertility associated with a 1 percent change in the independent variable. Table 8.2 translates this relationship into the percent change in each independent variable needed to effect a 1 percent change in fertility. The living standard constraints to which the variables are related are also listed.

The log-linear ordinary least-squares regressions in table 8.1 proved to be the best fit. The second equation with MPL instead of ENR has more degrees of freedom but a somewhat lower R^2. All variables in both equations are statistically significant. Infant fertility is lagged 3 years, and the change in GDP per capita covers the latest 3 years, moving with the associated fertility rate. Lags of up to 7 years were tested but performed somewhat less well, although the results were quite good, with correct signs and similar magnitudes for the coefficients. Notice that the equations with MPL give slightly higher coefficient for CHOP, DGDP3, and INF3.

The signs of all coefficients are as expected, and their magnitudes are *a priori* reasonable. About 75–90 percent of the change in

Table 8.2 Elasticities and constraint relationships between fertility and independent variables

Independent variable	Percent change	Fertility change (%)	Constraint relationship
INF3	2.5	+1	all child time norms
DGDP3	20–25	+1	goods time constraint
CHOP	12–25	−1	goods time norm and family time constraint
ENR	4.0	−1	education time norm and family time constraint
MPL	8.0	−1	education time norm and family time constraint

fertility rates is explained by the independent variables. As we will see later, inclusion of both MPL and ENR in the equation reduced sample size and affected the statistical significance of one or both variables.

Each country experienced a declining trend (but not a continuous decline) in fertility rates over the decades of the 1960s and 1970s. Data were collected for ten countries: Chile, 1976–7; Italy, 1970–9; Finland, 1970–80; Venezuela, 1975–6; Panama, 1970–9; Tunisia, 1975–6, 1980; Portugal, 1974–8; Japan, 1970–80; Puerto Rico, 1973–80; Costa Rica, 1978; for a total of 62 observations, ranging from 1 to 11 per country. Data availability imposed constraints on the time series. The regressions with ENR had fewer degrees of freedom, but the sample was less unbalanced. In this case observations numbered 35, ranging from 1 to 6 years per country. Fertility rates varied from a high of 166 live births per 1,000 women in Venezuela aged 15–49 to a low of 49 in Italy.

Gauged from the magnitudes of the variables, infant mortality has had twice the effect upon fertility as changes in secondary enrollment levels or its alternate, female employment as a percentage of total employment in organized labor markets. It exceeds the impact of changes in per capita GDP or housing by an even larger margin. The results show further that in the transition phase the increase in income raises fertility, offsetting approximately one-fifth of the decline due to the fall in infant mortality.

The fact that infant mortality (and by implication the closely tracked child mortality) has the greatest impact upon the drop in fertility is not surprising, since a change in the mortality rate affects all child time norms by affecting the expected time inputs needed per child. Constraints are eased by the anticipation that not all children will live through infancy and childhood. The tendency is to replace a deceased baby unless constraints have changed in the interim or the pregnancy was unplanned.

The spread between fertility and infant mortality rates enlarges and then declines over the transition. At high levels of fertility, infant mortality rates for the sample were about half fertility rates, while at low levels the percentage was only 16. The constant elasticities resulting from the log-linear regressions imply that, in absolute terms, fertility declines are less responsive to lagged declines in infant deaths toward the end of the transition. In earlier transition a decrease in infant mortality of 1 per 1,000 infant deaths lowers fertility by 0.8 per 1,000, with a 3-year lag. In late transition the reduction in fertility is only 0.4 per 1,000. Thus fertility rates become less sensitive to mortality changes once infant death rates and the number of children born per 1,000 women aged 15–49 are relatively low, and the chance of survival is more certain. This impact of uncertainty upon family size under conditions of high and variable mortality levels has been referred to as a hoarding phenomenon.

The living standards embedded in education and housing norms adjust over the transition, and family time for nurture and supervision decline as less housing is shared and more females are educated and enter the work force. Together, as represented by ENR (or MPL) and CHOP, these accounted for approximately half of the explained decline in fertility. The other half, as we have seen, results from changed estimates of constraints related to reduced expectations of infant (or child) deaths, which affect all time estimates for satisfying child norms. These magnitudes imply that over the transition, affluence leads to higher material and education norms and changed family work time. These more than offset the short-lived easing of the goods constraint upon fertility, which occurs as rises in goods norm standards lag those in income per capita. And there is an increase in expected time needs per child as death rates fall to a small fraction of their high initial levels. This raises the expected time allotments required per child to meet rising norms, thereby assuring the transition to lower birthrates.

It is interesting, and even somewhat surprising, that only four proxies explain 75 percent or more of the change in fertility rates. The change in housing space per annum seems to be a comprehensive proxie for material living standard norms and family time related to shared family living space. It was statistically significant, even though it does not show bivariate correlation with fertility. It was anticipated that both ENR and MPL would be significant in the same regression. The fact that they were not may be due to collinearity or the limited sample size.

Approximately 10–25 percent of the decline in fertility could be explained by variables for which data were generally not available. These might include government social expenditures upon families, family employment as a percent of total employment, and family wealth. (Attempts to use changes in personal savings as a proxie for wealth proved unacceptable in an equation which included changes in per capita GDP.) And while the rural vs urban split in the population did not prove significant in the pooled time series regressions, exploratory analysis suggests that it may be significant for time series of individual countries.

The fact that the rural vs urban population split is a poor cross-country proxie for family time-sharing may reflect the fact that urban centers in countries at different development levels can have quite diverse effects upon family time sets. In poorer countries or dual economies with high concentrations of population, the city is really composed of contiguous villages – the so-called informal sector – characterized by cottage industry, shared housing, and clan proximity. Family employment can be important, and under-employment may occur. Housing is shared readily with the extended family, especially recent migrants. This contrasts with the city in higher-income countries, where family time-sharing is very limited, and so-called premature urban concentrations of people did not occur (Singh and Casterline, 1985, p. 212).

Finally, pooled time series data aggregated at the national level must omit variables that would prove significant in more dis-aggregated data. In fact, the theory lends itself to historical and sociological exploration of the explanatory variables. Regression analysis is simply a first step.

INFANT MORTALITY

In the time constraint model, infant mortality affects expectations of how many children are affordable, because higher mortality rates reduce the expected time needed per child for all time input categories. Thus its impact is very broad. As expected, this variable is highly significant in both pooled and individual country time series regressions. The latter were estimated despite limited observations. Indeed, it was significant even in more advanced countries with lower fertility ranges such as Finland.

Variables that are presumed to determine fertility rates can also be predictors of infant mortality rates: education, as captured by ENR and MPL; living conditions, as measured by CHOP and DGDP3; and the urbanization level of the populace. However, when fertility is controlled for these variables, INF3 is still significant at the 1 percent or less level of confidence.

Both fertility and infant mortality rates are highly correlated with the median marital age, which may be considered a form of birth control. Somewhat troublesome is the fact that early marriage and closely spaced children can affect infant death rates. This means that there may be some causation running from fertility to infant mortality. It is difficult to determine if this causation would remain once poor education and living conditions are taken into account. Conceptually, the model views causation as running from living standard norms and time constraints to fertility. However, other independent variables could cause fertility to drop, thereby causing mortality to decline if there is greater spacing between births. For this reason, and to account for the time needed for replacement of lost infants by new births, infant mortality is lagged 3 years behind the fertility-rate year. This lag length was empirically determined.

The regression provides additional support for the long-held idea that infant and child mortality declines cause fertility declines. And it has been noted that many changes introduced by birth control programs, such as prenatal nutrition improvements, changed lactations practices, and infant care education, reduce mortality. This may explain a good part of the impact of such programs upon fertility.

EDUCATION NORMS AND FEMALE WORK FORCE LEVELS

The variables MPL and ENR are individually negatively correlated with fertility and infant mortality and positively correlated with each other. Their simple correlation with fertility has been discussed in the literature. Results reported in table 8.2 indicate that a 1 percent change in fertility is associated with a 4 percent change in ENR and an 8 percent change in MPL. Although they differ in magnitude, each produces a similar change in the number of births per 1,000 women aged 15–49. It would appear that either is proxie for the same set of factors relative to fertility. The impact of these factors on fertility is exceeded only by infant mortality.

Secondary education for women means greater work force participation and a large increase in child education norms. Once education of females is included in child education norms, this doubles the education needs per family size, constricting the capacity of the family to provide the normal lifestyle.

Females who are more educated participate in higher numbers in the work force. Female employment opportunities are greatest in urban areas. Here the family setting is more nuclear, with less proximity to relatives. This results in less family time available to help care for children and a constraint upon fertility. Education also raises health standards for both mother and child.

Today, education may also be a route for raising social awareness at the national level of the relationship between fertility and well-being of the populace. Once national leaders accept the idea, often internationally transmitted, that attained living standards may be threatened without additional limitations to family size, they use education to establish new norms and controls of fertility. This is illustrated by the case of Mexico (see Alba and Potter, 1986). Failure in some cases to obtain a statistically significant result may reflect a sample enlarged by countries that do not control fertility.

CHANGES IN PER CAPITA GDP

Even though changes in per capita GDP are measured in 3-year increments, there is some positive correlation with the annual change in housing space per capita. It is not pairwise correlated with any other variables, including fertility. This variable captures changes in the goods time constraint over a period too brief for changes in goods norms.

The change in per capita GDP must increase by 25 percent to effect a 1 percent rise in fertility. Thus, if GDP per capita had been growing at 1 percent per year, a rise to 1.25 percent for 3 years would raise fertility by 1 percent. Note that the *change* in GDP per capita will be a smaller number than GDP per capita. (The same is true for the change in housing per capita.) These magnitudes are reasonable in the sense that this rate of increase in the growth rate of per capita GDP would be large enough to ease the expected goods time constraint upon children. Similarly, a decline of this magnitude could forestall or prevent births. (These findings are consistent with individual country studies showing an impact of the business cycle upon fertility.)

Obviously, the higher per capita income, the greater the increase in income necessary to support another child at the experienced or normal living standard. This is consistent with the estimated log-linear relationship between fertility and DGDP3. For a log-linear equation the coefficient of determination is an elasticity coefficient – in this case the percentage change in fertility for a 1 percent change in DGDP3. Thus the coefficient is independent of absolute magnitudes. The same reasoning holds for the housing variable.

The literature often assumes that greater income per capita over lower income ranges reduces malnutrition and thereby raises fertility. Presumably, this posited relationship between nutrition and fertility would be strong in a situation where fertility is uncontrolled. Here, the value of DGDP3 needed to elicit a given change in fertility rises in absolute value as per capita income grows. Thus the relationship measured is not the one that would be expected if it were capturing the effect of reduced malnutrition upon fertility as income rises.

THE HOUSING STANDARD

Material living standards and family time-sharing are both reflected in the housing standard, so that as its magnitude rises, fertility falls. As with DGDP3, the relationship with fertility is expected to be log-linear; but the regression coefficient is negative for the log of CHOP. Although the annual change in housing space per capita and DGDP3 are positively correlated, their impact upon fertility has opposite effects.

Although this variable is not as important as others, it still has substantial impact. The education component of lifestyle standards, as captured by ENR, is more important than the material standard measured by housing. Housing standards were roughly one-fourth as important as infant mortality in reducing fertility, while ENR was over half as important. Taken together, they have about the same impact as changes in mortality on the fall in fertility rates. When MPL is substituted for ENR, sample size increases, and the coefficient for housing is somewhat higher. Overall, housing space per capita appears to be an adequate proxie for material living standards of families. Housing is important regardless of the development level, whereas items such as cars are not. And the ability to meet housing standards is often a precondition for marriage. The proxie might be improved on by a more comprehensive living standard index where available.

THE FERTILITY–MORTALITY LAG

It has been noted that in less developed countries today the onset of fertility declines lag those of death rates. And the rate of decline in mortality is greater over the first decades of the transition. The model developed here explains this by the relative timing of movements in other independent variables that affect fertility. During rapidly industrializing stages of development, there are accelerated changes in per capita income (Donaldson, 1984, chapter 12). This can change by as much as 6 percent per year for a decade or more, a rate which is more than twice long-term averages. At the same time, health care improvements and other factors are accelerating reductions in infant mortality rates. The decline in INF is half completed before CHOP, ENR, or MPL reach their midpoints.

In this phase of the demographic transition the positive income effects upon birthrates offset some of the negative effects of declining infant deaths. On the other hand, education and job opportunities for females remain limited until later in the development process. Recall that secondary education and female employment ratios are second only to infant mortality rates in their impact upon fertility. Enrollment rates jump once female education is instituted. Until this occurs, mortality declines are by far the major factor having a negative effect on birthrates. Their impact is reduced by positive income effects in the absence of other negative factors. Thus the lag is explained by the timing of the relative movements of other determinants, rather than a change in the basic relationship between fertility and mortality over the transition.

Typically growth rates slow in late stages of modernization as the growth base widens, living standards of more groups are adjusted to reflect experienced changes in income per capita, housing and education norms rise, and family time for nurture declines as women enter the work force. Fertility drops more precipitously as the impacts of norm and constraint changes are added to the effect of mortality declines. In other words, an accelerated middle phase of growth in GDP per capita and lagged female education and work force participation relative to males help to explain why fertility declines are slower than mortality declines in earlier phases of the demographic transition, even though infant mortality drops rapidly then. Growth in per capita GDP may also explain evidence showing that fertility rates rise in some countries before the permanent transition to falling rates (Dyson and Murphy, 1985; and chapter 6 above).

COMPARISON WITH WESTERN PATTERNS

The transition in the West did not produce as great a lag between fertility and mortality declines. Why? We would expect to find that the relative timing of housing and education norm changes, changing family time constraint patterns, and the behavior of per capita growth rates explain the differences in the gap between fertility and mortality in earlier and later transitions rather than any difference in the response of fertility to mortality declines. In the West, living standards rose moderately and gradually for the large percentage of the populace before major declines in infant mortality. Transition to controlled fertility began well before mortality's continuous decline, and fertility in the 1600s was lower than the high rates in today's less developed countries in early or pre-transition stages. The post-World War II developing countries have experienced higher continuous rates of per capita income growth than Western countries did.

Not only were changes more gradual in the West, but the composite variables had a different timetable. Housing standards were higher at an earlier stage of their development – in part because living space in colder climes is more expensive to construct and the need for shelter more demanding. In England by the eve of the industrial revolution, housing standards were relatively high, and birthrates below their maximum. Housing norms helped to set the age of marriage. Income increments were not as likely to be sufficient to support another child or two, and thus were more likely to lead to incremental increases in lifestyles. On the other hand, education needs were less likely to cause lower fertility. Rates of technical change did not require as much education for female labor force entrants as that required by today's technology. Moreover, there were more opportunities than today for sharp productivity improvements through emigration. In the new lands, labor productivity rose, income constraints lessened, and fertility levels were higher.

There were population surges in the West, but below the levels in the Third World today. In today's demographic experience two situations give rise to a burgeoning of infant and child populations over previous levels. Only one is traceable exclusively to mortality declines. And this occurs in countries where there is no purposeful social control of fertility for the vast majority. They are the countries that are economically and technically most underdeveloped. Often tribal killings and national warfare are common. Inoculations and internationally financed health measures are producing a one-time decline in infant mortality, but to a lower level that remains well above rates in advanced countries. Reproduction rates remain high, and population grows at relatively high rates unless crop failures, wars, or epidemics intervene. The level of technical advances in agriculture and the social structure do not result in the family being able to change very much the predictability or insecurity of their lifestyles, except the upper class perhaps. Social controls of fertility have not been introduced among the masses, and fertility rates do not adjust to mortality rates.

The other situation of rapid population growth occurs once the country is somewhat further along the development path. The rate of development is accelerating, causing income per capita to rise rapidly, while mortality rates have begun a quickening, continuous decline. Unlike the previous case, fertility rates are responsive to falling mortality, but the response is both lagged and less than equivalent. As explained, the population bulge is in part traceable to the relatively rapid rise in per capita income. Slower population growth must await the lagged effects of fertility-reducing factors such as rises in female education and employment and other living standard norms, particularly housing space. This rapid rise in per capita income sets the stage, though, for a relatively sharp increase in lifestyle standards that, once adopted, can lead to comparatively dramatic declines in fertility rates. This is particularly true once social perception of a relationship between living standards and fertility leads to population planning.

9
Policy Implications of the Lifestyle Approach

The living standard norm approach which I have developed here opens up various avenues for informed policies and gives insights into social and economic choices that affect fertility. The approach greatly broadens the scope for policy action. It also lengthens the time horizon of policies for changing fertility. Birth control information and health clinics gain stature when viewed from a broader policy perspective, where fertility is an integral part of government development or social policies in countries approaching or undergoing demographic transition. Many of the policy components will create an impact over the span of a generation, while others may have shorter-run effects.

Policy implications of the model must be viewed as experimental at this juncture, however. If further testing and examination of the approach fail to give evidence for rejecting the model, then the policy guidelines can be followed more confidently. At this stage, of course, policy implications must be adopted only after careful consideration, making sure that a policy is worth pursuing even if the fertility impact is negligible. Fortunately, there are important policy implications that are justifiable on grounds other than fertility change alone.

There are definite limitations to the scope and effectiveness of policies to reduce fertility. Governments only have resources commensurate with their country's tax-paying capacity. Laws must find acceptance with the populace in order to be enforceable. Even dictatorships are limited in their enforcement capacities. This means that marriage-age laws or land-tenure laws may be ineffective and that governments do not have resources to raise material standards, education, health, and so forth far beyond existing levels. Time taken in taxes limits the rise in standards in nonsubsidized areas. And it can take 10 years for lifestyle changes to affect fertility rates via higher norms for teenagers experiencing them. However, when standards are low, changes such as those for education and health norms can be significant enough to change family size to some degree. On the other hand, large changes in family size in short periods of time take draconian policies executed by overbearing dictatorships. There can be backlashes as policy controls become ruthless. In general, the time of greatest policy impact potential is when time productivity gains are rapid while lifestyles are still modest. This means that well-executed policies can reduce the increase in birthrates at onset and speed their decline at somewhat later stages.

POPULATION AND DEVELOPMENT

Unfortunately ideas about "vicious cycles" of poverty interrelated with population growth persist, even though our understanding of population's role in development has shown that this idea is severely overdrawn and even misleading. Frequently adherents strongly imply, if not state, that control of population in countries such as those of Africa is a necessary and sufficient condition for development. Yet current understanding refutes this.

The reference for the "vicious cycle of poverty" phrase is a 1956 article in the *American Economic Review* (Nelson, 1956). The analysis traces low saving to population pressures. It was written during the period when saving-centred growth models of the Harrod–Domar type were at their zenith of popularity. It was a time when Russian growth rates were high, and when it was thought that the Stalin growth strategy could be readily transplanted to less developed countries. The Communist Party chose a capital-intensive development path, extracting high savings from the populace to finance the capital formation. Vicious cycle ideas also appeared at a time when population growth rates in poorer nations were historically high, while economic growth was not. There was a ripeness for neo-Malthusian ideas. The Nelson model supplied an explanation for underdevelopment and poverty in these countries, based on a saving constraint related to rapid population growth. But the model was too singular in focus to survive a broadened understanding of the development process. Analysis, population behavior in less developed countries, and development experience have all passed the Nelson hypothesis by.

Over the past 30 years a more balanced treatment of population and development has emerged. Examination of data has failed to establish an inverse correlation between population growth rates and saving rates or GNP growth rates. Nor does there appear to be an inverse relationship between growth rates of per capita income and population density. In fact, there is no monotonic relationship between fertility rates and GNP per capita. Moreover, the data from the 1970s show incidences of transition in fertility from high to low rates that, once begun, appear to proceed at a much faster pace than occurred in Western demographic transition. In addition, it is believed that the world has already seen its highest population growth rates arising from the lag in fertility behind mortality declines.

Data collected over the postwar development decades show that there is only a very weak relationship, if any, between household saving and family size (Donaldson, 1984, chapter 4). Apparently, households clear additional land, work additional hours, and economize so that saving from household income is little affected by fertility. In studying households at various income levels, a trade-off between children and leisure is more likely to occur than one between children and saving.

Another point to be made is that the main source of saving in very poor economies is profits. Profits may or may not be affected by population growth. The most complete analysis treating a relationship between the two makes wages an inverse function of labor supply. High population growth produces an abundant supply of labor, low wages, and high profits, compared to lower labor force growth. Diminishing returns in agriculture can be overcome by technological change (Kelly, Williamson, and Cheetham, 1972).

Is it reasonable to downplay Malthusian models of agriculture and food supplies? Yes, it is. The Green Revolution, except in regard to African agriculture, has produced unprecedented growth rates in food crops. Those countries not sharing in this breakthrough generally have policies and politics that thwart transformation.

Even in Africa, a large part of the agricultural shortfalls are related to poor leadership and policies, particularly in regard to marketing board pricing, infrastructure development, and urban focus. As a continent, Africa is not densely populated. Lower population growth rates would do little to change the basic causes of poverty, in particular her capacity for technical change.

Returning to saving constraints, the level of saving needed for growth under well-designed development programs is not overwhelming. Less developed countries can achieve strong growth rates with average ratios of saving to GNP as low as 15 percent. Over the growth path, this ratio shows an elongated S shape (Chenery and Syrquin, 1975). In other words there is an acceleration, then a leveling off of the saving rate. Some of the saving increments come from fuller employment and more work days as workers enter the labor market and leave farm employment. The saving ratio varies considerably among countries. It depends on the capital intensity of the development path, the degree of specialization in production, and the efficiency of technically advanced capital used in the less developed economy. It is also affected by how much of savings go into housing and inventories, as opposed to more directly productive capital. Fortunately, newly developing countries do not have large capital stocks to replace, and obsolescence is not as high as in advanced countries. Saving needed to cover depreciation is more modest.

Today, emphasis is placed on conservation of capital and increasing its efficiency in infrastructure-poor environments, as opposed to the naive capital-intensive strategy of the growth models (Stewart, 1977; Donaldson, 1984). Countries may specialize and trade so that the product mix is less capital-intensive. Foreign investment may be allowed in more capital-intensive areas of production. Moreover, in warmer climates, saving for housing is lower, since costs of construction are less than in cold climates. And helpfully, the relative cost of capital goods falls with development (Kravis, Heston, and Summers, 1982).

It should be noted that the acceleration phase, when the saving to GNP ratio rises, is often a time of strong population growth associated with increasing prosperity, for this phase occurs fairly early in the growth process. In these early phases, demographic transition is only beginning among limited segments of the populace, and population growth remains high.

Is the neo-Malthusian paradigm completely irrelevant? Only if it places population growth in the role of the cause of stagnation, as opposed to a variable that can intensify poverty under certain conditions. These conditions would be situations where economies show no growth or development impetus, arable land is densely populated, and emigration blocked. A few countries come to mind here such as Bangladesh or Haiti. But even Bangladesh is struggling to introduce changes in agriculture to offset diminishing returns.

The important question is: What is the relationship between population density, population growth, and economic development? There are indeed important interrelationships. There is a general consensus that moderate population growth rates create the most favorable conditions for industrialization. This does not mean that high rates create vicious cycles of poverty, but simply that with them industrialization does not proceed as rapidly. Growth performances, such as those of densely populated Japan, are in part traceable to low rates of population growth (Kelley, Williamson, and Cheetham, 1972).

Two reasons are given as to why rapid population growth slows industrialization. First, demand patterns keep more resources in agriculture to feed a rapidly growing population. Also, education, housing, and health are needed in greater quantities as population expands rapidly. Second, rapid population growth increases the supply of labor, thereby lowering wages. Output responds more to lower labor costs in agriculture, because the production function technology is more labor-intensive. It absorbs labor more intensively as labor prices fall than does the more capital-intensive production function of industry.

Population, however, can have positive effects on growth. The low wages increase profits, and thereby investment and technological change, both financed from profits. Economies of scale are an important contribution of population density. Infrastructure such as transportation, utilities, and communications particularly achieves greater efficiency from scale economies. Firms in industry benefit more than farms.

On the negative side, unemployment and inequality may be worse under conditions of rapid population growth. Young people must be assimilated, apprenticed, and often relocated before they can settle into stable employment. The capital and other resources needed for this may lag when large numbers enter the labor force.

Inequality and dualism are worsened where the poor and the weathier classes have wide disparities in birthrates.

Countries densely populated and with high or even moderate growth rates of population undoubtedly need to curtail fertility in order to improve their economic performances. India and China come to mind. A country such as Brazil, however, has had very high growth rates of per capita GNP along with high rates of population growth; so has Mexico. A generalization about policy is not readily made outside the obvious cases. Often, however, population policies are pursued for reasons other than their impact on GNP per capita.

POLICIES FOR LESS DEVELOPED COUNTRIES

In the above discussion we have seen that population growth does not necessarily slow development. In some situations, moderate rates of population growth are helpful to economic performance. Nevertheless, the discussion with regard to less developed countries is caste in the framework of those policies that help to bring on transition and speed its pace. This is because policy is of greater interest to those seeking to curb birthrates.

Lifestyles are changeable in the absence of time productivity gains, but only to a certain degree – at least in the absence of disruptive social upheaval. The inability to redirect time use greatly without improvements in productivity places a limit on policy goals. Ambitious goals are more attainable when productivity and other changes set the stage for them. Plans that are overly ambitious and unattainable can cause failures that set back the opportunity for more realistic goals. Effectively designed policies will gauge the probability of success in the development context. Fortunately, many policies that achieve other important development or social goals can also lay the groundwork over time for fertility changes. Fertility goals, then, can be used as a bolstering argument for such policies. This means that many of the policies discussed below do not have to await further development and testing of the theory. They are justifiable on other grounds, and the predicted fertility results become a reinforcing argument for such policies.

Agricultural policies

The controllability of lifestyles is a prerequisite for fertility control. At early stages of development, a country's populace is mainly occupied in agriculture. Weather, pests, disesase, all beyond the control of the peasant, determine food supplies, fodder, and other basics. Famines and epidemics occur periodically and decimate populations. Until there is some degree of technical advance that allows the peasant to feel more in control and less threatened by starvation and plagues, there is no incentive to restrict births.

Going a step further, the greater and more secure the well-being of the peasant, the more fertility will respond to threats to an established living standard. Policies that promote a development in which the peasantry shares broadly will also be conducive to transition onset. Policies that neglect agriculture or allow a large proportion of farmers to remain technically backward, subject to the vagaries of rain-fed agriculture without basic farming advances, will stall the onset of the demographic transition among large segments of the populace in the rural sector.

The study of development since World War II has made it clear that neglect of agriculture will sabotage development strategies. Without productivity gains in this sector, the food needs, raw materials, exports, labor supply, and domestic markets needed for industrial growth will not be adequate (Kilby and Johnston, 1975). Some countries have tried a dualistic approach to agricultural development, targeting certain segments for modernization. This requires capital-intensive farms and is counterproductive. It fails to motivate subsistence farmers to raise their productivity, produce for the market, and free labor for industry. Goods markets are small because the masses remain poor. Firms need protection from imported goods to achieve scale efficiencies. Affluent sectors gain high purchasing power and demand advanced products, while masses of people subsist in poverty. Political unrest threatens stability as inequities rise. Food shortages occur in cities as the government controls prices, turning the terms of trade against agriculture. Foreign exchange shortages intensify as food is imported to the exclusion of capital goods, and agricultral exports suffer.

Often countries pursuing these policies also introduce inoculations and other health measures of a basic type which reduce mortality rates and lead to population increases among the poor. Fertility rates remain high, because the peasant's condition is still one of little control of his or her well-being.

In contrast to a dualistic development of agriculture, a unimodal approach can lead to a certain level of prosperity and security among rural peoples. Land reform or tenant reform, the introduction of Green Revolution technology, cooperatives, the right terms of trade, storage facilities and grain reserves, small-scale farm machinery and mass-market industrial goods, credit facilities, regional transportation, and so forth can create a sound basis for development.

Unimodal policies will also speed the onset and pace of the demographic transition. The high fertility rates of the rural populace will begin to decline eventually as the rural populace shares in the broad-based improvements of lifestyles and feels more in control of their lives. Broadly based productivity gains free labor from rural pursuits of farming to other sectors in which time constraints change and affect fertility. The differential between rural and other sector fertility rates will not be as large and will narrow more readily. Examples of such different approaches and their fertility impact might by unimodal Taiwan compared to dualistic Brazil. At the fertility onset, of course, fertility can rise as more equal income distribution reduces constraints. It will, however, set the stage for a more rapid transition to lower fertility.

Social threats to survival

Tribal or ethnic rivalry and wars can threaten group survival. Such challenges to survival are intensely present on the African continent today. Wars, killings, loss of political rights, create an atmosphere of great insecurity. Moreover, a larger-size group may be sought to diminish the insecurity. Fertility is usually high in such cases.

Policies that intensify rivalry are pro-natal. Tribal nepotism, army brutalities, apartheid laws, exclusive privileges, marriage laws limiting intermarriage, territorial divisions, government patronage, language barriers, and religious persecutions deepen the divisions. The theory of lifestyle norms is not applicable when survival is at stake. Groups threatened with annihilation will generally turn to high natality as a survival weapon.

What can be done to reduce social threats to groups survival?

Anything that will reduce the rivalry and distrust. This facile answer, of course, fails to address the great pitfalls that stand in the way of doing this. In the absence of reduced tensions, fertility is unlikely to moderate. Typically, however, the government is part of the social milieu giving rise to the divisions and may even be a cause of deepening rivalry.

Mortality

Countries differ in their ability to absorb and finance changes that can lower their death rates. However, reductions in mortality rates, in the absence of group rivalries, are usually goals of every state. And the reduction of infant and child deaths is generally a priority goal. A development pattern that avoids dualism is helpful in reducing death rates.

Declines in mortality precede drops in fertility today. This results in a burgeoning of population. At such time a rise in fertility rates will add to population increases. This may occur as economic growth raises productivity and constraints on lifestyles ease, while living standards are relatively low. The decline in mortality raises expected time needs per child only modestly when lifestyles are those of low development levels. It does not offset the positive effect on births of improved incomes as labor efficiency increases.

Generally mortality goals and fertility policy are not perceived to be related. However, there is a way in which fertility policymakers can capitalize on their success in lowering deaths. They can make sure that the improved survival probabilities are, first, made known to the public and, second, directly related to expected family size and family time needs to support children with higher survival rates. They can use this information in their family planning clinics. Gradually, as the mortality changes are perceived and living standards rise, mortality declines will play an increasing role in reducing fertility. But the impact will take hold more slowly without a public information effort. Moreover, if authorities do not attack causes of high mortality in all regions of the country, they will be confronted with its impact on high fertility. Optimally this should spur them on to attack mortality problems in backward regions. Of course, a decline in infant and child death rates may have limited consequences where fertility is concerned if adult survival is threatened by social conflicts.

Education norms

Education greatly changes time-use patterns and inputs into children. Work time is needed to supply the funds for education and to support children's lifestyles during longer dependency years. Time inputs into household tasks by children drops. When females are educated, then any newborn is expected to require education inputs, regardless of sex.

Government's greatest potential impact is probably in the area of rising education norms for both males and females. Both laws and subsidies come to bear here. A failure to enact and enforce education standards for females slows the transition to lower birthrates.

Education is expensive to both the household and the government and competes with other development needs that absorb savings. Governments must assess its opportunity cost, using carefully set-up cost–benefit analysis. One of the calculated benefits may be reduced fertility when an economy has high birthrates.

Another way in which education becomes relevant to fertility change is in its ideational impact. Informal education is important here, in birth control information and attitudes. Basic reading skills may be a prerequisite to following directions for use of contraceptives, medicine, and food and for engaging in other health-related activities. Education may also lead to changes in cultural values that will influence fertility levels.

Lifestyle norms within the home are greatly influenced by women. As a result, many lifestyle norm changes are related to the education level of females. Japanese society is an example of widespread education at relatively early stages for both sexes. Russian society also moved in this direction after the Bolshevik Revolution. The hand that rocks the cradle can also help determine its occupancy rate.

A woman's educational level and marriage age are also interrelated. In fact both sexes marry later as education norms rise. The female's age at marriage, of course, affects her fertility rate.

Technology advances, an enabling and integral factor of lifestyle changes, are dependent upon educational improvements. Today, rapid educational and technical advances give rise to more rapid growth rates than were possible in earlier development experiences. Sustained growth rates across generations are related to secular rates of decline in fertility.

In sum, educational goals and planning are central to economic development. Education requires inputs that gradually become sizeable. The pace of its advance is constrained by its costs relative to its benefits over each plan horizon. Countries seeking to reduce fertility will find that the level and distribution of education of the populace affect the transition, both directly and indirectly. The more widespread the education by region and sex, the higher the potential impact on fertility. Rural regions targeted for less education, based on economic criteria, may be upgraded somewhat, particularly in regard to the education of females, when there is a need to reduce fertility. In early stages of transition onset, education about health as well as the need for schooling could raise norms. If successful, higher norms would limit the rise in fertility at onset and the rate of population expansion.

Health

Governments play a major role in establishing and maintaining health norms. They may even force inoculations or other measures on people to assure their general welfare. Public informational campaigns introduce measures of preventive medicine.

It is not necessary for expenditures on children by households to be high for health norms to constrain fertility. Information about the optimal spacing of children and education about the effects of pregnancies at younger and older ages on child health can change fertility in receptive populations. So can vasectomies, abortions, and modern techniques of pregnancy prevention. Governments typically have influence over health information of this type that can affect norms.

Some aspects of improved health introduced by health agencies will be pro-natal at early stages of transition or development. Sanitation and nutritional standards reduce sickness; and healthier children absorb less adult time. Health improvements can reduce the incidence of infertility or change sex practices that reduce conception. Supply-side determinants of fertility in natural fertility regimes gradually change, in part due to health advances. These progressive health measures can then lead to higher birthrates.

Once health norms are high, and relatively expensive to maintain, they will be a major element of living standards constrained by family time. They will generally be supported, however, by public and private insurance so that the financial risks of health costs are spread across society. This reduces their impact on birthrates.

Overall, health policies may have offsetting effects on fertility, at least when their impact on mortality is not considered. Yet health agencies can miss chances for introducing health measures that tend to work against fertility rises. And the failure to introduce better health measures into poorer populations retards the decline in mortality, a necessary ingredient of the transition.

Employment

Family employment allows more flexible use of time and more family time interchange than market jobs of the corporate type. Hired employment has an impact on female time flexibility that is particularly constraining on child nurture and supervision norms. Thus the socialist policy of involving women as well as men in the hired work place at relatively early stages of economic development is anti-natal. Its impact on child time constraints is offset somewhat by day-care provisions and the increased household income of younger, child-bearing households. Nonsocialist economies tend to keep most workers in family or self-employment at earlier stages, and their absorption into market hirings is gradual. There is generally a considerable lag of females behind males into the work force of hired laborers. The fall of socialist systems into disfavor will increase the flexibility and interchange of family time in support of children.

Day laborers in poorer countries, whether rural or urban, with minimum income and no job security may not control their lifestyles or fertility. They can easily form an island of natural fertility in societies where most restrict births to some degree. Policies often exacerbate their situation. Governments seeking industrial growth often subsidize capital through low interest rates, favorable foreign exchange rates for capital imports, or in other ways. Firms respond to the capital subsidies by replacing laborers with machines, thus leading to less demand for unskilled and other labor. This perpetuates the oversupply of impoverished day laborers, whether rural or urban. Unenlightened land tenure and ownership policies can also help to create more unskilled day laborers in need of work. Such workers feel helpless to affect their own conditions. Controlling fertility would not change that feeling.

The more mobile the work force, the greater the time constraints on fertility. Mobility related to market employment opportunities separates families, reducing child time for nurture and supervision and shared housing. Even regional employment centers increase time constraints over those of the local immobile labor force. Governments are involved in transportation planning and regional development policies that affect population mobility. One benefit of such policies could be lower fertility.

The work day, week, and year affect lifestyles and time constraints. In some less developed countries, larger portions of time are traditionally given to family than in other countries of similar opportunities. There is a ceremonial flavor to family time interchange, and leisure hours are oriented toward these ceremonies. Culture undoubtedly plays a role here. In Africa, for example, the pull is so strong, that a worker will quit a job in a mine away from home to return to his village for a prolonged time to participate in family life. In such situations, work time constraints on fertility are less important or less likely to become binding than where longer work days or years are the norm. Moreover, productivity gains that set the stage for controllable lifestyle norms occur via work time efficiency gains as technology in production improves in agriculture and other sectors. The less work time, the less potential for gain.

In situations of population pressures on the land as in Asia, work time is often longer as more land is cleared and tilled, and conservation of the soil requires many hours. Work time productivity gains that then come with the Green Revolution agricultural practices can be quite dramatic. Rural lifestyles can change considerably when up to four crops a year are harvested instead of one.

Governments often legislate the work week or set an example by their employment rules or demonstration farms. They can easily influence hired workers in nonfarm employment. Where the work year is relatively short in rural cultures, regional factories may play a role that changes this and thereby affect fertility. Thus we return to the idea that a regionally balanced development pattern can affect fertility levels.

Child subsidies and charges

Government subsidies to lifestyles, and particularly child norms, affect time constraints. However, the effects of taxes on family resources and sharing have to be considered along with the effect of government family programs. The size of the child subsidy relative to lifestyle norms would influence the outcome as well as the degree to which the area subsidized is a binding constraint. Also, a subsidy to one type of expenditure on children could free time to be redirected to other constraint areas.

Subsidies to children that also mandate new child norms for health, nutrition, education, or housing can contribute over time to rising private norms once they have created the experience of higher standards. Many such standards are introduced with only partial financing via subsidies. The private sector must help finance the new norms set by government. Child time is constrained.

The impact of legislated norms with partial subsidy will depend on whether those to whom they apply control births or not. Forcing norms on the poor who do not control births will simply reduce their lifestyle in some other area. Health requirements for which the parents must pay can lead to children who have been inoculated suffering from malnourishment in natural fertility regimes.

The way in which a subsidy is financed can influence its impact. Taxes divert time from household support. They may reduce the flexibility or interchangeability of time. Subsidies may have a pro-natal effect when they are financed by taxes on more affluent households in their middle years and given to those in their fertile years. This redistribution then retards the upward movement of lifestyles in mature households sufficiently well-off to raise their living standards. At the same time it reduces child time constraints for fertile households.

The imposition of significant charges on children to penalize those having more children than a government-set family size norm is becoming more widespread. India and China have both used it, sometimes in draconian ways. Workers may even lose their jobs or half their salary as a penalty for excess births. One rationale for such an approach has been the utility theory of fertility. Children costing more will be less attractive compared to other commodities according to this theory.

Viewed from the perspective of the lifestyle framework, substantial penalties on extra children above government-set family size norms is a less than optimal approach. While it may constrain fertility to some degree, it does nothing to raise living standard norms. Moreover, for those not controlling fertility, it materially lowers living standards. Penalized households forced to pay more for education or health services will necessarily be forced to give less to each child. In addition, lowered health and education norms resulting from penalty charges for excess fertility reduce the potential work force contribution of the young. Growth is slowed, and so also is the transition in the long run. The cost of short-term birth declines may, in the long run, be a slower pace for the transition. The punitive approach to fertility control, then, can be counterproductive. This is especially true when the high-fertility, meager-income groups on whom it is imposed do not practice birth control. Nonpunitive programs, on the other hand, have the potential to reduce births, if well designed.

Housing norms

A large percentage of people in poorer countries live in warm climates. The need for shelter and artificial heat are modest. Housing standards and, as a result, costs can be relatively modest. Sharing of space is also easier when more of life is lived outdoors, rather than in cramped quarters trying to keep warm. The result has been more modest housing standards and a greater sharing of common family living space than in colder climates. Both outcomes are pro-natal.

Once birth control enters, an additional child is more readily housed at given standards than was the case in the history of Western development. Starting at modest living standards, housing norms are less likely to rise as fast as in cold areas. By contrast, in harsher weather conditions, housing can be a major component earlier on of lifestyle time needs. Moreover, in warmer climates there is more family time available to child-bearing couples to help care for children, since more kin share housing.

Governments generally have housing policies – everything from safety codes to government-provided living space. Probably one of the most anti-natal policies of the Soviet planners has been their denial of resources to private housing combined with the severe limitations of public accommodations. Housing in the main cities was particularly scarce and cramped as workers moved out of rural areas to form an industrial labor force. Under the socialist system the housing constraint became not a household time (income or wealth) constraint, but an actual physical constraint. Whatever living standards were overall, there was not room to raise many children in such a cold climate in the space provided.

Programs that succeed in raising housing standards in hot climates will result in time constraints on fertility. Unfortunately, they are costly and deny funds to investment in growth. This is why the Communists neglected housing. Policies should be designed to induce the private sector to devote off-work hours to home improvements to lessen their social cost. Particularly appropriate are self-help schemes in which indigenous materials are used in innovative ways by individual households or housing cooperatives formed in villages and towns. The government or co-op can provide a minimum of inputs and demonstration techniques. The government may also have an important role to play in financing the homes. Interest rates need not be below the opportunity cost of money in all cases. They can simply be much less than those of the curb-market moneylender.

Sociocultural traits

Cultures that allocate time (wealth or income) to children and families at the expense of other lifestyle components as the productivity of time rises will retard the transition. Such cultures generally allocate the time of those past child-bearing age toward supporting, directly or indirectly, the time needs of fertile couples, enabling them to overcome constraints. Moslem cultures are particularly noteworthy in this regard. Religion has also played a part in determining the percentage of the populace remaining celibate – from Buddhist monks to members of Christian religious orders. It gives a respected role to celibacy. Ireland in particular has seen this affect her fertility rates in a way opposite to Moslem countries. In this case, it greatly softened the Catholic pro-natal position. The time of nuns was directed toward education so that education norms rose relatively rapidly for women as well as men.

France has always had a relatively low birthrate, and culture is often thought to have played a role. Class and social standing influenced the choice of a mate and a lifestyle. Historically, men often chose a mistress as well as a wife to share their time and bed. In general the mistresses bore fewer children over their reproductive years. This double mating undoubtedly affected the size of the family for the wife as well, constraining time for its support.

Rigid caste or class systems such as that once found in India stratify societies, separating resources and limiting opportunities. They reduce the transfer of norms among reference groups. There is limited interaction, intermarriage, or social movement of the type that leads to ideational changes or time interchange. Lower strata can feel that they have no control over their well-being and must await the next life for an improvement in status and lifestyle. Such societies will have slower changes in fertility than more homogeneous societies.

Japan moved rapidly from her medieval stratification stage to a relatively homogeneous society with widespread uniformity of norms such as education. Her population expansion was very moderate by historical comparison with other countries of the Far East. Today, tribal divisions in Africa mimic some of the caste ideas of India. Should they so rigidify, they could slow the onset of fertility transition or slow its pace once started. On the other hand, policies developed early on to avoid segmented labor markets and other manifestations of tribal social stratification in Africa will modify fertility patterns. They would also reduce the survival threat associated with tribal rivalry.

Policies to reduce the cultural impediments to transition may have to originate with international agencies such as the World Bank. National governments will generally reflect the cultural values of their country. Their leaders do not readily go against these. However, there may be opportunities for change to occur in culturally affected norms and time use that are not threatening to social ideals. Marriage age could be an example. The approach taken here would focus attention on changing uses of time as productivity gains are made and on reducing threats to survival. The time use of women in particular is greatly influenced by culture. Male leaders may be insensitive to feasible, needed changes here.

Undoubtedly, international influence helped bring India to outlawing the caste system. After this, practices changed, albeit slowly. Policies were developed to give preferential treatment to those in the lowest caste. But despite this, their extreme poverty and precarious economic conditions meant that few had control over their living standards.

Overall, the Moslem culture stands out at this time as being particularly pro-natal. A deeper delving into reasons for this could be helpful in regard to devising anti-natal policies. Should there be feasible cultural changes that could lead to lower fertility, these would have a potentially large impact in today's developing economies. Once accepted, policies or cultural changes could spread from one country to another in the Moslem world. It should be pointed out, however, that in some areas Moslems feel that their survival is at stake and are unlikely to seek lower fertility.

POLICIES IN AFFLUENT ECONOMIES

It can be expected that constraining lifestyle categories differ somewhat between poorer and richer countries. In general, policy is not focused on lowering fertility, but may be aimed at raising it. For various reasons, governments are interested in knowing when policies can affect fertility. The need to plan for schools or housing are two examples of reasons why they would be of interest. Here some general areas of potential policy impact are pointed out. We begin with subsidies, since so often it is claimed that welfare and other subsidies are supportive of larger family size.

Subsidies

The impact of a subsidy on fertility will depend on its size relative to the constraints it relieves. A subsidy relieves the time constraint binding a category of time use and also frees time to be devoted to other lifestyle categories. Once lifestyles are high, modest subsidies to constraint categories such as health, education, or housing are unlikely to be sufficient to make another child affordable. It is unlikely that one or more norm categories will experience time shortfalls.

The main result of subsidies that are modest relative to norm levels could be to change the timing of births. Additional children may become supportable somewhat earlier. It is unlikely that such subsidies would increase overall fertility rates, especially when mortality rates are continuing downward. Not surprisingly, modest subsidies to children in societies with higher living standards have not worked. Their main outcome, if prolonged, may be to raise living standards over generations for younger-aged households.

Governments in advanced economies usually support lower-strata families so that they can maintain the society's minimum living standard. Typically governments make in-kind payments such as providing education, health, housing, or day care. Some of these families will never have known standards higher than the government welfare floor. A few will have known lower ones. The rest will be at a level below their minimum prior to their unexpected loss of earnings, health, and so on.

In the absence of government programs, all the recipients would experience lower living standards and would pass them on to the next generation. Now, instead, only the above-minimum group will do so. When government programs first start up, those below the floor will experience new, higher norms. Overall, the government programs support a lifestyle floor that would be lower in their absence. Taken alone, this is not pro-natal.

The form and conditions of the subsidy determine their more direct impact. It has already been noted that in-kind subsidies force certain category norms on recipients. They are unable to use them as they could cash to support spending in areas of adult choice while letting children experience norms below society's minimum. Of course, only a percentage with below-minimum norms would do this, since the rest share society's minimum standards or exceed them. Yet this may help explain why social agencies find in-kind payments useful. Economists, of course, point out that they abridge individual preferences. A cash approach, however, would not raise living standards of children whose parents are willing to accept levels below society's floor.

Are welfare subsidies pro-natal even though their support is limited to a floor? The answer turns on whether the subsidies are available to support those with minimum or below standards no matter how fertile they are. Generally, societies seek ways to limit support costs for welfare recipients. If subsidies are forthcoming for each child to maintain families at similar levels and there is nothing to deter acceptance of payments, then they would be pro-natal for a percentage of those receiving them. Usually eligibility requirements and public opinion restrict their ability to encourage births.[1]

There is in some cultures a public shame attached to being on the welfare roles and adding dependents to the household. Child payments often decline as family size grows. Work requirements may limit time for children if one or more parent can perform state-required tasks. Mothers may be required to work in public day-care facilities or hospitals. Fathers may be ineligible to receive the subsidy if they are able-bodied. Despite the harshness of the policy, states have been known to sterilize welfare mothers who are unusually fecund and inattentive to their large family's basic needs. States seeking to encourage higher fertility generally seek ways to encourage all families to raise births, not just the welfare recipients.

Social security for the elderly

Social security systems for old-age support in advanced economies reduce direct family time inputs to support elderly relatives. They can reduce the number of relatives who bond to each other to reduce risks of lowered lifestyles in a mobile society. This reinforces the shrinkage of the extended family and the time interchange of the family.

The security of family lifestyles is improved by a broadly shared support system that reduces risks for each family. By sharing broadly the risks that threaten the older generations, the chances lessen that one family will have to devote large amounts of time to their elderly.

The reduction of support time shared by a family resulting from social security for the elderly is anti-natal, while the increased expectation of greater security of family lifestyles is pro-natal. The manner in which taxes are distributed among contributing households must also enter the equation. The system is expected to reduce fertility overall, since family nurture time is generally a binding constraint in more affluent societies. The greater independence of the elderly lessens time interchange, including nurture time.

---

[1] *Wall Street Journal*, Sept. 5, 89, p. B1, reports that a survey by Mark Rank of Washington University reveals that US women on welfare have a fertility rate considerably lower than the national average. The study also finds that the rate drops the longer they are on welfare.

Divorce laws

Governments and the courts set the rules for divorce. These rules pay great attention to maintaining the lifestyle of the family broken apart and in particular seek to assure standards for children. There is a greater incidence and acceptance of divorce in richer societies, although it may occur among the wealthy in poorer states. Widespread acceptance of divorce in poorer societies could have harsh effects on family lifestyles. Moreover, it would leave large families without support, creating a burden for society. Where polygamy is accepted, as in some parts of Africa, maternal families and the tribe as a whole contribute to children's support. In some tribes, only wealthier males have several wives, and they support all families.

Swapping mates in affluent societies will have little effect if divorcées remarry readily, supporting dependents in their accustomed lifestyles. Fertility rates in advanced economies are low, and time between marriages will reduce the rates little. On the other hand, if divorce increases the time constraints of the family of remarried couples or if many do not remarry, fertility will be lower. Family sharing is undoubtedly affected as bloodlines are mixed.

Consider the case where divorce occurs, as it often does, prior to having children, or at least prior to having the number of children that would have been the case in the absence of divorce; this increases the incidence of single adults in the population of child-bearing age, thereby affecting fertility. Parents need not expect that divorce will lower their fertility. They may anticipate remarriage and feel that the bad marriage affects their welfare. Thus they divorce, being willing to tolerate lower lifestyles for a time in the hope that the situation will be short-lived. But then they may remain single. When there are offspring, lifestyles are then lowered, setting lower standards for the next generation. The low fertility of younger divorced women lowers the degree to which lifestyles fall in divorced households.

The effect of divorce on family time interchange leads to less efficiency of time use in support of lifestyles. When norms are breached, grandparents and others may be quite concerned. There have been growing demands on the courts to assure time interchange among family members, establishing grandparents' rights as well as those of parents in this regard. Nurture norms, education norms, and others are often at stake.

The acceptance of divorce, both socially and legally, leads to less security of lifestyles, lowers the family time available, and leaves a percentage of females without mates. It is thus anti-natal. Cultural changes, in particular those affecting traditional religious values, help to set the stage for divorce, along with economic independence of women.

CONCLUSIONS

The policy implications of the lifestyle–norm/time constraint framework are strong and far-reaching. This is true even if its applications are prudently restricted to policies that would be pursued independently of their effects on fertility transition, at least until further testing of the model. The transition, of fertility rates from high, fluctuating levels to lower rates is a lengthy process that typically occurs while states are changing technically, economically, and socially over a secular development path. The theory predicts that many policies which spur broad-gauged, equitable development paths will also foster transition, while those which encourage more narrowly based development springboards will retard the transition. In other words, dualism in agricultural and industrial development patterns retards fertility transition. A delayed or interrupted transition can lead to population density problems and create population growth rates that divert resources from industrialization.

In pre-transition countries the analysis identifies mortality rates and other threats to group survival as impediments to transition onset. It underlines the need to improve agricultural technology and secure living standards of populations dependent on rain-fed agriculture in order to set the stage for transition onset. Cultural changes that can support transition at this stage may have to originate from international sources.

The model's focus on family time opens up a new way for viewing the effect of various policies on fertility. An understanding of the role of time in constraining fertility provides policymakers in less developed countries with a lever for influencing fertility. There are many areas in such states where government policymakers help set new living statndards – for example, in health or housing. These standards can be introduced in ways that require household time inputs, perhaps supplemented by the carrot of some government subsidies. The new norms established in this way will become part of the family fertility equation. Education standards are especially far-reaching in their potential impact on time constraints that restrict fertility, especially those for females.

The analysis casts doubt on the wisdom of placing harsh penalty charges on "excessive births." Such a policy's longer-range impact is likely to be counterproductive. Yet this is an increasingly popular approach today. It reflects in part the utility model's view of fertility behavior but does not mesh with the norm framework.

Finally, the theory offers insights into the fertility impact of policies in countries with lower fertility rates. Some of these countries try to encourage higher birthrates. The model offers reasons why subsidies designed to do so generally fail over the long run. It also identifies time categories where constraints are typically binding in modern societies. Generally the model predicts that public and private policy changes sufficient to affect these binding time constraints enough to raise fertility are expensive and difficult to engineer socially. On the other hand, many aspects of modern life readily contribute to shortfalls of family time inputs needed to support children at established time norm levels.

In general, the framework developed broadens and lengthens the policy perspective for viewing transition, without losing sight of the contributions of traditional family planning policy efforts. In doing so, it adds new areas for family planning policymakers to pursue that will affect fertility. Since many of these policies involve norm changes, the time frame for assessing results lengthens over that of the traditional policy horizon. This means, however, that fertility policies can dovetail with many areas of longer-term development planning, adding another dimension to plan projects and perhaps tipping the scales weighing costs and benefits of the development strategy.

10
Agenda for Further Research

The agenda to be developed here highlights areas for testing the impact on fertility of the scissor blades of changing family time norms and shifting family time constraints. I will keep the discussion very general, however; for the design of research studies will differ depending on the disciplinary methodology used. In many areas that I will mention, research has already been done that pertains to the topic, though not always from the perspective of its impact on fertility transition. Some areas readily suggest literature surveys that use the lifestyle–norm/time constraint framework to organize the material.

Country studies and comparative studies can both be helpful. More refined generalizations about shifts in the categories of constraints that are binding over stages of the transition for the typical case can emerge from such studies. For example, they can reveal specifics about the binding restraints at onset, during stages of rapidly declining fertility and mortality, and during the concluding stage when fertility decline slows. Deviations from the typical constraint patterns offer an opportunity to see whether they are mainly traceable to social (cultural) or economic factors, and to what degree they reflect conditions that can be fostered or prevented. Insights can be sought with regard to threshold levels of variables related to fertility onset such as mortality rates and degrees of social and economic security.

Overall, of course, there is a need for more longitudinal data in order to design statistical studies that avoid the limitations of cross-country regressions. Since this need is not readily satisfied, a large number of agenda topics deal with studies that can test the theory in a more indirect way. Similarly oriented topics are grouped under general headings. First, though, I will say more about the need for time series data for today's transition countries.

DATA GENERATION STUDIES

The statistical forms chosen for tests of any model are constrained by data limitations, especially when many countries are involved. The empirical specifications of determinants of norms and time constraints in chapter 7 were selected with an eye to data sources and their reliability. Disaggregated data are not available for postwar transition countries, and thus aggregated proxie variables were used in chapter 8 to test the model. In fact, it was necessary to settle on fewer variables because of data limitations. The availability of better data sets, especially if they were household time-use data, would allow an improved specification of equations for testing the model. Here I will make some brief observations about data generation needs before dealing with specific areas of research that relate to conceptual aspects of the model.

There is a need for generation of longitudinal data on empirically specified determinants of changes in norms and time constraints. It would be helpful, for example, to be able to trace the effect of the difference in household per capita income of parents between the current period, PC, and the period of growintg up, $PC^\star$, on fertility, or $(PC - PC^\star)/PC^\star$. This is a rough proxie for the goods constraint assuming it reflects expected income flows. When this ratio equals or exceeds one, then fertility constraints are eased, assuming that other categories are nonbinding. This income measure must be adjusted for movements in the consumer price index. Not all countries have unbiased market basket estimates of price changes broken down by regions.

Over time, major components of the goods constraint may show discontinuous shifts, providing an opportunity to examine their impact on fertility. For example, large increases in housing costs relative to income such as occurred in the US in the 1970s and early 1980s might be sufficient to constrain fertility, or at least shift marriage age and family timing. The debt crisis in Latin America may have produced similar sharp, discontinuous shifts in fertility factors.

What would be ideal would be to have longitudinal time-use studies for fertility transition countries similar methodologically to those generated for the US at the University of Michigan. But, failing that, time-use studies from countries at different levels of fertility at particular points in time can also throw light on constraint determinants.

The World Bank's Living Standard Measurement Study, begun in 1980, is a source book for some types of investigations. The study has information usable for comparative and single-country research, including some time-use data. The US Agency for International Development also generates data through its Women in Development Office for a variety of applications, computerized by country.

TIME FLEXIBILITY

Not all constraint categories need be binding in the model throughout the transition. Time is imperfectly flexible, and there can be excess available for some norm categories, while others suffer shortfalls. Fertility is limited whenever transferring excess time from nonbinding to binding categories would not provide adequate relief for another child or in cases where the time cannot be shifted. The degree of flexibility of time varies with technological rigidities, economic institutions, social institutions, and cultural factors.

It would be helpful to have studies that trace specifically how specialization and division of labor and associated education needs, especially for women, affect time flexibility. These studies could throw light on questions such as the following: Are the increased dependency years of the young associated with education and specialization a major source of inflexibility? Once the majority of the work force is employed by others, is control of employees' time by employers the dominant source of time inflexibility, along with female entry into the job market? Or are there other – for example cultural – factors that have an important influence?

A possible example of the latter is the practice in Japan of the male working a long work week and then coming home late after work-related informal evening gatherings. Does the male's time inflexibility play a role in more women staying home than in modern societies? How does this time-use pattern affect Japan's binding time categories compared to other countries where the woman has a job?

What are the main sources of inflexibility arising in urban and rural situations? Does flexibility of family time vary under tenant farming from that under plantation or day-labor farming? Does day labor in rural or urban settings create time flexibility patterns that are pro-natal? Historically, did the transfer of female work from more rural putting-out or cottage systems to the factory introduce inflexibilities that affected fertility? How does family size affect time flexibility in agrarian or urban settings? Do older children in both settings provide supervision and other time inputs to younger children that relieve specific time category constraints on the *n*th child compared to the first child?

Does the need for developing countries to compete in the global economy force international time-use patterns with increasing rigidity on the national work force? Do occupational specializations arising from trade among nations vary much in their effect on time flexibility via work week, seasonality, night work, travel, or other aspects of work requirements? Hong Kong would make a good case study.

In situations where fertility rates in the society vary among ethnic groups, are there cultural, occupational, or other factors that create greater family time flexibility among high-fertility groups?

Does time flexibility of the father and mother vary with income? with wealth? If both, does time flexibility relate to income or wealth in the same way for both?

How does the imposition of Communist organizational techniques in the society and economy affect time flexibility? Do the demise of family farms and firms, the increase in female work force participation rates, the long hours spent in lines, and other such factors greatly reduce time flexibility in situations such as the Soviet Union after the Bolshevik Revolution or Chairman Mao's China? Does the impact vary from agrarian communes to industrial socialism?

What are the effects of the introduction of indoor plumbing, electricity, and household appliances such as stoves, refrigerators, and freezers on household time use and flexibility in transition fertility situations? What about the automobile or public transportation in this regard?

Does welfare support in modern societies that places no demands on recipients' time encourage fertility when lifestyle standards of recipients are low? Put another way, does the requirement that teenage welfare mothers finish school, provide labor hours to school-run nurseries, or similar time inputs reduce the probability that they will bear another child while receiving aid?

When the number of family hours exchanged is higher among extended family or there are more extensive family groupings, is the impact on child time of inflexibility reduced proportionately?

In the next section we will examine female employment, which is closely related to family time flexibility.

FEMALE EMPLOYMENT

Employment in the work force by females tightens the time constraint on fertility in the areas of nurture and supervision, while lessening it in the areas of goods and services, housing, and education. Even if the mother delays entry into the labor market until her children are older, there is less available and less flexible child time from female relatives who work. Thus the mother must choose the optimal work force participation rate over her work life so that the time constraint on children is minimized.

Comparative time allocation studies among countries dealing with the mothers' and female relatives' time decisions probably constitute one of the most interesting areas for further research. In many societies undergoing industrialization, women work before marriage but withdraw permanently to domestic work or family farm work when they marry. In other cases, women re-enter the work force after children are older. Today in advanced economies we see women making uninterrupted commitments to the work force over their adult work lives, while also raising children. Are there many different variations on these patterns? Are labor market commitments equivalent in all cases in their effect on the inflexibility of women's time?

Is the family business or cottage industry supportive of larger families than labor force jobs for women because of the effect on the flexibility of their time? Does it increase or decrease the flexibility of the male's time over labor force work? Does it tend to keep fertility from falling by satisfying rising norms for goods, while preserving family time for nurture and supervision? Does the impact of family business on time flexibility vary with the level of development of the economy? When the home is the work place, does it raise housing needs so that this constrains fertility, as it seemingly did in England in the 1700s?

Is female labor force participation among higher-norm families normally precipitated by specific constraint categories such as housing norm constraints or earnings needed to purchase education for offspring? In other words, once higher norms arise in these areas, are they typically the binding constraints that lead women to seek market jobs due to the considerable time inputs required to obtain income for them? Do subsidies in these areas reduce labor force participation rates of less affluent women?

How do work force participation rates of women change child time sharing in families among generations and between parents? Do older children take over some of the nurture and supervision time of adults?

NORMS

There is no one generally accepted theory of how norms develop or evolve. The working assumption adopted here is that there is an internalization of norms experienced in teenage years at home and among reference groups. The research I would suggest revolves around identifying norm specifics, tracing changes over time, and comparing norms of different societies, so as to establish a relation with fertility behavior. Often the methodology will perforce be that of sociologists and historians, although economists occasionally deal in behavior regularities that are socially established.

Some of the most challenging and potentially fruitful studies would focus on the Moslem culture, which pervades many areas of the globe. Fertility is high relative to per capita income and other measures of economic, if not social, security. Studies are needed to examine norms affecting male and female family time use, child norms, and other lifestyle norms, in search of the roots of the atypical fertility patterns found in this religious culture. Lifestyles in some oil-rich Moslem countries are changing rapidly and thus offer a laboratory waiting to be examined under a microscope.

Rural and urban fertility rates in the same society often differ, as do those among socioeconomic groups sorted by occupation or religion. It is expected that closer examination will show that location and so on are proxies for disparities in lifestyle standards and time-use constraints affecting fertility for the groups. Studies can shed light on why the proxies may vary in their ability to capture the underlying causes in different cases, and thus are not always associated with fertility variance.

It would be helpful to have a study of which norms prevail in households where parents come from disparate backgrounds. Does the higher norm raise family standards between generations, or is there a middle-of-the-road compromise? Or is the lower norm adopted?

Do the norms of reference groups affect lifestyle norms adopted by young parents, as well as the new family norms that evolve when productivity rises? Does their influence vary among cultures and/or stages of the fertility transition?

Rapid growth economies yield good data sets that show truncated cases of norm change. Studies of fast-track economies such as Taiwan, Korea, and Hong Kong could reveal how rapid labor productivity growth leads to quickly rising norms for goods and leisure and discontinuous shifts in time-use patterns.

Leisure norms may prove to be a productive area for understanding constraints on fertility behavior in transition societies. Leisure time norms in less rural, more technically advanced societies are seemingly less family time-oriented. How does the evolution of leisure norms affect family time constraints on fertility?

Studies of changes in child nurture and supervision norms over time and among cultures would be helpful. Are they a binding constraint only in modern societies? Do these norms in modern societies vary by ethnic groups, income levels, or other subgroupings?

The US today is undergoing an evolution of nurture and supervision norms as women flock to the work force and there are few relatives to provide child time. The changes are apparently leading to great soul-searching and ongoing tensions in society. The modifications of these norms appears to be an attempt to loosen binding fertility constraints for nurture and supervision time. Will an assault on the inflexibility of work time prove another route to loosening the bind? Is the divorce rate in modern societies having a major impact on these constraints? Does the experience of other countries suggest that successful pressures can be put on the state or business to provide more child supervision time to lessen the constraints? Does the indirect provision of more supervision time by the state gain legitimacy in the society that provides it because of its implications for modern family child-bearing?

Having sketched general areas for further study relating to norm changes and patterns, we will look at two norm categories separately – those for education and housing.

Education norms

Many child norms are maintained by women within the environs of the household. Examples are norms related to children's health and instruction. In what way or to what degree is the maintenance of family norms related to female education? At what point in the transition is female education a necessary ingredient for lifestyle changes of the fundamental type that affect time use and fertility? How much and what type of education are needed to reinforce the potential for lifestyle changes in developing economies to lower fertility as technology raises labor productivity? An examination of female education patterns among countries today and historically would help determine the importance and timing of their impact.

Do countries that lag in fertility transition also lag in regard to the progress of female education relative to male? Does this relative education level rise gradually or in discontinuous steps? Does its rise predict the timing of education as a binding constraint on fertility?

What is the relationship of female education to labor productivity of the family firm and thereby the goods constraint? Is female education a main determinant of labor force participation outside the family firm by women?

Do family education norms generally equal, exceed, or fall below government-set education norms? What are the support patterns during transition for these norms? What determines the percentages that governments and relatives contribute to support of education norms? Do these support patterns change as standards rise? Do the support patterns predict the timing of education as a binding fertility constraint?

Is loss of the work time of the young due to education a major cost to the family of extending education into teen and young adult years? Or are the school year and timetable flexible enough to allow continued work input by the young in family production or part-time labor market work? What effect does schooling of girls have on the mother's time inputs into nurture and supervision, food production and preparation, and other household time needs?

What is the role of relatively high male and female education standards in the Japanese society in keeping birthrates low by Asian standards over the development path? Does state provision of education in Communist societies greatly reduce the potential for this to be a binding constraint on fertility there? Or is it the prolonged dependency years and lost work time of the young at home and in the work place, rather than direct schooling costs, which cause education to constrain fertility?

Housing norms

Housing and accompanying land can be a limiting factor in the model due to their importance in the lifestyle of a family. This topic has already been mentioned in the section on data generation.

An interesting fact is that fertility tends to be higher in warmer climates. Do differences in housing-cost constraints, as they affect achievement of lifestyles, contribute to higher fertility in warmer climes? Generally housing costs, if not land values, are less in warmer climates, and shelter needs are more easily met. Less indoor space is needed if courtyards exist and outdoor living is more agreeable.

There is great scope for increases in housing norms in many Third World countries. What is the potential effect of rising shelter norms on fertility in such countries? Could it play a role similar to that hypothesized for colder climates of delaying marriage and limiting overall household size? Would government programs be able to help in raising norms in ways that do not offset their effect as a constraint? The approach to urban subsidized housing in Singapore or Hong Kong may give insights here. The experience of Habitat for Humanity could also prove useful.

What effect have the bureaucratic controls placed on housing in Communist societies had on the relatively low fertility rates in these states? Housing is generally an area where individual initiative and readily available inputs of home labor and indigeneous materials combine to ease constraints. And growing urban areas generally do not tightly control the space available per family as they grow from immigration. Yet Russia and other similar economies have set very tight physical limits on housing by thwarting decentralized response to space needs or norms.

Some high-density countries such as Haiti, Jamaica, and India have low fertility compared to other countries with similar per capita income levels. Does shortage of land, such as exists in India, where farm land seldom comes on the market, raise living costs and help explain the relatively lower fertility rate in these countries?

FAMILY SUPPORT OF LIFESTYLES

Direct and indirect family time-sharing greatly affect the time constraint on child-bearing. Data are not readily available or easily generated here. However, studies of income transfers within families such as the one by Kaufman and Lindauer (1984) can be readily adapted to test for fertility effects as well as lifestyle support flows. And this type of study could focus on direct time support as well as money or wealth flows.

Longevity can affect family sharing. How does an increase in the average life span due to a decline in adult as opposed to infant mortality affect the pattern of intergenerational wealth transfers? Longer life spans increase the need to retain more wealth in households of the elderly and/or to shift family time to elderly dependents. Do later inheritance and care hours for the elderly (or taxes to support nursing homes) inhibit fertility by restricting wealth-sharing of grandparents during the fertile years of parents?

On the other hand, under what conditions does greater adult longevity lead to a reduction in nurture and supervision constraints on children? Does this occur mainly when extended families live in close proximity and grandparents are relatively young on average due to early marriage age? Are nurture and supervision constraints likely to be binding at such time as greater longevity has an impact?

Another interesting area for study concerns the determinants of family ties and the degree of family time interchange. At one extreme is the tribal sharing in an African social system. What determines how societies gradually circumscribe their familial interdependence groupings from such broad mutual support systems? Are the changes both social and economic in origin? Work has been done in this area, but is not viewed within the lifestyle time model.

Is child fosterage such as exists in Africa a deterrent to fertility transition onset? Is it supportive of the very high birthrates in this area of the globe, rates that are historically high for pre-transition conditions in many cases? Is time interchange of this type that supports fertility a response to survival threats?

What is the effect of divorce on family support time, direct and indirect? Does less family support in divorced families lower norms for succeeding generations? Does it redefine behavior patterns of family support of lifestyles?

What is the level of intergenerational transfers within families in support of formal education of children? Does it vary by sex? Do children of a family where transfers per child are relatively high have more offspring, *ceteris paribus*?

LIFESTYLE SECURITY IN AGRARIAN SETTINGS

A better understanding of fertility in areas such as Africa requires an examination of levels of security. Security is related to group survival risks and to the securance of adequate food and other needs in a society subject to political upheavals or to threats from exogenous forces such as droughts, floods, and pests.

Certainly tribal warfare is rampant in regions of the African continent. There is a history of it in more advanced black nations such as Kenya, where fertility is high. It even lingers on to some degree among South Africa's black population. Combined with internecine warfare is the low technical level of rain-fed agriculture in Africa, where slash-and-burn procedures are used to clear fields and no soil conservation practices are followed. Storage and securing of food for shortfall years are also inadequate, in part due to technical limitations, in part to sociopolitical failings. The living standard is quite minimal by international comparison. It is not difficult to tip the economy to life-threatening conditions. Thus, despite the modesty of norms, many African nations are on the edge of deprivation, without the capacity to prevent sliding over that edge in some years.

It would be helpful to have in-depth understanding of the conditions necessary for families to view their survival and norms as within their influence. In particular, what economic and social conditions must emerge before there is a greater correspondence in such economies between fertility and security of lifestyle?

One way to understand the evolution to a different outlook on fertility is to examine the characteristics of more densely populated agrarian economies where birthrates are lower. What are the conditions that lead to a relationship between fertility and lifestyle maintenance in such societies? Certainly Asian agricultural and technology practices are more advanced than African practices overall. So is their social organization for securing lifestyles. Yet many segments within some Asian nations still live in high-risk situations and have high fertility. Can patterns be identified here, tying lifestyles security to fertility, and showing what conditions are needed for this connection to emerge? How did the Green Revolution figure in the patterns of Asian fertility within the framework of the lifestyle model?

The duality within some Latin American economies may offer other conditions where the same questions can be asked about agrarian fertility behavior. Generally land is more plentiful. But among Latin American Indian and other groups, technology can be very low, while fertility is high. They are usually not subject to tribal killings or famine conditions, however and mortality is lower than in Africa.

It is also important to study fertility in outlier less developed countries with mainly agrarian occupations, where fertility rates are falling or are relatively low compared to others in similar income ranges. Are there explanations to be found for atypical fertility cases within the analytical framework of norms and time constraints? Sri Lanka and Mauritius come to mind here. Sri Lanka, a country of ethnic diversity, experienced advances in living standards in earlier eras that placed her well ahead of most developing countries in the 1950s. Then her per capita income was about half of Japan's and much higher than Korea's or Thailand's. According to the World Bank "Living standards in terms of life expectancy at birth, school enrollment ratio, literacy, and infant mortality rates, were among the highest in the developing world" (World Bank, 1989, p. 420). Even as development faltered, an active government sought to secure and subsidize basic lifestyle components. Yet constraints tightened, due to the poor economic performance which, four decades later, placed her well below the per capita income levels of Japan, Korea, and Thailand. Did these constraints on Sri Lanka's experienced lifestyle lead to her relatively low fertility rate compared to other countries reaching her current per capita income level, countries which were not her equal in lifestyle norms at earlier time periods?

In order to examine fertility decline in agrarian settings, more information is needed about the impact of technological change in agriculture on time-use patterns of the household in different cultural settings at various levels of development. Does this vary when farming is more land-intensive at all stages of development due to better resource endowments? Does the impact of technical change on norms differ between plantation and tenant farming?

Studies of countries in pre-transition or transition onset can prove very helpful. They can uncover the many strands of changing conditions that eventually weave themselves into a regime of fertility control. Such studies can give a better feel for the time needed for societies to emerge from natural fertility states and the degree to which their transformation can be fostered or accelerated. Much information bearing on the subject exists and awaits being recast into a fertility framework.

MISCELLANEOUS

The research agenda items that follow either do not fit neatly into any of the other categories or encompass more than one of them.

What is the effect of government-decreed minimum standards plus government support for these standards on lifestyle norms and time constraints over the short and the long run? Have policies in a country such as Sweden, where standards and taxes are high, contributed to the highest female labor force participation rate in the world and relatively low fertility?

How can family planning policies raise norms and/or change time-use patterns so that fertility is nudged in the desired direction? Are child support policies designed to raise fertility, such as those of France or Quebec, counterproductive because they raise norms for the following generation? Do campaigns aimed at establishing a norm for family size fail because they are not oriented toward raising lifestyle norms first?

What has been the impact in the short and the long run of penalties designed to deter large families when assessed from the standpoint of the lifestyle framework? Such penalties include foreclosing education opportunities, job or salary loss, housing or health subsidy losses, and so forth. They have been used especially in Asia.

Raising health norms seems an especially productive route to lowering fertility and mortality in less developed countries. What is the optimal allocation of resources here and the most efficient way to promote health and moderate fertility? Can norms be raised in ways that change fertility constraints through requiring time inputs of the family? An aggressive pre-natal care program might be an example. What is the best way to disseminate information on falling mortality and what it means for the family's lifestyle maintenance? Should education time in the grade schools be allocated to raising health norms? Would not spending of this type pay off more than expenditures trying to convince parents simply that there is a bureaucratically determined optimal number of children per nuclear family unit? Movies, TV, and other educational media could be used instead to focus on major norm categories.

THE NEED FOR FURTHER STUDIES

Models carefully set up the logical consistency of cause and effect relationships and provide the basis for testable hypotheses. There are many challenges facing the model-builder trying to capture the complex forces at work leading to the secular process of fertility transition. The challenges of testing the models are even more daunting, in part because of the time span involved. Not surprisingly, different models may compete for primacy, because they have not been judged false by the empirical tests available. Or models may prove complementary within the framework of a more general theory, inspired perhaps as a result of insights from inconclusive tests of the complementary ideas. Generally repeated and different tests are necessary to establish confidence in the posited relationships. Certainly supplementary tests and studies of the lifestyle – norm/time constraint model are in order to examine more fully its explanatory or predictive powers. The general discussion in this chapter forms a basis for further testing and exploratory investigation of basic aspects of the analysis.

The model specifies the interrelations between the use of time and fertility over generations. The framework identifies categories of time use and living standard norms and relates them to fertility behavior. In the model, determinants of changes over long periods in time constraints and norms for these categories predict changes in fertility rates. These determinants are specified empirically by broadly based socioeconomic indicators. Their identification within the context of the general framework leads to an explanation of fertility transition that draws upon the cultural, social, and economic changes that feed into evolving time-use patterns and family time constraints. Suggested research topics are directed toward measuring and examining further these broadly based determinants of fertility transition.

The questions posed and the suggestions for research made in this chapter are also designed to demonstrate the flexibility and breadth of the theoretical framework, as well as to make its applications to fertility transition more explicit. The general living standard idea certainly has a long lineage, although not necessarily in the context of the transition. Usually when ideas survive academic scrutiny for centuries, there is substance to their insights. Recasting the living standard idea into a time-use framework and broadening the concept of lifestyle draw out further insights applicable to the transition and suggest new ways of testing the viability of the underlying concept. The model also indicates why some previous attempts to test the lifestyle concept were mis-specified in terms of the test itself and/or the appropriate statistical population for the test.

Finally, the agenda for further research suggests empirical work that can help in specifying the model more fully. The framework weaves together many seemingly diverse or contradictory strands of fertility determinants into a tapestry showing the intergenerational nexus of patterns of family support and reproduction. In some areas only the warp strands outline the picture in the tapestry. Further specification awaits a better assortment of threads to weave in details. In this chapter I have identified some of the research that can more firmly establish that the overall picture is representative of the transition and can also fill in some of the missing woof threads.

Bibliography

Alba, Francisco, and Potter, Joseph E. 1986: Population and development in Mexico since 1940: an interpretation. *Population and Development Review*, 12, 1 (Mar.), 47–75.

Andorka, Rudolf. 1986: The decline of fertility in Europe: review symposium. *Population and Development Review*, 12, 2 (June), 329–34.

Bagozzi, R. P. and Van Loo, M. F. 1980: Decision-making and fertility: a theory of exchange in the family. In T. K. Burch (ed.), *Demographic Behavior: Interdisciplinary Perspectives on Decision-Making*, Boulder, Colo.: Westview Press, 91–124.

Becker, Gary S. 1960: An economic analysis of fertility. In *Demographic and Economic Change in Developed Countries*, Universities–National Bureau Conference Series, no. 11, Princeton: Princeton University Press, 209–31.

—— 1965: A theory of the allocation of time. *Economic Journal*, 75 (Sept.), 493–517.

—— 1976: A theory of the Allocation of Time. In idem (ed.), *The Economic Approach to Human Behavior*, Chicago: University of Chicago Press, ch. 5.

—— and Barro, Robert J. 1988: A reformulation of the economic theory of fertility. *Quarterly Journal of Economics*, 103 (Feb.), 1–25.

—— and Lewis, H. Gregg 1973: On the interaction between the quantity and the quality of children. *Journal of Political Economy*, 81, 279–88.

—— and —— 1974: Interaction between quantity and quality of children. In T. W. Schultz (ed.), *Economics of the Family*, Chicago: University of Chicago Press, 81–90.

Beckman, L. J. 1978: Couples' decision-making processes regarding fertility. In K. E. Taeuber, L. L. Bumpass, and J. A. Sweet (eds), *Social Demography: Studies in Population*, New York: Academic Press, 57–81.

Ben-Porath, Yoram 1973: Economic analysis of fertility in Israel. In T. W. Schultz (ed.), *Economics of the Family*, Chicago: University of Chicago Press, 217–18.

—— 1982. Economics of the family – match or mismatch? *Journal of Economic Literature*, 20, 1 (Mar.), 52–64.

Berry, H. and Paxon, L. M. 1971: Infancy and early childhood cross cultural codes. *Ethnology*, 2, 10, 466–508.

Billings, John 1893: The diminished birth-rate in the United States. *The Forum*, 15, 4 (June), 467–77.

Blake, J. 1972: Coercive pronatalism and American population policy. In R. Parke Jr. and C. F. Westoff (eds), *Aspects of Population Growth Policy*, US Commission on Population Growth and the American Future, vol. 6 of Commission Research Reports, Washington, D.C.: US Government Printing Office, 85–109.

Boserup, E. 1965: *The Conditions of Agricultural Growth*. London: Allen Unwin.

Bowen, Ezra 1931: *An Hypothesis of Population Growth*. New York: Columbia University Press.

Caldwell, John 1965: Extended family obligations and education: a study of an aspect of demographic transition amongst Ghanian university students. *Population Studies*, 20, 5–26.

—— 1976: Toward a restatement of transition theory. *Population and Development Review*, 2, 3/4 (Sept./Dec.), 321–66.

—— 1983: Direct economic costs and benefits of children. In R. A. Bulatao and R. D. Lee (eds), *Determinants of Fertility in Developing Countries*, New York: Academic Press, vol. 1, 458–93.

Carver, Thomas 1904: *The Distribution of Wealth*. New York: Macmillan.

Chenery, Hollis and Syrquin, Moises 1975: *Patterns of Development 1950–70*. London: Oxford University Press.

Cleland, John 1985: Marital fertility decline in developing countries. In John Cleland and John Hobcraft (eds), *Reproductive Change in Developing Countries*, New York: Oxford University Press, 223–52.

—— and John Hobcraft (eds) 1985: *Reproductive Change in Developing Countries*. New York: Oxford University Press.

Coale, Ansley 1969: The decline of fertility in Europe from the French Revolution to World War II. In S. J. Behrman et al. (eds), *Fertility and Family Planning*, Ann Arbor: University of Michigan Press, 3–23.

—— 1979: The demographic transition: a summary, some lessons and some observations. In Lee-Jay Cho and K. Koboya Shi (eds), *Fertility Transition of the East Asian Populations*, Honolulu: University of Hawaii Press, 9–23.

—— 1986: The decline of fertility in Europe since the eighteenth century as a chapter in demographic history. In idem and S. C. Watkins (eds),

The Decline of Fertility in Europe, Princeton: Princeton University Press, 1–30.

—— and Watkins, Susan C. (eds) 1986: *The Decline of Fertility in Europe*. Princeton: Princeton University Press.

Cochrane, Susan H. 1979: *Fertility and Education: What Do We Really Know?* World Bank Staff Occasional Papers, no. 26. Baltimore: The Johns Hopkins University Press.

—— 1983: The effects of education and urbanization on fertility. In R. A. Bulatao and R. D. Lee (eds), *Determinants of Fertility in Developing Countries*, New York: Academic Press, vol. 2, 587–626.

Davis, K. 1945: The world demographic transition. *Annals of American Academy of Political and Social Sciences*, 237 (Jan.), 1–11.

—— and Blake, J. 1956: Social structure and fertility: an analytic framework. *Economic Development and Cultural Change*, 4, 211–35.

Donaldson, Loraine 1984: *Economic Development, Analysis and Policy*. St Paul, Minn.: West Publishing Co.

—— 1987: Economic constraints upon fertility: a survey of parental attitudes. Unpublished survey.

Dyson, Tim and Murphy, Mike 1985: The onset of fertility transition. *Population and Development Review*, 11, 3 (Sept.), 399–440.

Easterlin, Richard A. 1966: On the relation of economic factors to recent and projected fertility changes. *Demography*, 3, 1, 131–53.

—— 1968: *Population, Labor Force and Long Swings in Economic Growth*. New York: Columbia University Press for the National Bureau of Economic Research.

—— 1969: Towards a socioeconomic theory of fertility: a survey of recent research on economic factors in America fertility. In S. J. Behrman, Leslie Corsa, Ronald Freedman (eds), *Fertility and Family Planning: A World View*, Ann Arbor: University of Michigan Press, 127–56.

—— 1973: Relative economic status and American fertility swings. In Eleanor Sheldon (ed.), *Family Economic Behavior*, Philadelphia: J. B. Lippencott.

—— 1976: Population change and farm settlement in the northern United States. *Journal of Economic History*, 36 (Mar.), 45–75.

—— 1978: The economics and sociology of fertility: a synthesis. In Charles Tilly (ed.), *Historical Studies of Changing Fertility*, Princeton: Princeton University Press, 57–133.

—— 1980: *Birth and Fortune: The Impact of Numbers on Personal Welfare*. New York: Basic Books.

—— 1984: Reply to Rutten and Higgs. In T. P. Schultz and K. I. Wolpin (eds), *Research in Population Economics*, Greenwich, Ct: JAI Press Inc., vol. 5, 213–15.

—— 1986: Fertility. In John Eatwell, Murray Milgate and Peter Newman (eds), *The New Palgrave*, London: Macmillan, 302–7.

—— and Crimmins, Eileen M. 1985: *The Fertility Revolution, A Supply-Demand Analysis*. Chicago: University of Chicago Press.

—— Pollak, R. A. and Wachter, M. L. 1980: Toward a more general economic model of fertility determination: endogenous preferences and natural fertility. In Richard A. Easterlin (ed.), *Population and Economic Change in Developing Countries*, Chicago: University of Chicago Press, 81–149.

Ely, Richard 1893: *Outlines of Economics*. New York: Macmillan.

Fetter, Frank (1915): *Economic Principles*. New York: Century Co.

Freedman, Deborah S. 1963: The relation of economic status to fertility. *American Economic Review*, 53 (June), 414–26.

Freedman, Ronald, 1963: Norms for family size in under-developed areas. *Proceedings of the Royal Society*, 159, 13, 220–45.

—— 1979: Theories of fertility decline: a reappraisal. In Philip M. Hauser (ed.), *World Population and Development, Challenges and Prospects*, New York: Syracuse University Press, 63–79.

Giddings, Franklin 1898: *The Elements of Sociology*. New York: Macmillan.

Gille, Halvor 1985: Policy implications. In John Cleland and John Hobcraft (eds), *Reproductive Change in Developing Countries*, New York: Oxford University Press, 271–95.

Gomes, Melba 1984: Family size and education attainment in Kenya. *Population and Development Review*, 10, 4 (Dec.), 647–60.

Gray, Ronald 1983: The impact of health and nutrition on natural fertility. In R. A. Bulatao and R. D. Lee (eds), *Determinants of Fertility in Developing Countries*, New York: Academic Press, vol. 1, 139–62.

Greven, Philip J. 1970: *Four Generations: Population, Land and Family in Colonial Andover, Massachusetts*. Ithaca, N.Y.: Cornell University Press.

Gronau, Reuben 1977: Leisure, home production and work – the theory of allocation of time revisited. *Journal of Political Economy*, 85, 6 (Dec.), 1099–1123.

Hagan, E. E. 1984: *The Economics of Development*. Homewood, Ill. Richard D. Irwin.

Haines, Michael 1979: *Fertility and Occupation: Population Patterns in Industrialization*. New York: Academic Press.

Heckman, James J. and Hotz, V. Joseph 1987: An investigation of the labor market earnings of Panamanian males. *Journal of Human Resources*, 21, 4, 507–42.

Hill, R. 1974: Special lecture: the family and the regulation of population growth. In Fukuteke and K. Marioka (eds), *Sociology and Social Development in Asia*, Tokyo: Tokyo University Press, 3–16.

Hodgson, Dennis 1983: Demography as social science and policy science. *Population and Development Review*, 9, 1 (Mar.), 1–34.

Hollander, Samuel 1984: Marx and Malthusianism: Marx's secular path of wages. *American Economic Review*, 74, 1 (Mar.), 139–51.

Hollerbach, P. E. 1980: Power in families, communication and fertility decision-making. *Population and Environment*, 3, 146–73.

Isiugo-Abanihe, Uche C. 1985: Child fosterage in West Africa. *Population and Development Review*, 11, 1 (Mar.), 53–73.

Johnson, G. E. and Whitelow, W. E. 1974: Urban-rural income transfers in Kenya: an estimated remittance function. *Economic Development and Cultural Change*, 22 (June), 473–9.

Kaufman, D. 1981: Household income formation and expenditure behavior: issues and findings. *World Bank Staff Working Papers*, Washington, D.C.: World Bank.

—— and Lindauer, D. L. 1984: Income transfers within extended families to meet basic needs? the evidence from El Salvador. *World Bank Staff Working Papers*, Washington, D.C.: World Bank.

Keller, Albert 1917: Birth Control. *Yale Review*, 7, 1 (Oct.), 129–39.

Kelly, Allen, Williamson, Jeffrey and Cheetham, Russell 1972: *Dualistic Economic Development, Theory and History*. Chicago: University of Chicago Press.

Kilby, P. and Johnston, B. F. 1975: *Agriculture and Structural Transformation, Economic Strategies in Late Developing Countries*. New York: Oxford University Press.

Kirk, Dudley 1944: Population changes and the postwar world. *American Sociological Review*, 9, 1 (Feb.), 28–35.

Knodel, John and van de Walle, Etienne 1986: Lessons from the past: policy implications of historical fertility studies. In Ansley J. Coale and Susan C. Watkins (eds), *The Decline of Fertility in Europe*, Princeton: Princeton University Press, 390–419.

Kravis, I. B., Heston, A. and Summers, R. 1982: *United Nations International Comparison Project*. Baltimore: The Johns Hopkins University Press.

——, —— and —— 1982b: *World Product and Income*. Baltimore: The Johns Hopkins University Press.

Landsberger, M. 1971: An integrated model of consumption and market activity: the children effect. *Proceedings of the American Statistical Association*, 137–42.

Lee, R. P. L. 1974: Social change and changes in fertility motivation. In *Reports and Papers of the Expert Group Meeting on Social and Psychological Aspects of Fertility Behavior*, Bangkok: Economic and Social Commission for Asia and the Pacific, United Nations, 36–39.

Lee, Ronald D. 1978: Models of preindustrial population dynamics with application to England. In Charles Tilly (ed.), *Historical Studies of Changing Fertility*, Princeton: Princeton University Press, 155–207.

—— 1985: World development report 1984: review symposium. *Population and Development Review*, 11, 1 (Mar.),. 127–30.

—— and Bulatao, Rodolfo 1983: The demand for children: a critical essay. In R. Bulatao and R. D. Lee (eds), *Determinants of Fertility in Developing Countries*, New York: Academic Press, vol. 1, 233–87.

Leibenstein, Harvey 1974: An interpretation of the economic theory of fertility. *Journal of Economic Literature*, 12, 2 (June), 457–79.

—— 1975: The economic theory of fertility decline. *Quarterly Journal of Economics*, 89, 1 (Feb.), 1–31.

Levy, Marion J. 1965: Aspects of the analysis of family structure. In Ansley J. Coale et al. (eds), *Aspects of the Analysis of Family Structure*, Princeton: Princeton University Press, 1–63.

Liebowitz, A. S. 1975: Education and the allocation of women's time. In F. T. Juster (ed.), *Education, Income and Human Behavior*, New York: McGraw-Hill, 171–97.

Lindert, Peter H. 1980: Child costs and economic development. In R. A. Easterlin (ed.), *Population and Economic Change in Developing Countries*, Chicago: University of Chicago Press, 5–79.

—— 1983: Changing economic costs and benefits of having children. In R. A. Bulatao and R. D. Lee (eds), *Determinants of Fertility in Developing Countries*, New York: Academic Press, vol. 1, 494–516.

Lorimer, F. 1958: *Culture and Human Fertility*. New York: Greenwood Press.

Mason, K. O. 1983: Norms relating to the desire for children. In R. A. Bulatao and R. D. Lee (eds), *Determinants of Fertility in Developing Countries*, New York: Academic Press, vol. 1, 388–428.

McClelland, Gary H. 1983: Family-size desires as measures of demand. In R. A. Bulatao and R. D. Lee (eds), *Determinants of Fertility in Developing Countries*, New York: Academic Press, vol. 1, 288–343.

Mitchell, B. R. 1976: *European Historical Statistics, 1750–1970*. New York: Columbia University Press.

Moffitt, Robert 1982: Postwar fertility cycles and the Easterlin hypothesis: a life cycle approach. In J. L. Simon and P. H. Lindert (eds), *Research in Population Economics*, Greenwich, Ct: JAI Press, Inc., 237–52.

Mosk, Carl 1983: *Patriarchy and Fertility: Japan and Sweden, 1880–1960*. New York: Academic Press.

Mosley, W. H., Werner, L. H. and Becker, S. 1982: The dynamics of birth spacing and marital fertility in Kenya. *World Fertility Survey Scientific Reports*, no. 30 (Aug.), The Hague: International Statistical Institute.

Mueller, Eva 1982: The allocation of women's time and its relation to fertility. In R. Anker, M. Buvinic and N. H. Youssef (eds), *Women's Roles and Population Trends in the Third World*, London: Croom Helm, 55–86.

—— and Short, Kathleen 1983: Effects of income and wealth on the demand for children. In R. A. Bulatao and R. D. Lee (eds), *Determinants of Fertility in Developing Countries*, New York: Academic Press, vol. 1, 590–642.

Namboodiri, N. K. 1972: Some observations on the economic framework for fertility analysis. *Population Studies*, 26, 185–206.

—— 1980: A look at fertility model-building from different perspectives. In T. K. Burch (ed.), *Demographic Behavior*, Boulder, Colo.: Westview Press, 71–90.

Nelson, R. R. 1956: A theory of the low-level equilibrium trap in underdeveloped economies. *American Economic Review*, 46 (Dec.), 894–908.

Notestein, Frank 1945: Population – the long view. In Theodore Schultz (ed.), *Food for the World*, Chicago: University of Chicago Press, 33–62.

Oppong, Christine 1982: Family structure and women's reproductive and productive roles: some conceptual methodological issues. In R. Anker, M. Buvinic and N. H. Youssef (eds), *Women's Roles and Population Trends in the Third World*, London: Croom Helm, 133–50.

—— 1983: Women's roles, opportunity costs, and fertility. In R. A. Bulatao and R. D. Lee (eds), *Determinants of Fertility in Developing Countries*, New York: Academic Press, vol. 1, 547–89.

Pollak, R. A. 1976: Interdependent preferences. *American Economic Review*, 66, 3 (June), 309–20.

Repetto, Robert 1979: *Economic Equality and Fertility in Developing Countries*. Baltimore: The Johns Hopkins University Press.

Richards, Toni 1983: Statistial studies of aggregate fertility change: time series of cross sections. In R. A. Bulatao and R. D. Lee (eds), *Determinants of Fertility in Developing Countries*, New York: Academic Press, vol. 2, 696–736.

Robinson, Warren C. and Harbison Sarah F. 1980: Toward a unified theory of fertility. In T. K. Burch (ed.), *Demographic Behavior*, Boulder, Colo.: Westview Press, 201–35.

Rosenzweig, M. R. and Schultz, T. P. 1985: The demand for and supply of births: fertility and its life cycle consequences. *American Economic Review*, 75, 5 (Dec.), 992–1015.

Ross, Edward 1907: Western Civilization and the Birth-rate. *American Journal of Sociology*, 12, 5 (Mar.), 607–32.

Ryder, Norman B. 1974: Comment on "Economic Theory of Fertility Behavior," by Robert J. Willis. In T. W. Schultz (ed.), *Economics of the Family*, Chicago: University of Chicago Press, 76–80.

Samuelson, Paul A. 1958: An exact consumption loan model of interest with or without the social contrivance of money. *Journal of Political Economy* (Dec.), 467–82.

Schultz, T. Paul 1974: Birth rate changes over space and time: a study of Taiwan. In Theodore W. Schultz (ed.), *Economics of the Family*, Chicago: University of Chicago Press, 255–87.

—— 1980: An economic interpretation of the decline in fertility in a rapidly developing country: consequences of development and family planning. In R. A. Easterlin (ed.), *Population and Economic Change in Developing Countries*, Chicago: University of Chicago Press, 209–65.

Schultz, T. W. 1974: Fertility and economic values. In idem (ed.), *Economics of the Family, Marriage, Children and Human Capital*, Chicago: University of Chicago Press, 3–22.

Scott, Chris and Chidambaram, V. C. 1985: World fertility survey: origins and achievements. In John Cleland and John Hobcraft (eds), *Reproductive Change in Developing Countries*, New York: Oxford University Press, 7–44.

Simon, Julian 1977: *The Economics of Population Growth*. Princeton: Princeton University Press.

Singh, Susheela and Casterline, John 1985: The socioeconomic determinants of fertility. In John Cleland and John Hobcraft (eds), *Reproductive Change in Developing Countries*, New York: Oxford University Press, 199–252.

Smith, Adam 1937: *An Inquiry into the Causes of the Wealth of Nations*, (1776). New York: Random House, Inc.

Smith, Peter C. 1983: The impact of age at marriage and proportions marrying vs. fertility. In R. A. Bulatao and R. D. Lee (eds), *Determinants of Fertility in Developing Countries*, New York: Academic Press, vol. 2, 473–531.

Standing, Guy 1983: Women's work activity and fertility. In R. A. Bulatao and R. D. Lee (eds), *Determinants of Fertility in Developing Countries*, New York: Academic Press, vol. 1, 517–546.

Stewart, Frances 1977: *Technology and Underdevelopment*. Boulder, Colo.: Westview Press.

Sumner, William G. 1885: *Problems in Political Economy*. New York: Henry Holt and Co.

—— and Keller, Albert 1927: *The Science of Society*, vol. 1. New Haven: Yale University Press.

Taussig, F. W. 1911: *Principles of Economics*, vol. 2. New York: Macmillan.

Thorton, Arland 1978: The relationship between fertility and income, relative income and subjective well being. In Julain L. Simon (ed.),

Research in Population Economics, Greenwich, Ct: JAI Press Inc., vol. 1, 261–90.

—— and Kim, Joochul 1980: Perceived impact of financial considerations on childbearing in the United States. In J. Simon and J. DaVanso (eds), *Research in Population Economics*, Greenwich, Ct: JAI Press Inc., vol. 2, 351–63.

Watkins, Susan C. 1986: Conclusion. In Ansley J. Coale and Susan C. Watkins (eds), *The Decline of Fertility in Europe*, Princeton: Princeton University Press, 420–49.

Weisner, T. S. and Gallimore, R. 1977: My brother's keeper: child and sibling caretaking. *Current Anthropology*, 18, 2, 169–90.

Willcox, Walter 1906: The Expansion of Europe and Its Influence Upon Population. In *Studies in Philosophy and Psychology*, New York: Houghton, Mifflin and Co.

Willis, R. J. 1973: Economic theory of fertility behavior. In T. W. Schultz (ed.), *Economics of the Family*, Chicago: University of Chicago Press, 25–75.

—— 1982: The direction of intergenerational transfers and demographic transition: the Caldwell hypothesis reexamined. *Population and Development Review*, supplement to vol. 8, 207–34.

World Bank, 1984: *World Development Report 1984*. New York: Oxford University Press.

—— 1989: *Trends in Developing Economies, 1989*. New York: Oxford University Press.

Wrigley, E. A. 1978: Fertility strategy for the individual and the group. In Charles Tilley (ed.), *Historical Studies of Changing Fertility*, Princeton: Princeton University Press, 135–54.

Index